MULTICULTURAL EDUCATIO

James A. Banks, Series Edit

D0921330

(continued)

ASIANS IN THE IVORY TOWER

Dilemmas of Racial Inequality in American Higher Education

Robert T. Teranishi

Foreword by Marcelo M. Suárez-Orozco

Teachers College, Columbia University
New York and London

Published by Teachers College Press, 1234 Amsterdam Avenue, New York, NY 10027

Library of Congress Cataloging-in-Publication Data

Teranishi, Robert T.
 Asians in the ivory tower : dilemmas of racial inequality in American higher education / Robert T. Teranishi ; foreword by Marcelo M. Suarez-Orozco.
  p. cm.—(Multicultural education series)
 Includes bibliographical references and index.
 ISBN 978-0-8077-5130-5 (pbk.)—ISBN 978-0-8077-5131-2 (hardcover)
 1. Asian Americans—Education (Higher) 2. Pacific Islander Americans—Education (Higher) 3. Academic achievement—United States. 4. Racism in education—United States. 5. Discrimination in education—Education. 6. Multicultural education—United States. I. Title.
  LC2633.6.T47 2010
  378.1'982995073--dc22

                    2010023439

ISBN 978-0-8077-5130-5 (paper)
ISBN 978-0-8077-5131-2 (hardcover)

Printed on acid-free paper
Manufactured in the United States of America

17   16   15   14   13   12   11   10   8   7   6   5   4   3   2   1

Contents

Series Foreword

Asians in the United States have had a difficult time constructing a public image that describes them as human beings who experience the same struggles, pains, triumphs, and victories as other Americans. The Chinese sojourners who started coming to the United States in the 1850s became known as the "Yellow Peril," a term expanded to include the Japanese when they began settling in California after Chinese immigration was legally banned by Congress in 1882. "Yellow Peril" was also used to describe Japan when it began a military expansion that culminated in the attack on Pearl Harbor on December 7, 1941.

When the Johnson-Reed Act of 1924 virtually ended Japanese immigration to the United States, farmers in California and Hawaii recruited immigrants from the Philippines to satisfy their desire for cheap labor. The Japanese on the U. S. mainland were interned during World War II because they were considered a security risk, which history has revealed had no factual basis (Daniels, 2004). In the postwar years, Asian Americans largely faded from the public imagination until the 1960s, when a series of popular magazine and newspaper articles described them as the "model minority." William Petersen's article, "Success Story, Japanese-American Style"— published in *The New York Times Magazine* on January 9, 1966—is widely regarded as the first article that crystallized and initiated the popularization of the model minority stereotype. Petersen wrote, "By any criteria of good citizenship that we choose, the Japanese Americans are better than any other group in our society, including native born whites" (p. 21). Asian Americans became salient again in the public imagination when significant immigration from China, the Philippines, Korea, India, and other Asian nations began after the passage of the Immigration Reform Act of 1965 (Banks, 2009a).

As this informative and timely book reveals, Asian Americans are still grappling with institutional racism and the burdens of history while victimized by the model minority stereotype and perceived as causing an "Asian invasion" of America's most prestigious colleges and universities. They are also frequently used as an example for other marginalized racial and ethnic groups, such as African Americans and Latinos, to verify that a minority group of color can attain high levels of educational, occupational, and economic mobility if the American dream is diligently pursued.

In deconstructing the model minority stereotype and helping readers to grasp the complexity of the experiences of Asian Americans and Pacific Islanders

(AAPIs), Teranishi describes the enormous diversity within and across the ethnic groups that make up the AAPI population. In 2000, the AAPI population consisted of 24 different groups that varied greatly in time of immigration to the United States, languages spoken, facility in English, income status, educational level, as well as extent of cultural and structural assimilation.

Teranishi's demographic depiction of the diversity within the AAPI population strongly challenges the model minority stereotype, such as his description of the problems and challenges experienced by low-income and undocumented Asian Americans. Teranishi describes these differences in such compelling and graphic detail that the model minority stereotype will remain intact and unquestioned by few readers of this illuminating book.

Teranishi's demographic portrayal of the AAPI population complicates widespread misconceptions of Asian Americans. For example, he points out that many of the Asians in the United States are nonimmigrant workers and students, most of whom plan to return to their homelands. More than 800,000 Asian were admitted to the United States in these categories in 2007. These nonimmigrant students are often described in popular accounts as Asian Americans. Teranishi also describes why the inclusion of Pacific Islanders in the AAPI population makes it exceedingly difficult to make valid generalizations about AAPIs because of the enormous diversity within and across Pacific Islanders.

A singular contribution of this book is its descriptions of the experiences of the AAPI population and explanations of the unique challenges as well as the intricacy of the various ethnic and linguistic groups that make up AAPIs. Teranishi uses both quantitative and qualitative data to portray the neighborhoods and families of a sample of AAPI students, their schools, and the factors that influence their decisions and opportunities to pursue higher education. He provides fresh perspectives, research insights, and theoretical paradigms that will enrich the understanding of educators and policy makers about the higher educational needs, challenges, and possibilities for Asian American and Pacific Islander students.

This adept and informative book will help P–12 educators as well as higher educators to develop sophisticated understandings of AAPI students as well as work more effectively with the diverse student population in U. S. schools, colleges, and universities. American educational institutions are experiencing the largest influx of immigrant students since the beginning of the twentieth century. About a million immigrants are making the United States their home each year (Martin & Midgley, 1999; Roberts, 2008). Between 1997 and 2006, over 9 million immigrants entered the United States (U. S. Department of Homeland Security, 2007). Only 15% came from European nations. Most came from nations in Asia, from Mexico, and from nations in Latin America, Central America, and the Caribbean (U. S. Department of Homeland Security, 2007). A large but undetermined number of undocumented immigrants also enter the United States each year. In 2007, *The New York Times* estimated that there were 12 million undocumented immigrants in the United States ("Immigration Sabotage," 2007). The influence of an increasingly ethnically diverse population on U. S. schools, colleges, and universities is and will continue to be enormous.

Schools in the United States are more diverse today than they have been since the early 1900s when a multitude of immigrants entered the United States from Southern, Central, and Eastern Europe. In the 34-year period between 1973 and 2007, the percentage of students of color in U. S. public schools increased from 22 to 55% (Dillon, 2006; National Center for Education Statistics, 2008a, b, & c). If current trends continue, students of color will equal or exceed the percentage of White students in U. S. public schools within one or two decades. In the 2007–2008 school year, students of color exceeded the number of Whites students in 11 states: Arizona, California, Florida, Georgia, Hawaii, Louisiana, Maryland, Mississippi, New Mexico, Nevada, and Texas (National Center for Education Statistics (2008a & b).

Language and religious diversity is also increasing in the U. S. student population. English Language Learners (ELLs) is the fastest growing group of U. S. students (Suárez-Orozco & Suárez-Orozco, 2001). In 2000, about 20% of the school-age population spoke a language at home other than English (U. S. Census Bureau, 2003). The Progressive Policy Institute estimated that 50 million Americans (out of 300 million) spoke a language at home other than English in 2008. Harvard professor Diana L. Eck (2001) calls the United States the "most religiously diverse nation on earth" (p. 4). Islam is the fastest-growing religion in the United States as well as in several European nations such as France, the United Kingdom, and the Netherlands (Banks, 2009b; Cesari, 2004). Most teachers and professors are likely to have students from diverse ethnic, racial, linguistic, and religious groups in their classrooms during their careers. This is true in the United States as well as in most other nations, as is amply documented in the *Routledge International Companion to Multicultural Education* (Banks, 2009b).

The major purpose of the Multicultural Education Series is to provide educational practitioners, graduate students, scholars, and policy makers with an interrelated and comprehensive set of books that summarizes and analyzes important research, theory, and practice related to the education of ethnic, racial, cultural, and linguistic groups in the United States and the education of mainstream students about diversity. The dimensions of multicultural education, developed by Banks (2004) and described in the *Handbook of Research on Multicultural Education,* (Banks & Banks, 2004) provide the conceptual framework for the development of the publications in the Series. They are: *content integration, the knowledge construction process, prejudice reduction, an equity pedagogy, and an empowering institutional culture and social structure.*

The books in the Series provide research, theoretical, and practical knowledge about the behaviors and learning characteristics of students of color, language minority students, and low-income students. They also provide knowledge about ways to improve academic achievement and race relations in schools, colleges, and universities. Multicultural education is consequently as important for mainstream White students as it is for students of color. Multicultural education fosters the public good and the overarching goals of the nation.

The thick descriptions of high school students grappling with decisions about going to college enrich this incisive book and vividly convey the diversity within the AAPI student population. Pang (Hmong), Tony (Chinese), Trung (Vietnamese), and Lilly (Filipino) are high school seniors wrestling with the decision about where they will go to college and how they will pay for it. The powerful stories of these four students—which Teranishi spreads across this book—strikingly illustrate how difficult it is to generalize about AAPI college-bound students. These engaging stories, the descriptions of the complexity of the AAPI population, and the novel analyses and theoretical perspectives that enrich this book make it an essential source for comprehending the experiences of Asian American and Pacific Islander students as they navigate the sometimes arduous path to higher education.

—James A. Banks

REFERENCES

Banks, J. A. (2004). Multicultural education: Historical development, dimensions, and practice. In J. A. Banks & C. A. M. Banks (Eds.), *Handbook of research on multicultural education* (2nd ed., pp. 3–29). San Francisco: Jossey-Bass.

Banks, J. A. (2009a). *Teaching strategies for ethnic studies* (8th ed.). Boston: Pearson.

Banks, J. A. (Ed.). (2009b). *The Routledge international companion to multicultural education.* New York and London: Routledge.

Banks, J. A., & Banks, C. A. M. (Eds.) (2004). *Handbook of research on multicultural education* (2nd ed.). San Francisco: Jossey-Bass.

Cesari, J. (2004). *When Islam and democracy meet: Muslims in Europe and the United States.* New York: Pelgrave Macmillan.

Daniels, R. (2004). *Prisoners without trail: Japanese Americans in World War II.* New York: Hill and Wang.

Dillon, S. (2006, August 27). In schools across U. S., the melting pot overflows. *The New York Times,* vol. CLV [155] (no. 53,684), pp. A7 & 16.

Eck, D. L. (2001). *A new religious America: How a "Christian country" has become the world's most religiously diverse nation.* New York: HarperSanFrancisco.

Immigration sabotage [Editorial]. (2007, June 4). *The New York Times,* p. A22.

Martin, P. & Midgley, E. (1999). Immigration to the United States. *Population Bulletin, 54* (2), pp. 1–44. Washington, DC: Population Reference Bureau.

National Center for Education Statistics. (2008a). *The condition of education 2008.* Washington, DC: U. S. Department of Education. Retrieved August 26, 2009, from http://nces.ed.gov/pubsearch/pubsinfo.asp?pubid=2008031

National Center for Education Statistics. (2008b). Public elementary/secondary school universe survey, 2007–2008. *Common core of data.* Retrieved January, 20, 2010, from http://nces.ed.gov/ccd

National Center for Education Statistics. (2008c). State nonfiscal survey of public elementary/secondary education, 2007–2008. *Common core of data.* Retrieved January, 20, 2010, from http://nces.ed.gov/ccd

Petersen, W. (1966, January 9). Success story, Japanese-American style. *The New York Times Magazine,* pp. 20–21, 36, 38, 40–41, 43.

Progressive Policy Institute. (2008). *50 million Americans speak languages other than English at home.* Retrieved September 2, 2008, from http://www.ppionline.org/ppi_ci.cfm?knlg AreaID=108&subsecID=900003&contentID=254619

Roberts, S. (2008, August 14). A generation away, minorities may become the majority in U. S. *The New York Times,* vol. CLVII [175] (no. 54,402), pp. A1 & A18.

Suárez-Orozco, C., & Suárez-Orozco, M. M. (2001). *Children of immigration.* Cambridge, MA: Harvard University Press.

U.S. Census Bureau. (2003, October). Language use and English-speaking ability: 2000. Retrieved September 2, 2008, from http://www.census.gov/prod/2003pubs/c2kbr-29.pdf

U.S. Census Bureau. (2008, August 14). *Statistical abstract of the United States.* Retrieved August 20, 2008, from http://www.census.gov/prod/2006pubs/07statab/pop.pdf

U.S. Department of Homeland Security. (2007). *Yearbook of immigration statistics, 2006.* Washington, DC: Office of Immigration Statistics, Author. Retrieved August 11, 2009, from http://www.dhs.gov/files/statistics/publications/yearbook.shtm

Foreword

A substantial body of economic, psychological, and sociological research has mapped the effects of education on socioeconomic mobility, social cohesion and citizenship, and health and well being. The preponderance of evidence is hardly surprising; schooling tends to generate powerful virtuous cycles (Bloom, 2004; LeVine, 2007). There is, however, less research on the relevance of higher education in a world transformed by the dual synergetic forces of mass migration and globalization of economy, society, and demography. In this ground-breaking book, Robert Teranishi tackles these issues by making the case for thinking carefully about the interplay among the issues of mass migration, race, and higher education. If we are to understand our increasingly complex present and inevitable future as a pluralistic society, this is an essential undertaking.

Asians in the Ivory Tower once and for all does away with the tired old clichés about Asian American and Pacific Islander (AAPI) populations that are long reduced to the symbolic violence of caricature, silence, and invisibility. It shatters the "model minority" myth for what it is: a lazy excuse not to do the hard work that the new hyperdiversity requires of engaged and intelligent citizens in the twenty-first century. Teranishi counters facile stereotypes with a magnificently crafted towering edifice, building accurate depictions of today's hyperdiverse AAPI universe that defy previous generations' notions of Asian Americans. To bring together the breathtaking range of humanity contained in the AAPI experience is a considerable achievement, one that Teranishi accomplishes with an intelligent, persuasive, and compassionate voice.

Asians in the Ivory Tower covers so much critical territory and shatters so many myths, prejudices, and misunderstandings that I simply cannot do justice to all it achieves. While the putative focus of the study is the vertiginous growth of our AAPI population, the book accomplishes much more: As a paradigm of mixed methods in basic research, it weaves together the hard numbers behind the colossal changes that have taken place in the AAPI population with the unique individual voices of informants clamoring to tell their stories. Through this beautiful tapestry Teranishi creates, the AAPI population can finally be acknowledged and seen beyond the distortion of stereotypes and racial splitting games pitting "model" minorities versus other "problem" minorities.

Comprehension of these issues is an endeavor that requires an integrated perspective through the narrative of individual stories and hard numbers. Only such an approach can capture the complex issue of global migration—a problem that defines an era in which immigrants (and in many countries other minorities) simultaneously belong and do not belong in the same social landscape. Diverse nation-states throughout the world, particularly the United States, now experience a schizogeneric duality: Glossy-eyed, we lovingly celebrate the triumphs and travails of past immigrant generations, but in the here and now, plurality and difference call forth deep anxieties and ambivalence in the face of inevitable change. Currently, immigration and difference evoke the unmaking of home, inducing a disturbing, unsettling, and misshapen sense of something at once familiar yet utterly foreign: Freud's *Das Unheimliche*—literally, the "un-homely."

Capturing the lives and experiences of AAPIs in their pursuit of mobility is at the heart of *Asians in the Ivory Tower*. In the spirit of the best sociological imagination, Teranishi weaves essential threads among agency, social conditions, and the organizational structures and practices that shape the lives, dreams, and deeds of our rapidly growing and ever more diverse AAPI population in the world of U.S. higher education. *Asians in the Ivory Tower* explains the contemporary and historical underpinnings of how AAPIs have navigated America's catastrophic fears of mass invasions, broken borders and, above all, panic of the balkanization of a fatigued nation. This social landscape has resulted in robust architectures—institutional, psychological, and sociocultural—that, alas, act as powerful constraints on the movement of populations worldwide (Zolberg, 2001).

Indeed, how AAPIs navigate the multifaceted contours of global migration is central to this book. It places higher education opportunity and social mobility in the broader context of the most notable features of global migration in the last two generations: stability and sobriety. For all the fear and anxiety, the story of global migration at the beginning of the twenty-first century is the story of the unbearable normalcy of human movement. While more people are now on the move than ever before in terms of sheer numbers (214 million, according to data from the United Nations Department of Economic and Social Affairs, 2009), the *rate* of international migration has remained remarkably stable over the last 50 years, with roughly 2.5 to 3.1% of the world's population living beyond their country of birth. Additionally, the rate of U.S. migration today is lower than in the last wave of mass migration. Put another way, approximately 97% of the human population remains in the confines of the national territory of their birth, and it typically requires a shock to the biosocial system to induce mass transnational migration (Suárez-Orozco & Suárez-Orozco, n.d.).

It is within this context that Teranishi positions the participation of AAPIs in U.S. higher education. *Asians in the Ivory Tower* captures the contemporary educational mobility of AAPIs within the historical legacy of inclusion and exclusion of minority populations in American society. Among these histories are stories of complex and multiple origins, beginning with the U.S. appetite for Chinese laborers in the early decades of the nineteenth century as a result of the Gold

Rush and the building of the transcontinental railroad (there are now 2.7 million Chinese Americans), and the arrival of Japanese agricultural workers in Hawaii and California (today there are over 1.4 million Japanese Americans). The Spanish American War and the subsequent U.S. occupations of Cuba, Puerto Rico, and the Philippines set the stage for Filipino Americans to become the third largest group of immigrants in the United States (there are now over 2.3 million Filipino Americans). The end of the British Raj and the partitioning of the Indian subcontinent led to the relocation of over 14 million people away from their birthplaces and to the newly formed countries of India and Pakistan, also beginning a steady and growing pattern of Indian and Pakistani migration (the United States now has over 1.8 million Asian Indian Americans and over 200,000 Pakistani Americans). The Korean War is why the United States today has over 1.2 Korean immigrants and their descendants, and the Vietnam War largely accounts for the influx of Vietnamese (1.2 million), Cambodians (over 200,000), and Laotians (over 190,000) now living in the United States.

In the best tradition of C. Wright Mills, Robert Teranishi brings into focus the human agency behind these massive historical events. More precisely, *Asians in the Ivory Tower* shares global migration's most important story at the dawn of the new millennium—the story that is missing in the policy briefs, in the think-tank study groups, and in the headlines: Where migrant workers are summoned, families and children will follow. The children of immigrants are a fast-growing sector of the child and youth population in nearly every country of immigration today, including Australia, Canada, Germany, Italy, The Netherlands, Spain, and Sweden. In the United States, approximately a quarter of all youth are of immigrant origin (16 million in 2010) and it is projected that by 2040 over a third of all children will be growing up in immigrant households. Because of migration, by the year 2030 less than half of all children in the United States will be of White European origin.

Schools in cities all over the world—from Sydney to Beijing, from Barcelona to Toronto, from Los Angeles to Reggio Emilia, Italy—are being transformed by growing numbers of immigrant children. In New York City, for example, children from over 190 countries and territories, speaking over 170 different languages, go to school every morning. Just as schools face the challenge of educating linguistically, culturally, and racially diverse students, the global integration and disintegration of economies imposes yet another challenge on education—nurturing ever more complex skills, competencies, and sensibilities on students to equip them to engage in the globally linked economies and societies and to become globally conscious and competent citizens in the twenty-first century.

It is imperative for schools to respond to the challenges that Teranishi captures in these nuanced stories of the pursuit for American higher education by AAPIs. *Asians in the Ivory Tower* tells the story of Pang, a young woman born without a country to call home, who valiantly struggles while pursuing her dreams of higher education seemingly against all odds. It also tells the story of Tony, a young man for all seasons who "does his own laundry, cooks his own food, and does his own homework without anybody keeping track of him," while nurturing the right networks to pursue the pathway of college for a better tomorrow. It tells the story of Trung, the newly arrived kid from Vietnam with a formidable mother and two college-savvy sisters setting a high standard for him. It tells the story of Lilly, a vivacious Filipina, managing the difficult balancing act between the "traditional" expectations of her fiercely loyal family that would keep her close to the hearth and her own ambition to explore wider horizons in multiethnic California. It is these stories, coupled with the broader context of the human condition in an immigrant America, that tell the tale of the sacrifices behind each and every human journey. *Asians in the Ivory Tower* is a gift to all American citizens who struggle to understand their rapidly changing world. It is a must read for anyone interested in the contemporary world as it is—and not on the myths and dated tales that continue to delude so many of our citizens.

—*Marcelo M. Suárez-Orozco*

REFERENCES

Bloom, D. E. (2004). Globalization and education: An economic perspective. In M. M. Suárez-Orozco & D. Qin-Hilliard (Eds.), *Globalization: Culture and education in the new millennium* (pp. 56–77). Berkeley, CA: University of California Press.

LeVine, R. A. (2007). The global spread of women's schooling: Effects on learning, literacy, health, and children. In M. M. Suárez-Orozco (Ed.), *Learning in the global era: International perspectives on globalization and education* (pp. 121–136). Berkeley, CA: University of California Press.

Suárez-Orozco, C., & Suárez-Orozco, M. M. (n.d.). *Immigration's echo: Family dislocations and the new immigrant generation.* Manuscript submitted for publication.

United Nations, Department of Economic and Social Affairs, Population Division (2009). *International migration to and from selected countries: The 2008 Revision.* Retrieved June 22, 2010 from http://www.un.org/esa/population/publications/2008ittmigflows/2008ittmigflows.htm

Zolberg, A. (2001). Beyond the crisis. In A. Zolberg & P. Benda, (Eds.), *Global migrants, global refugees problems and solutions* (pp. 1–16). London: Berghahn Books.

Acknowledgments

This project spanned nearly a decade of my life and involved many people to whom I am grateful. I begin by thanking Pat McDonough, Walter Allen, Danny Solorzano, and Mitch Chang for their guidance at the beginning stages of this project. Their generous support and mentorship have been critical for my development as a scholar.

I am also indebted to the many colleagues who have given me input and feedback during various stages of this research project. Special thanks are due to Margaret Spencer, Estela Bensimon, Jack Tchen, Shirley Hune, Helen Zia, Miguel Ceja, Jamie Lew, Dina Marumba, Sam Museus, Don Nakanishi, Robert Underwood, Carola Suarez-Orozco, Will Perez, Debbie Wei, Pedro Noguera, Karen Yoshino, Sunil Chand, Liz OuYang, Frank Tang, Jim Trent, Kamilah Briscoe, Tara Parker, Laurie Behringer, Emily Grey, Shaila Mulholland, Chera Reid, Daniel Choi, Oiyan Poon, Julie Park, Tu Lien Nguyen, Mark Carolino, Annie Bezbatchenko, Suzie White, Gniesha Dinwiddie, and Ann Tiao. This is an extraordinary group of individuals from whom I have gained insight during my research and work on this book.

There are other individuals and organizations that played an integral part in this book. My thanks to Neil Horikoshi, Gale Awaya, and the whole team at the Asian Pacific Islander American Scholarship Fund; Doua Thor, Soumary Vongrassamy, and Monica Thammarath at the Southeast Asian Resource Action Center; Vanessa Leung and Wayne Ho at the Coalition for Asian American Children and Families; Peter Gee at Asian Americans for Equality; Khin Mai Aung at the Asian American Legal Defense Fund; Jim Montoya, Steve Handel, Alan Heaps, Selena Cantor, and Ron Williams at the College Board; and at the Ford Foundation, I am thankful to Jeannie Oakes, Alison Bernstein, Gregory Anderson, and Leslie Williams.

I also appreciate the support of my colleagues in the Higher Education program and the Department of Administration, Leadership, and Technology at New York University. The Steinhardt Institute for Higher Education Policy provided key core support for the past 5 years and the Steinhardt School of Culture, Education, and Human Development allowed me the flexibility in my teaching schedule that gave me much-needed time to finish the writing of this manuscript.

The research for this book was funded by USA Funds; the College Board; the Mellon Foundation; the W. E. B. DuBois Research Institute at the University of Pennsylvania; the University of California Office of the President; and the University of California All Campus Consortium on Research for Diversity (UC ACCORD). This funding also helped to support research assistants at UCLA, the University of Pennsylvania, and New York University, all of whom have been deeply involved in this project.

For their time, patience, and insight, I am especially grateful to the student respondents in this project. Their willingness to open up and provide a glimpse into their lives made this work possible. I am also thankful to the school personnel at the various sites where the research was conducted for providing me access to their schools.

With regard to the publication process for this work, it is important that I give a special acknowledgment to James Banks, who graciously worked with me to publish this book with Teachers College Press, and my colleague Marcelo Suárez-Orozco, who introduced me to James as I sought out a publisher for this book. It was only fitting to ask Marcelo to write the foreword for this book so the project could come full circle. For their support during the publication of this work, I am also indebted to Brian Ellerbeck and Lori Tate at Teachers College Press, who were instrumental in aiding me through the editorial process.

Finally, I wish to express my gratitude to my family, who has provided me with unwavering love and support throughout this project.

ASIANS IN THE IVORY TOWER

Dilemmas of Racial Inequality in American Higher Education

Introduction

Race remains one the most important historical and contemporary issues in American society—rightfully so, considering the extent to which it has been a cause for and consequence of stratification in the United States. Perhaps nowhere else is the struggle against racial stratification more prominent than in America's system of education. This is not surprising inasmuch as educational attainment is a prerequisite for social mobility in the United States, with opportunities and outcomes in education being a major determinant for gaining and maintaining social status (Blau & Duncan, 1968). Although America's schools are more diverse today than at any other point in history, there continue to be disturbing gaps in educational mobility that are divided along racial boundaries. Students of color are more likely than Whites to attend racially segregated schools with poorer funding, fewer college-preparation courses, and less educated and less experienced teachers. They also face other social conditions and organizational contexts that negatively affect their ability to learn and succeed academically (Darling-Hammond, 2010; Gandara, 1995). The differences in access to and opportunity for quality schooling create severe gaps in postsecondary educational participation and attainment, which have several implications for our nation as a whole.

Accordingly, education is central to our national conversation about race. How and with what urgency America deals with racial stratification, among other forms of subordination, will determine its position in our global society. It is widely recognized that achieving a high-quality workforce is predicated by a more educated workforce (Holzer, 2008). In her new book, *The Flat World and Education,* Linda Darling-Hammond (2010) describes how the United States must respond to data that suggest that three-quarters of the fastest-growing occupational sectors require a college education (p. 3). But the United States, which once led the world in educational attainment, has now been surpassed by at least 10 other developed nations (Goldrick-Rab et al., 2009). These trends have implications for competition in science productivity: Between 2002 and 2007 the U.S. share of the worldwide research population fell to 20.3% from 23.2%, compared to an increase in China to 20.1% from 14.0% (UNESCO Institute for Statistics, 2009).

Trends in the K–12 education sector in the United States are not encouraging. A 2006 report from the National Center for Education Statistics (NCES) found that the average scores of 15-year-old students on combined science and mathematics literacy scales for the United States fell below the average for all of the countries

1

involved in the assessment, including major competitors such as the United Kingdom and Japan (Baldi, Jin, Skemer, Green, & Herget, 2007). In order for the United States workforce to maintain its status as a top competitor in the world market, it is imperative for our nation to close the gaps in college participation and degree attainment, which is at the center of our national priorities.

Despite the volume of research devoted to the decades-old debate about the causes of and solutions for the racial divide in American society, Asian Americans and Pacific Islanders (AAPIs)[1] remain in the margins, as an outlier in our national conversation about race. In the rare instance when AAPIs are included in the racial discourse about access to and equity in higher education, they have been reduced to a single, stubbornly persistent narrative—as a "model minority"—a group with "stellar educational achievement" whose students do not have needs or concerns worthy of attention by researchers, policy makers, or practitioners. From the viewpoint of mainstream society, AAPIs are perceived as a minority group that has amassed an "Asian Invasion" (Hwang, 2005) in America's colleges and universities, even a threat to our national goal of increasing minority participation in higher education.

Recent trends in educational attainment and college enrollment among AAPIs have become the contemporary foundation for the perception of the "Asian Invasion" in U.S. higher education. According to analysis of data from the U.S. Census Bureau, 49.8% of Asian Americans, 25 years or older, completed 4 years of college, compared to 30.6% of Whites, 17.6% of Blacks, and 12.0% of Hispanics in 2005. Not only are AAPIs more likely to attend and complete college, they have also been found to do so in some of America's most elite and selective universities. In 2005 AAPIs made up 14.1% of California's high school graduating class, but they comprised 41.8% of the freshman class at University of California (UC) campuses; at seven of the nine UC undergraduate campuses, AAPIs were the single largest racial group. In the zero-sum game of selective college admissions this has been translated into an idea that AAPIs are succeeding to such an extent that it is occurring at the expense of other minorities, even at the expense of Whites. With affirmative action at a major crossroads now and in the years to come, AAPIs have been dubbed the "conspicuous adversaries to diversity."

The idea of the model minority is not a new one; in fact, the proclamation of AAPIs as the model minority is at the eve of its fiftieth anniversary. The December issue of *U.S. News and World Report* in 1966 ran an article titled "Success of Chinese Americans," which proclaimed, "At a time when Americans are awash in worry over the plight of racial minorities, one such minority is winning wealth and respect by dint of its own hard work—not from a welfare check" (p. 73). This article helped to solidify an idea that was coined earlier that same year by William Petersen (1966), who described Asian Americans[2] as a racial group who had achieved success in the United States despite many obstacles. Helping to further the idea of the model minority in the minds of Americans were two additional mainstream news stories, focused more specifically on educational achievement: *Newsweek* touted that Asians are "Outwhiting Whites" (June 21, 1971) while *Time Magazine* declared that Asians are "The New Whiz Kids" (Brand, 1987). At the dawn of the twenty-first century, the idea of the model minority student persisted in the mind of mainstream America. In a *New York Times* column in 2006 entitled, "The Model Students," Nicolas Kristof wrote that "stellar academic achievement has an Asian face" and that others would be "fools" not to learn from these "perfect" students. Indeed, the image of the model minority is alive and well as we enter this new millennium.

WHAT'S WRONG WITH A POSITIVE STEREOTYPE?

The face of "stellar academic achievement" has become synonymous with the AAPI population, and this stereotype has become deeply engrained in the American vernacular. In my many conversations with people about Asian American stereotypes, I often ask, "How do you know what you know about Asian Americans?" I often get the response, "I know that it is based on stereotypes, but I do know successful Asians so the stereotype must be true." Coupled with this type of statement is often the question, "What's wrong with stereotypes, especially if they are positive ones? After all, isn't a *good* stereotype better than a *bad* one?"

The stereotypical depiction of AAPIs as the model minority is not just relegated to the mainstream public. In a talk I recently gave at the NYU Law School, I was asked to debate a political scientist from Princeton on the social science implications of race-based jurisprudence for policy debates, including affirmative action and the admissions policies of selective universities. Our debate turned to Asian Americans and their apparent success in accessing Ivy League universities, including his own. In our debate about this topic I was compelled to refute much of what he said by asserting that his ideas about Asians seemed to be entirely based on stereotypes. His response to me was simply that—and I'm paraphrasing—stereotypes are based on generalizations, generalizations are grounded in facts, and thus there is truth to all stereotypes.

Stereotypes have been described as fixed impressions, exaggerated or preconceived ideas about particular social groups (Steele & Aronson, 1995). Put another way, they are generalizations that lead to a reduction of complexity. American journalist Walter Lippmann (1922) coined the concept, calling a *stereotype* a "picture in our heads" and saying "whether right or wrong . . . imagination is shaped by the pictures seen. . . Consequently, they lead to stereotypes that are hard to shake" (pp. 95–156). Thus stereotypes become deeply engrained in the ethos of members of society. Unfortunately, the monolithic model minority image is a perception that does little to capture the reality of the AAPI educational experience.

There is a need for research that transcends the model minority myth and recognizes the uniqueness of the educational experiences and outcomes among the AAPI population through an approach that focuses solely on AAPIs as the unit of analysis. With the exception of a few notable studies (Chou & Feagin, 2008; Kim, 1999; Lee, 1996; Louie, 2004; Takagi, 1992), the focus on AAPIs as a racial minority population with distinct educational needs and issues is seldom pursued in academic research. Oiyan Poon (2006), a graduate student at UCLA, conducted an unpublished study on the representation of Asian Americans or Pacific Islanders in higher education research journals.[3] Between 1996 and 2006, these journals published 2,660 articles in total, but only 13 articles were based on the study of Asian Americans or Pacific Islanders. Two journals had not published any articles on AAPIs. Similar trends can be found in the search of literature databases. A graduate student working with me looked for literature on AAPI students in the Education Resources Information Center (ERIC) database, which is recognized as the largest digital library of education literature. She found that out of over 40,000 articles that focus on academic achievement and attainment, articles on Asian Americans or Pacific Islanders (as a whole or subgroups within the population) constituted less than 250 articles combined (about one-half of one percent of the total).

The representation of AAPIs in academic journal articles does not necessarily mean that research is not being conducted on AAPIs; in fact, there is a great deal of research that can be found in theses, dissertations, research reports, and papers presented at conferences. Often, many studies on the AAPI population do not pass the peer-review process of academic journals because the topic is seen as "not relevant to the field" or having "low audience appeal," two criteria that are critical to the selection process of academic papers. Because much of this work is not accessible to the field through academic journals, they have been of little impact on the consciousness of researchers, policy makers, and the mainstream public about the population and its needs.

There is a timely and compelling need for an examination of the AAPI population relative to their educational mobility, especially in the context of how AAPIs are treated as a model minority in research, including: (1) the extent to which it is a factor in how social scientists, policy makers, and educational practitioners position AAPIs within debates about access to and participation in higher education; (2) what knowledge and empirical evidence actually exist that can be used to interrogate it through the study of the educational mobility that occurs within the population; and (3) how it is a factor in the lived experiences among AAPI individuals and communities as students develop and pursue their goals and aspirations. In this book I critically examine and transcend the narrow model minority concept to capture the relationship between who AAPIs are as a population, where they live, and what schools they attend, and how these factors translate into a range of postsecondary opportunities and outcomes, both in terms of their relative social position in America's stratified society, as well as how we capture their actual lived experiences within this journey. With these perspectives taken into account, perhaps the "too good to be true" model minority mantra fails to be either good or true when it comes to the education of Asian American and Pacific Islander students.

PURPOSE OF THE BOOK

Social scientists have long been concerned with how distinctions of race, ethnicity, language, and other cultural factors play out in the day-to-day operations of America's system of education. As the United States continues to become more racially diverse, there is a much-needed demand for empirical research to inform educational practice and policy on key issues and trends for the access, participation, and outcomes of various student populations. It is for these reasons that researchers, policy makers, and practitioners can no longer overlook the AAPI population.

While the title of this book can trigger one's imagination to envision the sizeable presence of AAPIs in colleges and universities throughout the country, for others the image may be their high concentration in the science and technology fields. Certainly this book is concerned with and sheds light on both of these trends relative to the participation of AAPIs in U.S. higher education, but it also addresses other issues that may be counterintuitive to what is associated with *Asians in the Ivory Tower*. I explore when, why, and how AAPIs are relevant to our nation's higher education priorities. I also problematize how the treatment of AAPIs in educational research and policy are affected by existing theoretical perspectives on the stratification of college opportunities, while simultaneously responding to the need for a focus solely on AAPI students and families as they navigate the United States educational pipeline. Generally, I place the study of AAPI college participation within a broad set of conditions through which all students must navigate as they pursue higher education. Two levels of contextual factors—societal and organizational—are the focus of this book, both of which are examined in terms of how they operate separately and cooperatively. This integrated perspective captures the intersections of individual agency, social conditions, and organizational structures.

The analyses in this book are informed by the following previously unanswered research questions: How are AAPIs positioned within broad debates about access to and equity in U.S. higher education, and how, if at all, is this a factor in what we know and don't know about their educational mobility? What are the demographic characteristics of and social conditions among AAPIs, and in what way, if at all, do these factors have implications for their educational and social mobility in American society? Among AAPIs who do go to college, are there particular characteristics of AAPI students that correlate with attending certain sectors of higher education? Do AAPIs have similar or different college outcomes with regard to mobility beyond the baccalaureate, including their occupational trajectories? Responding to these questions leads to a more informed discussion about the population and its unique educational needs, and the extent to which AAPIs have a place within discussions about equity and opportunity in American society.

The research pursuits of this book rely on both quantitative and qualitative data sources (see Appendix A). On one hand, the quantitative data captures the demography of and social conditions among the AAPI population, including their relative position within communities and institutions. This analysis is consistent with the approach of most equity studies that focus on end points and outcomes along educational pathways, such as standardized test scores, GPAs, and completion rates. On the other hand, the qualitative data provides a portrait of the educational process, which is an invaluable and essential perspective in order to grasp an understanding of the processes through which students and their families navigate the educational system. Bankston and Zhou (2002) refer to this as "being well" versus "doing well," or the difference between capturing the ends as opposed to the means. Annette Lareau (2003), in her book *Unequal Childhoods: Class, Race, and Family Life*, describes how she set out to capture the "large and seemingly invisible ways that the social context impacts students' life experiences and outcomes" through the study of "pleasures, opportunities, challenges, and conflicts in the daily lives of children and their families" (p. 13).

Although I rely on the use of a number of data sources as the foundation for inquiry in this book, I recognize that the usefulness of the data depends on questions, interpretation, and judgments (Argyris & Schon, 1996). Thus the data do not have their own explanations and are highly dependent on the lens through which the data is examined (Alford, 1998). Therefore, I couple data with key theoretical propositions from sociology and education about race, race relations, social inequality, and other perspectives I have gained as an educator and scholar interested in understanding and challenging racial inequality in higher education.

The lens that I apply to the research in this book is guided in part by insight I have gained through my work as codirector of the CARE Project, a 4-year collaborative effort between the Steinhardt Institute for Higher Education Policy, the Asian/Pacific/American Institute at New York University, and the College Board.[4] One of the most important insights I gained from my work with the CARE Project is the need to be critical of how achievement and mobility in the United States are conceptualized and how these paradigms influence our understanding of AAPIs and their educational achievement and attainment. For my own particular interests in this topic, the CARE project generated a great deal of insight on the conceptual, analytical, and methodological challenges that have prevented AAPIs from being a part of discussions on equality and social mobility in American society.

ORGANIZATION OF THE BOOK

To provide a greater context for the contents of this book, I begin the book by challenging the notion that a single story can represent the range of experiences and outcomes of individuals and communities that comprise the AAPI population. I also discuss the literature from which I formulated research questions, including the terrain for how AAPIs are positioned in discussions about race, equity, and social mobility in American society. Chapter 2 gives an overview of the theoretical perspectives that were guiding tenets for the research in this book. Building on alternative conceptual framing, I provide a portrait of the AAPI population, which challenges the idea that AAPIs are a monolithic population with similarities in experiences, opportunities, and outcomes in American society. In Chapter 3 I examine issues of ethnicity, language and language policy and immigration and immigration policy, and position these demographic distinctions within the context of residential patterns and the influence of ethnic enclaves that exist as social networks and socializing agents for different AAPI ethnic populations.

The next three chapters delve into the organizational contexts within which AAPIs are educated. The first organizational setting I focus on in Chapter 4 is the K–12 setting and examine how the arrangements and processes within institutions mediates opportunity, the shaping of aspirations, access to resources, and differential postsecondary outcomes for AAPI students. Chapter 5 considers AAPIs within the organizational context of higher education and examines how opportunities and barriers faced by subpopulations within the AAPI population translate into differential postsecondary outcomes. Of particular interest is examining the ways in which AAPI participation in United States higher education is unique with regard to how their college participation has changed historically, what variations exist in terms of their participation throughout the American system of higher education (2-year and 4-year institutions; public and private institutions; selective and nonselective institutions; and so on), and the intersection between demographic characteristics among AAPIs and its relationship to different patterns of college participation. In Chapter 6 I discuss how the needs of AAPIs have been affected by and can be responded to with attention to human capital and the education pipeline for AAPI educators and administrators in K–12 and higher education. I focus most intently on how opportunity structures are a factor in the distribution of AAPIs in the field of education and how the poor representation of AAPIs among educators and administrators is a critical factor for repositioning AAPIs within broader discussions of equity throughout the education pipeline.

I conclude the book by offering a reconceptualized approach for research, policy, and practice that repositions AAPIs within the narrative of equity and higher education. Specifically, I describe the future direction of inquiry-based research and policy for AAPIs and education and provide ideas for how to find relevance for the AAPI community in America's equity agenda.

DATA SOURCES AND METHODOLOGY

Throughout this book the story of the pursuit of college for AAPIs is situated in both quantitative and qualitative data (see Appendix A). The quantitative data, which is situated in a nested-case design of multiple units of analyses, capture the demography of AAPI students, families, communities, and institutional contexts. While the use of numbers present one set of opportunities, they also have their limitations. Thus qualitative methods are also utilized to give voice to the lived experiences of AAPI students and families. These analyses are focused most intently on the formation of AAPI students' educational aspirations, how they perceive and experience opportunities and challenges, and the role of their families and schools in facilitating the transition from high school to college. These layers of data offer an interrogation that is rich with comprehensiveness and complexity, offering both depth and breadth of analysis.

As a whole, these data provide a complex story that lends itself to an alternative perspective on the AAPI student experience through a comprehensive examination of the factors that contribute to the educational mobility of AAPIs. Through an investigation of empirical evidence, along with new theoretical framing of comparative research, the ideas in this book about AAPIs and their educational achievement can lead to policy, service, and treatment of AAPIs that is informed by an alternative story, a story that is more accurate in reflecting and portraying the population to the public and to itself.

AAPIs have a rightful place in conversations about racial equality and opportunity in American society. This book demonstrates the ways in which the experiences and outcomes of AAPIs can and cannot be comparatively measured against other racial groups. The research in this book also sheds light on the structural barriers faced by AAPIs, as opposed to focusing on the mere outcomes compared to other racial groups. This will illuminate actual opportunity for AAPIs, rather than focusing on the status of Asians in America as measured by outcomes. Finally, this book sheds light on issues of race and race relations in American society. Specifically, a major thrust of this book is to move beyond stereotypes as a guiding tenet to scholarship, policy making, and educational practice.

CHAPTER 1

Transcending Conceptual Blockages

Social scientists have long been concerned with the causes and consequences of racial stratification in our society. A fundamental interest is to examine the conditions through which opportunities and mobility occur for different populations, and the ways in which race is a factor in these processes. Prior to the 1960s, racial and ethnic minorities were substantially excluded from higher education through a combination of overt (legal) and covert (social and political) mechanisms. The civil rights movement of the 1960s created a profound change in America's opportunity structure, with access to higher education (as well as with employment opportunities) being among the primary catalysts for the integration of minorities into mainstream America. As a result, the rate of Blacks, 25 years or older, who completed 4 years of college or more[1] increased from 2.2% to 14.3% between 1950 and 2000 (United States Census Bureau, 2000b).

The gains in college participation among non-Whites have certainly been substantial since the 1960s, which speaks to the extent to which equality of opportunity has taken hold in American society. Yet there continue to be concerns about equality of condition at the dawn of the twenty-first century. Between 1960 and 1980, aggressive desegregation efforts resulted in a decrease in the rate of southern Black students attending racially segregated schools from approximately 99% to 54%. By 2003, however, the trend had reversed, with 71% of southern Black students again relegated to segregated schools, while the average White student nationwide attended a school that was nearly 80% White (Orfield & Lee, 2005). That same year, Black and Latino fourth graders were nearly 10 times more likely than White fourth graders to attend a school where more than 75% of the students were eligible for free or reduced-price lunches (NCES, 2005). Indeed, while "America may be a land of opportunity. . . it is also a land of inequality" (Lareau, 2003, p. 3). There remains a stubborn and persistent relationship between race, class, and the quantity and quality of resources and opportunities relative to educational mobility.

Since W. E. B. Du Bois's groundbreaking sociological work, *The Philadelphia Negro* (1899), there have been a plethora of studies on racial stratification, with a great deal of research devoted to the study of educational opportunity and mobility. While there is greater consensus on the extent to which racial gaps exist in

9

such places as America's education system, there is less agreement on what determines disparities along the color line. However, most social science research tends to acknowledge that perspectives on the causes for and consequences of racial stratification is not complete without describing the ecological configurations of race, ethnicity, and class, or the influence of the intersection between these social constructs (Anderson & Massey, 2001). Additionally, advantages and disadvantages that groups experience because of race, ethnicity, and class are accentuated by these very social constructs, resulting in disparities in the distribution of resources, opportunities, and educational outcomes. This book is an attempt to capture the ecological conditions and organizational arrangements that enable or constrain educational mobility for AAPIs.

Positioning AAPIs within the research on how and why racial inequality manifests itself in social and educational mobility is challenging considering that most of this research defines the boundaries of race in America as a Black-White construct. Until recently there has actually been very little research that considers how and where AAPIs fall along the color line and how race, ethnicity, and class, among other ecological factors, play out in terms of the mobility of Asian Americans and Pacific Islanders. In fact, AAPIs are often treated as though they are invisible—irrelevant in the many important discussions that exist about educational and social mobility in America. In the few instances when AAPIs are included in important research and policy debates, it is typically to make a point about the relative position of other groups; the AAPI population has simply served as a reference point against which the needs of others can be compared. These delimitations require further deconstruction, particularly with regard to their relationship to broader paradigms that guide how and why AAPIs are positioned in our understanding of how race is a factor in the stratification of educational and social mobility in American society.

AAPIs AND AMERICA'S EQUITY AGENDA

The unique and relative position of AAPIs along the color line and within the equity agenda is predicated upon the confluence of key conceptual problems. At the most basic level, normative framing is often the basis for examining equity in America, invoked to identify populations that may warrant resources or services that can help close the gap identified in the research. Essentially, the goal of normative framing is to identify how different racial groups are unevenly distributed across a particular outcome (i.e., participation, graduation, GPA, and so on). Within this framework, the experiences, outcomes, and representation of AAPIs are examined vis-à-vis Blacks and Whites, which often results in the conclusion that problems related to race in American society are dichotomous, with Blacks at one end of the racial spectrum and Whites on the other (Chang, Witt-Sandia,

Jones, & Hakuta, 1999). This conceptual framing is designed intentionally to close the achievement and attainment gaps between the low performers (Blacks) and high performers (Whites). Within the Black-White paradigm, AAPIs—along with Latinos and Native Americans—have vicarious and problematic positions.

Consider that in a 1927 Supreme Court ruling[2] on how to position Asian Americans in racially segregated schools, the court ruled that Blacks and Asian Americans were "equivalent and interchangeable" (Wu, 2002). This historical frame is defined by Whites versus non-Whites, which places AAPIs in the latter grouping. More recently, we find the placement of AAPIs on the other end of the racial spectrum. According to sociologist Andrew Hacker (2003), in *Black and White, Separate, Hostile, and Unequal*, AAPIs symbolically fall under the "White umbrella" in a racial paradigm that continues to be reduced to two groups, Whites and non-Whites. His claim is based on a belief that AAPIs do not fall within the "out-group," which he defines as those groups that face structural barriers.

In the recent book by William Bowen, Martin Kurzweil, and Eugene Tobin, *Equity and Excellence in American Higher Education* (2005), as in many other important scholarly debates about access and equity in higher education, Blacks define the "minority" category, which is where you will also find Latinos, while Whites define the "nonminority" category, which is where Asian Americans and Pacific Islanders are situated. Doug Massey has even stated that "Whites and Asian Americans are jumbled together in a way that is making the distinctions between the groups less obvious" (Massey, 2008).

The position of AAPIs as a "nonminority" minority group has come to define the contemporary model minority concept with their vicarious position within the Black-White paradigm enabling them to be a wild card in debates about equity issues in America (Takagi, 1992). In many cases of this instance, AAPIs are simply selectively included in analysis that helps to make a point about the relative disadvantage of "minority" groups. Put another way, discovering and disseminating knowledge about AAPIs is often not a goal, but rather the population serves as a reference point within which the needs of others can be compared. This has been particularly pronounced in debates about selective college admissions and affirmative action, which began with inquiries into UC Berkeley's admission policies in the 1980s (Takaki, 1998), became even more heated with Proposition 209 in California, and continued through the most recent Supreme Court decisions on affirmative action (National Commission on Asian American and Pacific Islander Research in Education, 2008).

In contemporary affirmative action debates, we find AAPIs positioned as a group that is adversely affected by affirmative action, and that it is AAPIs, not Whites, who have the most to gain with ending affirmative action. Essentially, with affirmative action, AAPIs are the biggest "victims." Ward Connerly, architect of the California Civil Rights Initiative, made a similar point about AAPIs reacting to the number of Black students admitted to UC Berkeley and UCLA, which appeared to be rebounding from the damage caused by Proposition 209. He claimed that the increase in Black enrollment at these campuses has meant "kicking out" Asian students (Connerly, 2006). The perspective was further popularized by a number of news stories about Jian Li, an applicant to Princeton University who filed a civil rights complaint with the Office for Civil Rights for not being admitted to the institution despite being in the top one percent of his high school class.[3]

In 2009 the University of California approved a new admission policy—one of the most dramatic changes since 1960—which intended to eliminate the requirement that applicants take two SAT subject tests and reduce the number of students guaranteed admission. Ling-Chi Wang called the change, "affirmative action for Whites" (quoted in Chea, 2009) because internal research by the UC system projected a 20% decrease for AAPIs with most gains found among Whites. Ward Connerly (2009), in wake of a considerable outcry from AAPI advocacy organizations, reached out to the community through newspaper commentaries. He wrote:

> There is one truth that is universally applicable in the era of "diversity," especially in American universities: an absolute unwillingness to accept the verdict of color-blind policies. . . . The proposed UC admissions policies are so egregious and so dramatically discriminatory against Asians. . . . Please join Mr. Ward Connerly and other community leaders to put together a plan to fight against this new proposal.

Connerly (2009) also took aim at AAPI advocacy organizations directly who opposed his outreach to the community, saying, "The so-called Asian civil rights groups, such as Chinese for Affirmative Action, that purport to represent the interest of Asians have not served their communities with distinction."

The inclusion of AAPIs within affirmative action debates hasn't just been relegated to politics and what can be found in mainstream media; it has also been the focus of a number of empirical studies. Daniel Golden (2006), in *The Price of Admission*, says that AAPIs are deliberately held to a higher standard in selective college admissions to maintain an acceptable level of AAPI enrollment. Espenshade and Chung (2005) says that if Princeton University were to end affirmative action, AAPIs would be the "biggest winners" occupying four out of every five seats created by accepting fewer African American and Latino students. The decline of Black and Latino students throughout selective colleges that do not consider race for admissions decisions has resulted in AAPIs assuming the identity of conspicuous adversaries of diversity in higher education.

Beyond the discourse of selective college admissions and affirmative action, we also see AAPIs selectively included in studies that have posited a cultural explanation for the racial achievement gap in America's schools. Anthropologist John Ogbu's (1991) theory of oppositional culture posits that Blacks experience *low-effort syndrome* as an oppositional response to subordination and oppression. In mainstream society this theory is often viewed as a Black "attitude problem." In order for there to be a true correlation, the Black attitude problem/low achievement hypothesis requires that a good attitude/high achievement hypothesis also hold true. However, when AAPIs perform well in school they are generally considered to be "acting White"; yet when behavioral problems arise among AAPIs, these individuals are seen to be "acting Black" (Coloma, 2006). AAPIs often straddle two "peg holes" depending on the issue at hand, depending on how they are perceived relative to "Black" in one regard and "White" in another.

Put another way, how AAPIs are positioned in debates about racial stratification in United States society depends largely on interest convergence (Bell, 1987), which is defined by how they can support or refute the position of the interests of others. Thus AAPIs are examined within these paradigms, not to explain AAPI achievement, but to provide an example of why these theoretical propositions hold true for others. In the context of Ogbu's theory of opposition, if it can be validated by the study of how culture operates among AAPIs, then the theory has greater validity in, and is not an anomaly for, explaining the underachievement of Blacks.

Despite the selective inclusion of AAPIs in certain equity debates, most likely they will not be found in national discourse on educational equity. Because of the normative racial paradigm it is evident that it is widely acceptable to exclude them in policy discussions about race, omitted by scholars and policy makers in their pursuit of the equity agenda (Teranishi, 2007; Kiang, 2006). In many cases, this is because the inclusion of AAPIs does not help in the final conclusion, which is ultimately about the ways in which Blacks and Latinos are deficient compared to Whites. This was even true for the report produced by the the the Council of Ecnomic Advisers for the President's Commission on Race (1998), *Changing America: Indicators of Social and Economic Well-Being by Race and Hispanic Origin*. Despite the goals of this report, which were in part to "to educate Americans about the facts surrounding the issue of race in America" (p. 1), the AAPI population was almost completely excluded from the analysis.

The exclusion of AAPIs in equity policy debates is problematic and noticeable in our nation's higher education priorities. There is almost no recognition of AAPIs in the community college sector, which is where AAPIs have their highest enrollment in United States higher education (National Commission on AAPI Research in Education, 2008). This is problematic as President Barack Obama, the United States Department of Education, and a number of education foundations are making substantial investments in this sector of higher education with little input on how AAPIs fit within and are affected by these higher education priorities. Another area of interest where AAPIs are excluded is in the efforts to support the work of Minority-Serving Institutions (MSI), which includes Historically Black Colleges and Universities, Hispanic-Serving Institutions, and Tribal Colleges, even though there is "Asian American Native American Pacific Islander Serving Institution" (AANAPISI) legislation. Unfortunately, without a connection of these institutions to the MSI program, it is difficult to demonstrate the relevance of the AANAPISI program to the success of low-income AAPI students and other underrepresented student populations to policy makers, institutional leaders, researchers, and the public. This book calls into question this blatant exclusion in some instances and ambiguous positioning in other instances, when it comes to the inclusion of AAPIs in important equity debates in higher education. To bring clarity to these issues, I begin with a critical examination of the conceptual framing that is often the culprit for how AAPIs are positioned with the American racial paradigm.

RACE IN COMPARATIVE RESEARCH

Understanding the position of AAPIs within the racial frame of the United States begins with an understanding what defines race. As discussed earlier, race is a relative concept. There can only be a minority group with a majority group. The social position of a White majority—the privilege and normative position—is only possible through the existence of non-White minority groups. Race is a concept that exists through, and has meaning because of, differences between groups. Thus it is the gap between groups, when it comes to status attainment and other social indicators, that largely defines the social boundaries of race. It is these concerns among sociologists—the causes and consequences of racial stratification in our society and the conditions through which opportunities and mobility occur for different groups—that make comparative research essential to social science on racial inequality.

Although there is certainly a place for the use of comparative research, it should not be the only basis for understanding race in American society. Historically, in fact,it is exactly an overreliance on comparative race research that has concerned scholars in the past, who have noted that this perspective can lead to a system of deficit thinking. Richard Valencia (1997) states that deficit thinking is a narrow set of assumptions about marginalized groups that is "tantamount to 'blaming the victim' . . . [and is] founded on imputation, not documentation" (p. xi). Blacks and Latinos are viewed as a problem in comparative research, while Whites, and in some cases Asians, are viewed as a solution. I argue in this book that the gap in educational outcomes between groups—certainly an indicator that should be addressed—does not necessarily reveal what the problem is. Nor do the education achievement and attainment gaps necessarily represent where solutions can be found.

For AAPIs, normative framing can lead to problems regarding the conceptualization and positioning of the population in America's equity agenda. It has been well documented, for instance, that the inclusion of AAPIs in research and policy is challenged by inaccurate, incomplete, misleading, and often unreliable information that does not represent the population well relative to other groups.

Many studies have been found to poorly accommodate distinctions within the AAPI population. In terms of data itself, even the U.S. Census Bureau has faced many challenges in finding ways to more accurately collect data from and describe the Asian American and Pacific Islander populations (Omi, 2000).[4] The trends in how AAPIs are treated in research and policy that are emerging are disturbing. In addition to being mischaracterized in comparative racial analysis, or worse, excluded from analysis, AAPIs are often also mixed with "other" or "international" categories (Teranishi, 2007). Very few studies and policies acknowledge the ethnic, language, and other unique demographic distinctions within the population, and how these affect their comparability to other racial groups in the United States. The limitations and treatment of data are just the tip of the iceberg when it comes to the inclusion of AAPIs in discussions about race, equity, and opportunity in American life.

Problems of comparisons between racial groups arise when researchers, policy makers, and practitioners attempt to find solutions for the racial gap by drawing inferences from the size and magnitude of the racial achievement gap. Higher education policy has been driven by untested assumptions about the validity of racial factors, with conclusions about the effect of these factors based solely on cross-sectional, normative framing. More specifically, results of cross-sectional research are commonly used to reach conclusions about the relative differences that exist between groups, and the between-group differences are often used to determine the treatment of a particular group (Teranishi, 2007). Walter Allen (1999) cites this paradigm commonly applied to educational research as an often "misguided and counterproductive game of 'oppression sweepstakes'" (pp. 206–207), whereby various groups are pitted against one another in competition for the dubious status of "Year's Most Oppressed."

In many cases, studies are not designed to critically examine, acknowledge, or appreciate the heterogeneity that exists within a racial category. Rather, comparative racial frameworks assume that racial categories as a whole are consistently homogeneous across groups with regard to their characteristics. As a result, the actual educational experiences and processes of students from different racial groups as a whole, and as distinct parts, are often concealed. By adopting a comparative racial framework that combines broad racial groups, we assume that there is enough consistency in the homogeneity inside racial groups that they are equally comparable and the instruments used to measure differences across groups are universally applicable. I argue that racial groups are neither equally nor consistently comparable and that the approaches to studying differing student populations are not universally applicable.

Positioning AAPIs within America's equity agenda requires transcending the intellectual boundaries that have severely limited—and even undermined—the knowledge about the intersection of race and educational opportunities and outcomes generally, and for the AAPI experience specifically. Existing research paradigms that are commonly applied to the study of Black, Latino, Native American, and AAPI students neither promote a better understanding about any individual racial population nor provide a perspective that allows us to constructively improve their educational experiences or outcomes. What makes it particularly difficult is the fact that race in itself is a complex social phenomenon that is difficult to define and conceptualize.

DESTABILIZING CONCEPTUAL BLOCKAGES

There are promising new theoretical frameworks in the social sciences and education that have emerged in recent years that provide alternative perspectives for examining the AAPI educational experience. These theoretical propositions challenge our understanding of the relative effects of racial stratification on post-secondary preparation, participation, and outcomes—social and organizational problems that have challenged scholars and policy makers for several decades. The age-old problem is simply this: Although a persistent gap exists across groups on a variety of measures of academic achievement and outcomes, policy makers and educational researchers have not come to a consensus about why the gap exists or what the gap represents. In other words, despite the significance of race in higher education research, policy, and practice, there is still a great deal that is unknown about the complexity of America's problem with race, such as the extent to which race works in similar and different ways for different racial groups. Consider the studies that have examined the differences in the educational experiences and outcomes of native-born and immigrant Black populations (Bowen & Bok, 1998; Massey, Mooney, & Torres, 2007; Sutherland, 2008). Other research has challenged the notion that the Black population is homogeneous in terms of social class and residential patterns by pointing to the growth among Black middle-class and suburban residents in America (Ascher & Branch-Smith, 2005; Ferguson; 1999; Teranishi & Briscoe, 2008).

Research on Latinos and Native Americans has also identified ways in which treating these populations as monolithic groups is problematic. Recognizing that Latinos represent a complex and ethnically diverse population with unique immigration histories, William Perez et al. (2009) has examined the educational pursuits of high-achieving, undocumented Latinos who face a number of unique challenges in their pursuit of higher education. Miguel Ceja (2001) has paid particular attention to the ways in which gender is a factor in the college aspirations and choices of Chicanas in Los Angeles. Native Americans and Alaskan Natives represent one of the most heterogeneous racial categories in the United States, consisting of more than 560 distinct federally recognized tribes and at least half as many more distinct unrecognized tribal groups (U.S. Department of the Interior, 2008), each with its own history, culture, and language. Amy Fann (2009) has examined how these distinctions within the population create complex challenges when positioning the Native American population in comparative research and policy perspectives on race and equity in higher education.

These studies are complicating many long-standing assumptions about the compositions and conditions of racial groups in America, which have too often been oversimplified and generalized socially and politically (Allport, 1954). In the context of education, intergroup comparisons often conceal the distinctions between groups, including what we know about individual groups or the differences between groups. Jencks and Phillips (1998) describe *labeling bias* as the mismatch between what an indicator (e.g., test scores) claims to measure and what it is actually measuring. Race, as a predictive variable, is often used to explain variation in educational outcomes (e.g., "controlling for other background characteristics, being Black predicts . . . "). In some instances, researchers and policy makers have asserted that the effects of race are really a representation of the effects of social class. In other words, policies that help low-income students are good for addressing racial inequality because Blacks and Latinos have the most to gain through such an approach. However, results of studies indicate that so-called race-neutral, class-based approaches have shown little progress in closing access and attainment gaps between racial groups (Holley & Spencer, 1998; Tiendes, Cortes, & Niu, 2004). These approaches also do not recognize or appreciate the salience of race in the stratification of American society.

These various perspectives on race point to the need for research to continue to grapple with what "race" is capturing as a socially constructed concept in American society. The study of AAPIs requires careful consideration of what the AAPI category represents demographically, socially, and politically, and the ways in which labeling bias is a factor in comparative research. Attention to these distinctions raises awareness to important, but often misunderstood problems in research on the population, particularly when researchers try to make sense of "being Asian" as an independent variable. Simply put, the AAPI population is categorically unique with heterogeneity within the population that is difficult to capture comparatively with reference to other racial groups.

Driven by the need for alternative approaches to thinking about race and educational policy, I argue that current policy research is limited in its ability to understand the ways in which differences within race and class groups have implications for what we know across groups, as well as within any particular group. Thus there is a need for new ways of thinking about and engaging race in research and policy in a manner that captures the multiple, nuanced, and complex features of different subgroups within each racial category. The desired outcome of this work is to find ways for research and policy to be informed by better information about racial stratification, including how it is conceptualized, measured, and applied in research, policy, and practice relative to access to higher education.

Racialization and Rearticulation

Omi and Winant (1989) coined the term *racial formation* to describe the process by which social, economic, and political forces determine the meaning and importance of race in society. They state: "Race is pre-eminently a *sociohistorical* concept. Racial categories and the meaning of race are given concrete expression by the specific social relations and historical context in which they are embedded. Racial meanings have varied tremendously over time and between societies" (p. 15). As Frank Wu (2002) has pointed out in his book *Yellow*, race is meaningless in the abstract; it acquires its meanings as it operates on its surroundings.

The concept of race has evolved over time, demonstrating the complexity of the term and the varied ways in which its definitions have been used in scientific, social, and legal arenas. This theoretical framing moves the conceptualization of race beyond the biological arguments that have been invoked to define race (i.e., the insistence that physical characteristics are accepted as proof of racial membership). According to the American Anthropological Association's (1998) *Statement on Race*, genetic evidence of major variations *within* "racial" groups as opposed to *between* them has contributed to a determination that "race" is indeed a social construct that masks itself as a biological one. In other words, these biological distinctions (e.g., hair type, skin color, and facial features) are arbitrary and subjective. Omi and Winant (1994) further explain the conceptualization of race:

> Although the concept of race invokes biologically based human characteristics . . . selection of these particular human features for purposes of racial signification is always and necessarily a social and historical process. . . . Indeed, the categories employed to differentiate among human groups along racial lines reveal themselves . . . to be at best imprecise, and at worst completely arbitrary. (p. 55)

Similar to other racial populations, the historical positioning of AAPIs within the racial frame is indeed unique and arbitrary. Massey, Charles, Lundy, and Fischer (2003) in *The Source of the River* wrote, "The United States now houses a variegated population characterized not by a single, all-encompassing racial duality, but by a multidimensional intersection of changing racial and ethnic continua" (p. 4).

Omi and Winant (1994) describe *rearticulation* as the process through which existing social meanings reorganize into new forms. The new social meaning does not displace the original, but rather "resituates it on a new horizon that includes new methods and new objects of study" (Lowe, 1995). Rearticulation of race can be considered a useful and constructive step toward a shifting consciousness around race to think of it in new, more complex ways. This can lead to more than one interpretation of a group, including how they are categorically unique and possess multiple, nuanced, and complex features. However, the rearticulation process may also be problematic from the perspective of the group itself, as it is often the result of race being invoked by others through social and political processes that may or may not be in the best interest of the group. Although Asian Americans were originally viewed as a "yellow peril" threat in the early part of the twentieth century and later a danger to national security during World War II, they have since been lauded as the model minority with a narrow focus on exceptional studiousness, diligence, and intelligence. Relative to contemporary equity debates in higher education, the position of AAPIs has often been invoked, not by AAPIs themselves, but to make a point for others. These are important propositions about race as we continue to strive toward solving our problem with the color line, and as the racial tapestry of American society becomes increasingly intertwined and complex.

Critical Race Theory

Critical race theory (CRT) has been applied to the study of racial stratification in higher education challenging dominant paradigms and placing the educational experiences of students of color in a broader context of social, institutional, legal, and historical contexts (Delgado, 1995; Solorzano, Villalpando, & Oseguera, 2005). Solorzano (1998) explains that "critical race theory in education challenges the traditional claims of the educational system and its institutions to objectivity, meritocracy, color and gender blindness, race and gender neutrality, and equal opportunity" (p. 122). Thus an understanding of the educational experiences of the Asian American and Pacific Islander population requires a framework that acknowledges the unique racialized status of the population, including their social, political, and structural positions in society.

Conceptually, critical race theory in education challenges ahistoricism and the unidisciplinary focus of most analyses and instead centralizes race and racism in education by placing them in both historical and contemporary contexts using interdisciplinary methods (Delgado, 1989, 1995; Garcia, 1995; Harris, 1994; Olivas, 1990). CRT challenges the dominant discourse on race and racism in education by examining how educational theory, policy, and practice have been used to subordinate certain racial and ethnic groups (Solorzano, 1998). CRT is an effective lens for problematizing traditional notions of race by examining the intersections of ethnicity, social class, and immigration among the AAPI population (Bell, 1987; Carrasco, 1996; Delgado, 1995, 1989; Olivas, 1990).

Critical race theory has also been found to be an innovative interpretive framework for researchers, policy makers, and practitioners to challenge mainstream approaches to higher education policy analysis (Solorzano & Villalpando, 1998; Solorzano et al., 2005; Tate, 1997). CRT asserts that the needs of marginalized populations are often overlooked by the agenda served by normative frameworks. Therefore, CRT is an effective lens for examining and challenging normative paradigms, which define mainstream policy problems and determine appropriate concerns for research in education. Moreover, CRT can be used as a way not only to understand policies and decision making and their impact on a population but also to look critically at the very presumptions and reasoning that underlie them. These presumptions often go unquestioned and unchallenged.

Categorical Inequality

Sociological theory on social stratification also has useful concepts for understanding the position of AAPIs within discussions on social mobility. First, sociologists are interested in the categorization of individuals and groups, which are socially defined in nominal and ordinal terms. *Nominal categories* are ascribed qualitative attributes, like race and gender. *Ordinal categories* are the rank of persons along some quantitative continuum of social structures (e.g., income, occupation, and education attainment) (Blau, 1977). Second, individuals and groups within categories are often examined in the context of *stratification,* which is the uneven distribution of ascribed groups along the continuum of ordinal social structures. Stratification is measured by examining the degree of variability in the distribution of individuals and groups (i.e., nominal categories) across ordinal categories (i.e., ranked social structures). *Inequality* is the extent to which groups distribute unevenly within ordinal categories. Thus a larger uneven distribution of individuals across nominal groups represents greater inequality.

According to Charles Tilly (1998), stratification and inequality, at their most basic levels, come down to the relationship between two mechanisms: (1) the distribution of people to ordinal categories, and (2) the institutionalization of practices (and policies) that allocate resources unequally across these categories. Tilly refers to this as *categorical inequality.* He posits that categorical inequality is "durable" and reinforced by design to maintain opportunity structures that benefit one category over another. Categories are reinforced through societal boundaries that are unique for different groups, with categorical stratification and inequality being defined and controlled through scripts. The dominant script is often as simple as a generalization or stereotype that determines the treatment of different groups. The scripts that are associated with groups represent "accepted knowledge" until it is mitigated by an alternative perspective of the group.

A *categorical lens* is a useful conceptual tool for at least two reasons. First, it moves discussions about race beyond what individuals and groups are able to accomplish by accounting for the systemic nature of how race operates in society. As Tilly (1998) says, "Large, significant inequalities in advantages among human beings correspond mainly to categorical differences . . . rather than to individual differences in attributes, propensities, or performances" (p. 7). This is an important point, considering that higher education literature often attributes inequality to group characteristics and does not account for the explanatory power that is added by considering the extent to which systems, practices, and policies reinforce such inequality. Thus, for AAPIs, the discussion of education and achievement needs to move beyond the dominant scripts of hard work, strict parents, and other factors that are attributed to what occurs among AAPI individuals and families. A categorical lens is critical of individual explanations of achievement or mobility and places inequality across groups within the context of institutional systems and practices.

Second, a categorical lens is useful for critically examining what we know about differences that exist within broad racial categories, including subgroups along ethnic, class, and other demographic distinctions. These distinctions that exist within racial groups are often overlooked when the focus on groups is from a comparative perspective. Research and policy need to be shaped with careful consideration of the limitations of between-group differences for an understanding of any one group. Capturing categorical inequality can result in new perspectives on policies and practices that are driven by the needs for different groups within categories because larger systems, practices, and policies work in unique ways for each group. It is a rare occasion to focus on how these mechanisms affect the AAPI population when the dominant narrative about race is defined in Black and White terms. In this book I demonstrate that not only is race more than just Black and White, it is a reality in all of our lives and operates in complex and meaningful ways. In describing the need to transcend race in America beyond Black and White, Frank Wu (2002) writes, "My premise is straightforward. Race is more than Black and White, literally and figuratively. Yellow belongs. Gray predominates" (p. 18). Indeed, there is a lot of gray in between Black and White.

THIS BOOK RESPONDS to the need for AAPIs to be positioned within the interest of social scientists related to two fundamental aspects of race. First, building on the concept of racial formation (Omi & Winant, 1994), I set out to capture an accurate rendering of the AAPI population, as well as what defines the boundaries of the racial category. Second, in the context of categorical inequality (Tilly, 1998) I attempt to more fully articulate the conditions through which opportunities and mobility occur for AAPIs, and the ways in which race is a factor in these processes.

Given these goals, I have begun this book with a critical systematic examination of the existing theoretical propositions that have served as the basis for the assumptions about AAPIs and their participation in United States higher education, replacing them with conceptual perspectives that challenge and rearticulate the socially defined categories that have been applied to the study of AAPIs. Doing so challenges the extent to which AAPIs as a whole can be used to represent the population in its parts. This is made possible through a rearticulation of the categorical boundaries of AAPIs with regard to their unique demographic features and through an investigation of how their population characteristics are tied to their position within the stratification of educational mobility in American society.

From the perspective of critical race theory, challenging and reconceptualizing narrowly defined categories can move research, policy, and practice from a mode of generalized thought about race, class, and other social structures to a more granulated and contextualized treatment of inequality of educational mobility for all students. A reconceptualized perspective on how AAPIs fit within the boundaries of race is central to the ideas and perspectives that are offered in subsequent chapters on the educational experiences and outcomes of AAPIs who are indeed a part of a categorically unique community.

CHAPTER 2

Students, Families, and the Pursuit of College

For some, Pang and Tony may not seem that different; both are Asian Americans in the 12th grade, with nearly the same 3.4 and 3.5 GPAs and high aspirations to attend college after high school. Pang and Tony have been diligent students, always making sure their homework gets done each night, and both of their parents insist that their child goes to college to pursue an opportunity to earn a level of education that they were not afforded. Despite the similarities between Pang and Tony, their upbringings and the social conditions through which they have navigated to get to this point have been quite different. Most relevant to this book is the unlikely event that they will have the same educational trajectory from this point forward in terms of college.

Pang, who is Hmong, was born in Thailand. Her parents ended up in Thailand as refugees, fearfully driven out of Laos following America's withdrawal from Vietnam in the first half of the 1970s. Pang's parents lived in a refugee camp for many years before Pang was born, and Pang spent the first five years of her life there. After being displaced for nearly 2 decades without a country to call home, the family was admitted to and settled in the United States as refugees. The U.S. government told them they would be relocated to Fresno, California.

Fast-forwarding 10 years after her arrival to the United States, Pang, now in 12th grade, lives with her husband and his family. Also living with her husband's family is the wife of her brother-in-law, who is no longer enrolled in school. Pang says that she is lucky because she is still enrolled in school. She tells me that her education comes first, so "on holidays and weekends, there's lots of payback" for what she doesn't do for the in-laws during the week. Pang talked about juggling school, living with her in-laws, and trying to help out her immediate family. "I feel bad sometimes. I feel like I cannot take care of my own family." Her parents are now separated and Pang's four younger siblings live with their mother, an aunt, and two cousins. Pang also has two older brothers who recently moved to Minnesota to live with relatives. Neither of Pang's brothers finished high school. Pang says that her younger sisters complain that her mom is strict with them because Pang fights with her mom too much. Pang did not have a lot to say about her father, although she seemed to still have contact with him. A lot of pressure rests on Pang's shoulders as she will be the first in her family to go to college, let alone finish high school.

23

Tony was born in San Francisco, California. His parents immigrated to the United States in the mid-1960s by way of Hong Kong, following the advent of the Cultural Revolution in China. Tony's parents ended up in the United States through sponsorship from a Christian church, which settled them in Detroit, Michigan. Tony says that his parents described Detroit as being very cold and not a good place for work. Through secondary migration, Tony's parents were able to connect with other family members in the United States and moved to China-town in San Francisco; this was all before Tony and his only sister, who is older, were born. When Tony talks about his childhood, he says moving around a lot stands out in his memory: "I think it was probably three or four times." The family eventually ended up in the Richmond District of San Francisco when Tony was in middle school, which he describes as being diverse—predominately Chinese, Jew-ish, and Russian. Tony says that he does not see his parents a lot because they are "always working," so he spends a lot of time at home alone. This does not bother Tony; he does his own laundry, cooks his own food, and does his homework with-out anybody keeping track of him. Tony's sister attends a selective public univer-sity in California. She gives him a lot of advice about college, as do other members of his extended family who have gone to college. Although Tony doesn't live in Chinatown, he still goes there for church and is involved with a lot of community activities.

Of Pang and Tony, it would be easy to assume that Pang's story would align more closely with that of a third student, Trung, given that he is Vietnamese, which makes them both Southeast Asians. Actually, Trung would likely disagree. Where Trung lives in San Jose, California, he says that many of his friends, neighbors, and classmates are Chinese. Trung says that he and his friends have a healthy competi-tion for who will end up at the best university.

Trung's parents came to the United States 6 years ago when he was 11 years old. Trung says that after they arrived, his dad left immediately and went back to Vietnam. Trung lives with his mom, two sisters, aunt, uncle, and two other cousins. Trung's mom has a college degree from Vietnam, which he describes as "a big deal" since most education is costly, including grade school. In Vietnam his mom was a banker, but she could not find a comparable job in the United States. He takes pride in the fact that his mom went back to school when she was 40 years old to get another degree. But Trung adds that his mom is disappointed with the education she received from the for-profit technical college she attended because "it didn't end up getting her a better job." Trung hopes to follow in the footsteps of his two sisters who both attend public 4-year colleges in a neighboring city.

Lilly, a Filipina, lives in Daly City, California, where her parents settled upon their arrival in the United States. Lilly's parents were born and raised in Luzon, the northernmost region of the Philippines, and came to the United States along with many other Filipinos following the 1965 Immigration Act. Lilly and her three siblings were all born in this country. Lilly now lives with her mother and two younger brothers. Lilly's dad works in Las Vegas, where he holds a job in retail, so she only sees him on holidays when he returns to the family home. Lilly's older sister moved away for college when she finished high school; Lilly says that her mom has a lot of plans for her sister after she graduates and returns home. She says that her mom is often sad because of her sister's absence. "It's kind of a double standard . . . if my sister was a boy, it wouldn't be an issue." Lilly says that there is a lot of tension in the home because of "tradition." She says that she and her siblings are "Americanized," but her parents are still very traditional. She gives the example of "the last supper in the kitchen, and the big spoons and forks on the wall—you know the traditional Filipino stuff." Lilly adds that she is embarrassed telling her friends who are not Filipino that they need to take their shoes off before they enter the house.

The particulars of these four high school students' stories are uniquely their own. Nevertheless, they serve as portraits of the varied immigration histories that represent the Asian American experience. These backgrounds, coupled with the powerful social forces of social class, language, and cultural traditions, play out in unique ways for communities within the AAPI population and ultimately become significant factors in the educational opportunities and trajectories among these students. As C. Wright Mills (1959) said, "The life of an individual cannot be adequately understood without references to the [social settings] within which his biography is enacted" (p. 161). The premise for this chapter is that a proper account for the mobility of a population is not complete without consideration of the ecological configuration in which it occurs.

Given that race, ethnicity, and social class are key factors that influence the type of college a student attends if a student attends college at all, it is essential that these social conditions be taken into account when examining the educational opportunities and outcomes of a population—AAPIs notwithstanding. Consider the relationship between socioeconomic status (SES) and the likelihood one will graduate high school, enroll in college, or earn a degree. Among U.S. high school graduates in 2003, only 54% from the lowest income quartile enrolled in college, compared to 82% of high school graduates in the top quartile (Bowen et al., 2005).

In addition to how ecological conditions operate independently, it is equally important to take account of how they intersect, working as a collective force. This point is captured succinctly by research that has found that the effects of race on educational mobility are dramatically obscured by the impact of class dynamics and economic resources (Wilson, 1987). Dalton Conley's (1999) research has examined class inequality within the context of race, asking, "to what extent can class explain racial inequality?" He posits that, "while the sorting of social positions may occur predominately within the process of formal schooling, the socioeconomic endowments that each child brings to the educational system powerfully predict that individual's chances for academic success" (p. 55). Thus some of what we see in terms of intergroup differences in educational outcomes can be explained by the context of social conditions that happen to be more prevalent among some groups than among others. We find that these same dynamics also exist with regard to the effects of nativity, language ability, and other factors associated with particular populations. Accordingly, an examination of AAPI educational mobility must be informed in part by an accurate rendering of the ecological conditions through which their postsecondary educational mobility occurs.

THE DEMOGRAPHY OF THE AAPI POPULATION

The stories of Pang, Tony, Trung, and Lilly are illustrative for how difficult and problematic it is to generalize a "typical" AAPI experience. In other words, if you choose an AAPI student at random, one should not expect, with any degree of certainty, that he or she is representative of all AAPIs. Accordingly, the universal success story of AAPIs, which has been described as having a high degree of generalizeability throughout the population, needs to be examined in the context of their demographic features, such as their complex and sorted history of immigration and settlement. Although few would argue that the AAPI population is not a definable racial category, it is important to recognize that the boundaries that define *Asian American and Pacific Islander* are socially constructed, and need to be placed in a social, political, and institutional reality (Omi & Winant, 2003). While the population represents a single entity in certain contexts, such as for interracial group comparisons, it is equally important to understand the ways in which the demography of the AAPI population represents a complex set of social realities for individuals and communities that fall within this category. Barringer, Gardner, and Levin (1995) in *Asian and Pacific Islanders in the United States* said of the AAPI population, "practically or theoretically, it makes little sense to lump together Americans of Asian origin, much less those of Asian and Pacific origin" (p. 2). The rest of this section considers the population both as a single entity and also in distinct parts.

Immigration

The United States has always been a population fueled by immigration. Waves of immigration have fluctuated historically, resulting in varying degrees of impact on population change in the United States. From around 1850 to 1910 the net gain in population growth due to immigration steadily increased from 20% to 50% of the population. The net gain in total population due to immigration began to subside around 1910, a trend that lasted until the 1950s. After the 1965 Immigration Act the net gain in total population due to immigration picked up again and has been increasing steadily since. At some point, all immigrant groups have encountered a distinct racialization process that places them into racial categories. This has

Figure 2.1. Asian Population in the United States, 1860–2020

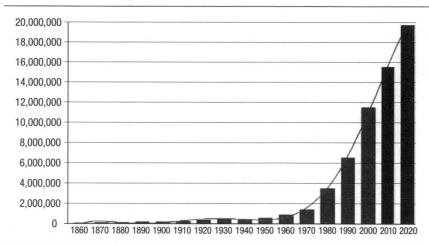

Note. Data for 2010 and 2020 are projections.

Source. Adapted from Barringer et al. (1995); U.S. Census Bureau (2008).

been particularly pronounced among European immigrants whose White identity was formed through the process of distinguishing them from non-Whites. Today, ethnic Whites are comfortably White, possessing the option to choose whether or not, or to what degree, ethnicity is a part of their lives (Waters, 1990).

For AAPIs, immigration has also been a central component for population change and the creation of the AAPI racial category. The presence of AAPIs in the United States can be traced back to the early part of the nineteenth century. Going back as far as 1820, there were data collected on U.S. immigration from Asia, mostly from China. This immigration occurred despite limited U.S. access for Asians until the middle of the twentieth century due to restrictive quotas and discriminatory legal exclusion. Nearly all immigrants up to this point in America's immigration history were from Europe. As recently as 1955, in fact, the Asian American population was significantly less than one percent of the total U.S. population (Daniels, 1997). Exceptions to this trend could be found in Hawaii, which was then a territory and therefore excluded from U.S. population figures. In Hawaii, 58% of the people in 1940 were of Asian descent (Tamura, 2001).

The slow trickle of Asian immigrants began to change significantly following the passage of the 1965 Immigration Act, which created many new opportunities for immigrants who were formerly excluded; immigrants from Asia and Latin America made up the majority of immigrants to the United States following this change in immigration policy. Between 1960 and 2000, the Asian American and Pacific Islander population grew tenfold from approximately 1 million to over 10 million (see Figure 2.1). During this same time period, Asia was the source of nearly 40% of new immigrants to the United States. Fueled by immigration and a growing sector of second, third, and fourth generation AAPIs, the population has been projected to increase to nearly 20 million by 2020. The growth among AAPIs is estimated to occur at a higher rate than other racial groups in the United States, increasing their proportional representation in future population projections.

The sheer growth in the AAPI population has resulted in a similar sharp upswing in college enrollment. During the period 1970–2000, the enrollment of AAPIs in college increased fourfold from about 200,000 to more than 800,000. While the growth and representation of AAPIs nationally has changed dramatically in recent decades and has been a key factor in the rise in college participation among AAPIs, it is important to also consider the settlement patterns of the population across different regions of the country. The regional distribution has also had implications for college participation.

The AAPI population has historically been particularly pronounced in the West and Northeast. In 2000, approximately 65% of all AAPIs lived in just five states: California, New York, Hawaii, Texas, and Illinois. The level of concentration of AAPI residents is actually less now than in previous decades. Between 1980 and 2000, there was a high rate of growth among AAPIs outside the West and Northeast, with the fastest rate of growth occurring in the Midwest and South. The regional representation of AAPIs has had implications for the regional distribution of college students throughout the United States. Consider that in 2000, nearly half of all AAPIs enrolled in college could be found in California alone. However, growing representation outside the West and Northeast coasts has also led to an increase in AAPI college enrollment in a broader group of institutions in the Midwest and the South, which is where college enrollment among AAPIs is increasing at the fastest rate. Trends in the growth and distribution of AAPI college students are discussed further in Chapter 5.

While the population growth and regional concentration of AAPIs are certainly notable and by themselves have been a significant factor in the participation of AAPIs in United States higher education, it is also important to recognize other demographic trends that occurred throughout their history in the United States, including the increasing demographic heterogeneity across subpopulations within the population. There are a number of distinctions within the population that have implications for how we understand educational mobility for AAPIs as whole, as well as for subgroups. Consider that the dominant script of the AAPIs remains rooted in perceptions about the descendants of immigrants from Asia who were almost exclusively Chinese and Japanese Americans whose families arrived prior to the 1965 Immigration Act. Changes in immigration policy, along with simultaneous changes in the opportunity structure in America, have created a much more heterogeneous population of Asian Americans and Pacific Islanders. The diversity of the AAPI population includes differences across ethnic groups, social class, timing of immigration into the United States, and differences in cultures, languages, and dialects. Quite simply, in contemporary American society, there is no single story that represents the AAPI experience in a contemporary portrait of the population.

Ethnicity and Varied Immigration Histories

One key characteristic of the contemporary AAPI population is the tremendous ethnic diversity that exists within the larger aggregated category. The differences in the history of Asian Americans and Pacific Islanders are quite unique and are discussed separately in this section. Starting with the Asian American population, there were 24 ethnic subpopulations based on analysis of data from the 2000 Census (see Table 2.1). That same year, there were between 10.5 and 12.2 million Asian Americans in the United States, depending on if they are counted as "ethnicity alone" or "ethnicity in combination with another race."[1] The largest ethnic groups were Chinese (2.5 million), Filipino (1.9 million), and Asian Indian (1.7 million), which together made up nearly 6 out of 10 Asian Americans in the United States. Korean and Japanese comprised another 18% of the Asian American population, with Southeast Asians, which include Vietnamese, Hmong, Cambodian, and Laotian, comprising another 16% of the total population.

Asian American ethnic subgroups vary greatly across a number of population characteristics, with patterns of immigration being an essential component for these differences. Analysis of data from the 2000 census indicates that among contemporary Asian Americans some ethnic groups have a very large portion of their population comprised of foreign-born immigrants, including Chinese (70.8%), Asian Indian (75.4%), Pakistani (75.5%), Vietnamese (76.1%), Korean (77.7%), and Thai (77.8%). For these groups, the proportion of the population that was foreign born was greater than for the Asian American population overall not including Pacific Islanders (68.9%), and far greater than for the United States total population (11.1%).

Both the number of immigrants and the timing of immigration have been directly influenced by complicated U.S. immigration laws. Prior to WWII, immigration from China, Japan, and the Philippines was mainly restricted to men who were allowed in the United States to work in mining, agriculture, and on the transcontinental railroad (Kitano & Daniels, 1995). After WWII, various factors led to the restructuring of U.S. immigration policy. Immigration among South Asians began to occur following the independence of India and Pakistan in 1947, and Korean immigration was sparked by the end of the Korean War in 1953. Additionally, the United States was emerging as a world superpower, the country was experiencing economic expansion, and there was a structural shift from an emphasis on manufacturing employment to demand in skilled labor. There were also racial conflicts, the civil rights era, and more liberal views in Washington (Barrin-

Table 2.1. Asian American and Pacific Islander Population by Ethnicity, 2000

Asian American	Asian American Subtotal	Pacific Islander	Pacific Islander Subtotal
Asian Indian	1,899,599	Carolinian	173
Bangladeshi	57,412	Chuukese	654
Bhutanese	212	Fijian	13,581
Burmese	16,720	Guamanian or Chamorro	92,611
Cambodian	206,052	I-Kiribati	175
Chinese (except Taiwanese)	2,734,841	Kosraean	226
Filipino	2,364,815	Mariana Islander	141
Hmong	186,310	Native Hawaiian	401,162
Indo-Chinese	199	Ni-Vanuatu	18
Iwo Jiman	78	Marshallese	6,650
Japanese	1,148,932	Palauan	3,469
Korean	1,228,427	Papua New Guinean	224
Laotian	198,203	Pohnpeian	700
Malaysian	18,566	Saipanese	475
Maldivian	51	Samoan	133,281
Nepalese	9,399	Solomon Islander	25
Okinawan	10,599	Tahitian	3,313
Pakistani	204,309	Tokelauan	574
Singaporean	2,394	Tongan	36,840
Sri Lankan	24,587	Yapese	368
Taiwanese	144,795	Other Polynesian	8,796
Thai	150,283	Other Micronesian	9,940
Vietnamese	1,223,736	Other Melanesian	315

Note. Ethnic subtotals are reported alone or with any other racial group.

Source. Analysis of data from U.S. Census Bureau (2000), Summary File 1.

ger et al., 1995). These factors culminated in the passage of the 1965 Hart-Cellar Act,[2] which abolished the quota system, replacing it with preferences for trained professionals that would benefit the labor needs of the U.S. economy. This greatly facilitated the entry of health care professionals, engineers, technicians, computer scientists, and other immigrants from the eastern hemisphere.

A sizeable share of immigrants from Asia today gain access to the United States as permanent residents, admitted via employment preferences, which include "priority workers," "professionals with advanced degrees or aliens of exceptional ability," "skilled workers," "special immigrants" (e.g., employees of the United States government abroad)," and those individuals able to invest a significant amount of money to create a new business (U.S. Citizen and Immigration Services, 2008). Immigrants admitted under employment preferences are comprised of highly educated and skilled professionals, "often representatives of the best their countries have to offer" (Barringer et al., 1995). The capital that these individuals possess is often correlated with educational and social mobility in the United States. In 2005, 34.1% of Asian immigrants granted permanent residence were admitted via employment preferences, compared to admits from Europe (20.8%), the Middle East (18.8%), Latin America (15.9%), Africa (9.7%), and the Caribbean (3.2%) (U.S. Department of Homeland Security, 2005). Thus a large portion of the permanent residents admitted from Asia are indeed highly educated elites with a great deal of opportunity for mobility.

While more than a third of permanent residents from Asia are admitted based on their education, skills, and other forms of capital, the rate of admits among immigrants from different countries of origin varies greatly. For some groups, the proportion of new immigrants admitted via employment preferences is far greater than the average for all new immigrants from Asia. Consider the large proportion of admission under employment preferences among immigrants from Singapore (72.3%), Korea (58.2%), India (54.6%), Japan (40.8%), China (37.7%), and Taiwan (30.0%) in 2005 (Office of Immigration Statistics, 2005). In that year alone, these six countries accounted for nearly 85,000 new permanent residents from Asia admitted via employment preferences, which constitutes 76% of the 111,947 total from Asia.

In addition to the immigrants from Asia admitted under employment categories, a surge of immigration from Southeast Asia also occurred starting in 1975 under refugee and asylee status.[3] These categories represent individuals and families who are "unable or unwilling to return to his or her country of origin because of persecution or a well-founded fear of persecution on account of race, religion, nationality, membership in a particular social group, or political opinion" (U.S. Citizen and Immigration Services, 2008). Refugee and asylee legislation began in the mid-1940s and resulted in nearly 500,000 refugees from Eastern Europe up until 1960. The number of refugees admitted to the United States decreased between 1960 and 1970 and increased again in the mid-1970s following the end of the Vietnam War. During a 15-year period between 1975 and 1990, there were more than one million new Southeast Asian immigrants to the United States, nearly all of whom arrived under refugee status. Southeast Asian refugees arrived in two phases. First, a large number of admits from Southeast Asia arrived prior to 1980. These were of individuals who assisted the United States during the Vietnam War and also individuals and families with influence in their homeland (Barringer et al., 2005). A large portion of these refugees were from Vietnam (205,800) with a smaller number arriving from Laos (50,300) and Cambodia (13,900) (Office of Immigration Statistics, 2005). Among new arrivals from Southeast Asia during this time period, nearly all (92.1%) were admitted via refugee status.

A second wave of refugees from Southeast Asia arrived after 1980. These refugees, often referred to as "boat people," were individuals and families who fled their countries in large numbers by any means available to them. In contrast to the first wave of Southeast Asian refugees, the second wave was larger and included more individuals and families with few possessions, few financial resources, and low educational attainment. From 1980 to 1985, the number of new arrivals from Cambodia (96,900) and Laos (94,700) increased significantly, again with nearly all of the new admits from Southeast Asia (96.5%) arriving via refugee status (Office of Immigration Statistics, 2005). The proportion of new Southeast Asian immigrants admitted via refugee status began to decrease in the period between 1985 and 1990. This was mostly due to a decrease in the proportional representation among new arrivals from Vietnam, which decreased from 94.5% during the period 1980–1984 to 69.0% during the period 1985–1990. In 2005 the number of new admits to the United States via refugee and asylee status was reduced to below one hundred thousand (Office of Immigration Statistics, 2005).

Two additional groups of people in the United States from Asia complicate our understanding of the Asian American population. First, there are large numbers of highly skilled, nonimmigrant students and workers visiting from Asian countries on visas at any given time. In 2007 alone, there were 870,661 nonimmigrant admissions to the United States from Asian countries under student and employment categories (Office of Immigration Statistics, 2007).[4] New arrivals from Asia represented nearly half of all nonimmigrant admissions in these student, scholar, and employment categories. Similar to the categories for permanent resident status, preferences for nonimmigrant students and employees favor particular skills, experiences, and backgrounds. In *The World Is Flat*, Thomas Friedman (2005) talks about the 1.2 million science and engineering degrees granted to students by Asian universities in 2003, compared to the 400,000 by institutions in the United States. He states that "in China, where there are 1.3 billion people . . . when you are one in a million—there are 1,300 other people just like you" (p. 265). Indeed, there is no shortage of qualified students seeking college outside of Asia. The nonimmigrant skilled workers employed in the United States are indeed the cream of the crop of their intellectual and human capital pool. These individuals are often categorized as "Asian Americans" even if they are in the United States temporarily, challenging us to ponder the questions, "Who are Asian Americans?" and "What is their status in America?"

If the composition of Asians and Asian Americans in the United States is not complicated enough, there is yet another category of people from Asia in America that is often the most marginalized: the undocumented immigrant. In 2000 the U.S. Immigration and Naturalization Services (INS)[5] defined undocumented residents as "foreign-born persons who entered without inspection or who violated the terms of a temporary admission and who have not acquired permanent residence status or gained temporary protection against removal" (U.S. Immigration and Naturalization Service, 2003). That same year, the INS Office of Policy and Planning estimated that there were between 470,000 and 500,000 undocumented immigrants in the United States from Asia (U.S. Immigration and Naturalization Service, 2003). While this number is much smaller than the estimated 5 million undocumented immigrants from Mexico, it does represent a 91.1% increase from 1990. The three largest groups of undocumented immigrants are from China (115,000), the Philippines (85,000), and India (70,000), three countries that are also the source of highly skilled workers. This paradox underscores that generalizing the immigration status of any one ethnic group may lead to generalizations and false conclusions that are problematic for the treatment of the group.

The complex immigration rules throughout U.S. history, coupled with a "flatter" global society, have had many implications for the composition of Asian Americans. On the one hand, there are many foreign-born Asian Americans in the United States who have been admitted under preferential conditions because of the political, financial, or intellectual capital that they could bring. The children of these immigrants enjoy access to resources, opportunities, and capital that significantly advantages them in the pursuit of college. On the other hand, there are sectors of the Asian American foreign-born population that arrived under refugee and asylee status or as undocumented residents who do not have access to the same assets, resources, and capital. The children of these families face socioeconomic situations that are among the lowest levels of any population in the nation. The differences between these two groups of foreign-born Asian Americans in the United States have contributed to a wide distribution in socioeconomic status among subpopulations, which is discussed later in this chapter.

Adding to the complexity of the contemporary history of Asian Americans is the Pacific Islander population, also known as "Native Hawaiians and Pacific Islanders." These are people whose origins are Polynesia, Micronesia, or Melanesia. Determining foreign-born status among Pacific Islanders is a more difficult assessment. Some argue that Pacific Islanders cannot be foreign born because they do not immigrate to the United States; rather, the United States has immigrated to them.

Analysis of data from the 2000 Census identifies 24 ethnicities within the Pacific Islander category (see Table 2.1). That same year, there were between 408,000 and 888,000 Pacific Islanders in the United States, depending on if they are counted as "ethnicity alone" or "ethnicity in combination with another race." The largest Pacific Islander populations were Native Hawaiians (401,162), and Samoans (133,281), which constituted almost 60% of the population. Other categories that captured a large share of the Pacific Islander population were Guamanian or Chamorro, Tongan, and those who identified as "Other Pacific Islanders."

Native Hawaiian and Pacific Islanders have a very different "Asian" experience than Asian Americans. Even the boundaries of "America" and the Pacific Islands are quite blurred if one takes into account the United States Virgin Islands, American Samoa, and the Commonwealth of the Northern Mariana Islands, which includes Guam, Saipan, Tinian, and Rota—all of which are "unincorporated" territories of the United States. Guamanian immigration was aided by military service and the 1950 Organic Act, both of which conferred U.S. citizenship to Guamanians. However, their status as an "unincorporated" U.S. territory is different from Puerto Rico in that residents of Guam hold U.S. citizenship, but cannot vote in United States presidential elections. Residents of Guam, among other U.S. Pacific Island areas, are sometimes included and sometimes excluded from U.S. population statistics.

Native Hawaiians also have a unique position relative to the U.S. government. Some scholars position them closer to Native Americans because of the history of colonialism in the Pacific Island region that has been a key factor in their relationship to the United States. Native Hawaiians are recognized as having a "special relationship" with the United States government, which is similar to Native Americans and Alaskan Natives in terms of access to special resources and programs. Additionally, there has been a movement from within the Native Hawaiian population to seek sovereign status equal to Native Americans, which would enable them to pursue self-determination and self-governance. These population distinctions, including their unique position relative to the United States, make them quite unique relative to Asian Americans, even though "Asian American and Pacific Islander" is the group to which they are designated racially. In fact, if the model minority myth has misrepresented any group of AAPIs, Native Hawaiians and Pacific Islanders would be at the top of the list.

Beyond Ethnicity:
Socioeconomic Status and Language Background

In addition to the varied immigration histories among AAPIs, which contributes to the heterogeneity within the population, there are dramatic differences within the population with regard to socioeconomic status and language backgrounds. Socioeconomic status and ability to speak English are key factors associated with education and social mobility among immigrant populations in the United States (Rumbaut & Ima, 1987), and AAPIs are not impervious to these social realities (National Commission on AAPI Research in Education, 2008; Teranishi, 2005). Socioeconomic status is a measure of a person's position in society, otherwise known as an indicator of economic and social position relative to others (Jencks, Bartlett, Corcoran, & Elder, 1979). The criteria of socioeconomic status are typically income, education level, and occupation. Also referred to as financial and human capital, these factors are positively correlated with access to information, knowledge, and resources, which cumulatively provide opportunities that are often not afforded to individuals who lack these forms of capital. Research has identified a number of ways that socioeconomic status is a factor in the college destination of students. Across all achievement levels, students from lower socioeconomic status are less likely to apply to or attend college (McDonough, 1997). Students from lower socioeconomic backgrounds disproportionately attend less selective institutions, 2-year institutions, and public institutions (Hearn, 1991; Karen, 1988; McDonough, 1997).

When discussing socioeconomic status among AAPIs, it is useful to focus on poverty, which is an income threshold that varies by family size and composition.[6] If a family's total income is less than the prescribed threshold, that family and every individual in it is considered impoverished. Given this definition, AAPIs exhibit wide variations in poverty rates that distribute unevenly across ethnic subpopulations (Table 2.2). In 2000, Filipinos (6.3%), Japanese (9.7%), and Asian Indians (9.8%) had poverty rates that were far below the national average of 12.4%. On the other hand, other AAPI ethnic groups had poverty rates that far exceeded the national average. For Hmong (37.8%), Cambodians (29.3%), Laotians (18.5%), and Vietnamese (16.6%), their poverty rate was one and a half to three times the national average. High poverty rates often translate to a lack of access to various instruments that can assist in students' preparation for and access to higher education, including tutoring, extracurricular training, and counseling, not to mention access to comfortable housing, good nutrition, and access to physical and mental health care (Massey, 2003).

Educational attainment, a form of human capital, is another common measure of socioeconomic status. Parental education is an important factor for the mobility of students because it affords them with access to the knowledge, skills, and experience of their parents. Similar to poverty rates, AAPIs ethnic subgroups vary widely in educational attainment. Some Asian American subpopulations have high levels of educational attainment; particularly those who were admitted precisely because of their education and training. This is particularly evident among the rate of Asian Indians (63.9%), Chinese (48.1%), Koreans (43.8%) and Filipinos (43.8%) with an educational attainment rate of a bachelor's degree or more (see Table 2.2). On the other hand, other Asian Americans, such as Southeast Asians who almost exclusively arrived under refugee status, exhibit very low levels of educational attainment. Indeed, the rate of educational attainment that is less than high school is disproportionately high among Hmong (59.6%), Cambodian (53.3%), Laotian (49.6%), and Vietnamese (38.1%). Variation in educational attainment among parents has some practical implications, including the ability for parents to help their students with their homework and provide their children with guidance, support, and involvement (Lareau, 2000; McDonough, 1997). Additionally, parental education has also been found to be linked to cultural capital, or the norms, values, and practices that are comprised by cultural knowledge.

Among Asian Americans, differences in timing of immigration and the country of origin have also had implications for language ability in the United States (see Table 2.2). Asian Americans and Pacific Islanders have exhibited a wide range of native languages and English-language abilities; Asian Americans and Pacific Islanders spoke more than 300 languages in 2000 according to analysis of data from the U.S. Census Bureau. While some ethnic groups, including Japanese (52.7%), Filipinos (29.3%), Thai (19.2%), and Koreans (18.1%) had high rates of "speaking English very well," other groups, including Vietnamese (62.4%), Hmong (58.6%), Cambodians (53.5%), and Laotians (52.8%) all had high rates of not speaking English very well. Pacific Islanders also spoke a range of languages and dialects, including Carolinian, Chamorro, Fijian, Hawaiian, Marshallese, and Samoan.

Some AAPI populations acquire a number of languages prior to their arrival to the United States. A study of newly arrived Hmong residents in St. Paul, Minnesota, found that a large proportion of the adult Hmong population spoke Lao, Vietnamese, and Chinese, in addition to their native Hmong language (McNall et al., 1994). Many of the adults that arrived in the United States via refugee camps in Thailand also spoke Thai. Their language acquisition occurred despite little or no formal education. With a great deal of secondary migration that occurs among AAPIs, the prevalence of multilingualism is quite high within the population relative to other immigrant populations in the United States.

The language ability of parents has several implications for the educational opportunities and outcomes of their children. AAPI parents with poor English-language ability often face challenges working with their children's teachers, counselors, and administrators. They are also often at a disadvantage for advocating for their children, or face difficulties asking questions that require a response to the specific needs, challenges, or skills that their children may have. The children of parents with limited-English ability are often put in a position where they have to translate for their parents, or are responsible for other daily tasks, such as paying bills or helping to manage a family-run business (Suarez-Orozco & Suarez-Orozco, 2001).

Many AAPIs arrived in the United States between the ages of 5 and 18, which often translates into challenges with language at school. Among AAPI children and youth ages 5–18, nearly one out of four (24%) was an English Language Learner (ELL) in 2000 (Asian American Legal Defense and Education Fund, 2008). This is more prevalent for AAPI students in some states than is the case for others. Among

Table 2.2. Socioeconomic and Language Indicators Among Asian Americans, 2000

	Chinese	Japanese	Korean	Filipino	Asian Indian	Vietnamese	Hmong	Cambodian	Laotian	Thai
POVERTY STATUS										
Percent below poverty	13.5	9.7	14.6	6.3	9.8	16.6	37.8	29.3	18.5	14.4
EDUCATIONAL ATTAINMENT										
Less than high school	23.0	8.9	13.7	12.7	13.3	38.1	59.6	53.3	49.6	20.9
BA degree or greater	48.1	41.9	43.8	43.8	63.9	19.4	7.5	9.2	7.7	38.6
ENGLISH-LANGUAGE ABILITY										
Only English at home	14.6	52.7	18.1	29.3	19.3	6.9	4.4	8.4	7.2	19.2
Less than very well	49.6	27.2	50.5	24.1	23.1	62.4	58.6	53.5	52.8	46.9

Note. Poverty status was determined for everyone except those in institutions, military group quarters, or college dormitories. Educational attainment rates are for individuals between the ages of 18 and 64.

Source. Analysis of data from the U.S. Census Bureau (2000), Summary File 1.

just five states (California, New York, Texas, Minnesota, and Washington), the ELL population was more than 250,000 in 2000 (AALDEF, 2008). Among certain AAPI ethnic groups, the ELL rate among children and youth is quite significant. Hmong (52%), Vietnamese (39%), and Cambodians (33%) have particularly high rates of ELL children and youth. Other AAPI subpopulations have a high number of ELL children and youth (e.g., Chinese: 115,000, Vietnamese: 95,000, Korean: 51,000), even though the number might not constitute a high proportion among the 5–18-year-old population. These indicators related to language background have several implications for their educational success in the United States, given that English ability is often a key factor in educational mobility, including the ability to comprehend lessons in all subject areas, transition from one grade to the next, graduate from high school, or to perform on college entrance exams (e.g., SAT, remedial exams, and so on). Clearly, the ELL rate across AAPI subpopulations is quite disparate and is affected by ethnicity, timing of immigration, and the language(s) spoken in the country of origin among immigrants.

The statistical portrait provided thus far demonstrates the ways in which ethnicity, immigration histories, social class, and language backgrounds vary widely across AAPI subpopulations. While these quantitative indicators are instructive for establishing a pattern of social indicators and their connections to key factors that influence AAPI educational outcomes, it is also necessary to consider the more nuanced, qualitative aspects of how these social forces play out in the lived experiences of Asian American students and families. A qualitative perspective of the Asian American educational experience brings the voices of individual lives to the fore, which is essential for diminishing the extent to which these individuals are misunderstood and misrepresented in social and institutional research and policy. The following section captures the ways in which Asian American students described their own processes of navigating various relationships and organizational settings as they formulated and pursued their educational aspirations. Working with a team of researchers over a 3-year period, we listened to the stories of over 300 Asian American seniors from 10 high schools in California about the ways in which their various demographic characteristics and backgrounds had implications for their educational mobility (see Appendix A). How the students expressed their dreams and aspirations, sources of support and guidance, and their challenges and barriers enhances our understanding of the ways in which Asian American students pursue higher education within the context of immigration histories, social class, and language background, among other social indicators.

PERCEPTIONS OF OPPORTUNITIES AND CHALLENGES

It is instructive to revisit the lives of Pang, Tony, Trung, and Lilly, whose educational trajectories are as diverse and complex as their demographic backgrounds.

Examining how they describe their lived experiences helps reveal how they each make sense of their postsecondary plans differently, despite the homogeneity in their academic backgrounds, which was achieved by delimiting the selection of individuals for high academic achievement.[7]

Whether or not Pang attends college right after high school will depend on how she is able to negotiate the expectations of both her parents and her in-laws, with whom she and her husband live. At the center of the decision for both families is money, or the lack there of. She says that there is a high likelihood that she will need to find a job soon. "I need to help out with the family; both my parents and my in-laws are constantly worrying about money."

Pang's concerns about college are very different from Tony's, which revolve more around which college he will attend as opposed to if he will attend college at all. While his parents have little experience with the American system of higher education and have little command of English, he is confident about plans to attend a selective private university on the East Coast, "probably in the Ivy League." He has a lot of guidance from his sister, cousins, and peers who are keeping him on the right track. He proclaims, "My parents put pressure on me to attend college, but other people give me guidance and help me navigate the process."

Tony's confidence for attending an Ivy League university across the country is far more ambitious than is the case for Trung or Lilly. Trung has ambitions to follow in the footsteps of his two older sisters who attend public 4-year colleges in a neighboring city, but he observes their struggles trying to balance their coursework and the college experience while working and living at home. Trung understands these challenges firsthand, working 19 hours a week, mostly on weekends but also a couple of days a week after school, to help out with his own expenses. Trung's mom has also made it clear that he will need to pay for at least half of his college tuition, which has him putting away as much money as possible before he applies for college. How much he saves will determine if he will be able to enroll in college full-time or part-time, or if he will be able to attend a 4-year college, which costs more, or a community college, which is more manageable financially.

Lilly is equally as qualified to attend a 4-year university, but is also uneasy about her postsecondary educational plans. She is torn between staying home and attending a college nearby to please her mother, and leaving home to attend a more selective university, as her sister has done despite her mother. Lilly says that her mom wants her to be a "good daughter," and not abandon the family by moving far from home like her sister, who only visits the family on holidays. "In fact, my mom said she'll buy me a car if I live at home—not a new one, but still, that would be cool."

Learning from Pang, Tony, Trung, and Lilly about how their lived experiences shape their college aspirations is a revealing endeavor. In some ways, how they describe their educational goals is seemingly consistent with the model minority stereotype—a deep desire to attend colleges that are "famous," "top-tiered," and "prestigious." These students set their sights on America's most selective and prestigious public and private universities. As Tony says, "I want to get into a good college, and the colleges that I'm expecting myself to get into are the top ranked—I mean, the greatest colleges there are. I'm shooting for a Harvard or an MIT or something, something within like the top 50, or like, first tier."

Conversely, there is a narrative about college among Asian Americans that is wrought with confusion and a lack of information on how to choose a college, and with concerns about whether or not the student will be admitted to any selective college if they submit an application. According to Pang, one of her biggest fears about college is that she will not be able to keep up with college-level coursework and will fail in her first semester. Trung is concerned, first and foremost, with cost, but he also doesn't know when a college is too big or too small, if he will fit in socially, or if he will be able to make friends. Lilly has a similar concern with the social aspect of college. She said:

> My biggest worry about college is just fitting in, just because it takes me a while to get comfortable with people. But I mean academically I think I'll do good anywhere I go—I hope. But it's just socially, I just want to make sure I can fit in.

For both Trung and Lilly, their racial and ethnic backgrounds were a factor in their concerns about fitting in. Trung wants to be able to find friends with whom he can communicate and feel comfortable. More specifically, it comes down to being able to find a college where he can form friendships with other students with whom he can talk in his native language, Vietnamese. Growing up in the Bay Area, Lilly says that she has an appreciation and preference for diversity. She says, "Students like me, Asian or Filipino, but also a mix of students of other racial backgrounds." She adds:

> When I go to college, I want some Filipinos there. Blend it in as long as I can communicate with them. But, if it's all White students, I would feel a little awkward. I wouldn't want them to look at me all weird or treat me bad because I'm the only Asian there.

The wide range of goals and preferences related to these students' college aspirations is quite revealing. The variation in the factors that contribute to the construction of their aspirations, however, and how they connect with their ethnic, language, and cultural backgrounds, is also insightful for understanding Asian American postsecondary outcomes. This relationship reveals that while there were certainly students who want to and eventually do attend prestigious universities, there are also just as many if not more students who pursue and enrolled in nonselective 4-year colleges, public 2-year colleges, or end up with other postsecondary outcomes (e.g., the military and vocational schools that train students in trades such as auto mechanics, technology, and various visual, performing, and culinary art programs). The following section explores further the educational aspirations of Pang, Tony, Trung, and Lilly in the broader context of the social forces of immigration histories, social class, and language backgrounds.

College Is "The Immigrant American Dream"

While the aspirations of AAPI students range from wanting to continue their education beyond high school to wanting to attend America's most selective universities, the consistent narrative of the role of the immigrant drive as a factor in college predisposition is remarkable. Between 82.2 and 83.9% of Asian American children under the age of 18 lived in households headed by foreign-born parents in 2000.[8] Given the role of parents in the predisposition of students regarding college, Asian American students' college aspirations are driven in large part by an immigrant experience. Tony is representative of this story. He says, "I know my parents sacrificed a lot to get us here. And I don't want to show that their sacrifices were in vain. I want to show them that I can actually get an education and go further than they did." Tony adds that in his Chinese family there has been a consistent message to him and his sister that "from the time [we] were born, we were expected to go to college." Tony's parents have been adamant about the importance of going as far as he possibly can because a good education is the only means for mobility, and "a college degree opens doors to opportunities in America. It's the immigrant American dream."

With four out of five Asian American youth having foreign-born parents, there is an abundance of storytelling by students' parents about the immigrant experience. For many students, their parents tell a story that places their education at the center of the conversation. Put another way, the family immigrated to the United States specifically to give their children a better life—a chance to have opportunities that were not available to them in their homelands. Trung says that his parents told him to take advantage of higher education in the United States, which is a system that is very different than in Vietnam. His parents tell him that access to higher education in Vietnam is limited to privileged families who are wealthy. He says:

> My parents [would tell] me and my sisters about how they came [to the United States] to give us a better education, and we need to take that to the limit. And in Vietnam, you had to pay for your education. Some people didn't have enough money to pay for books and stuff, so they had to drop out of school early. And here, in the United States, we have a free [public] education and they believe that we should use it for our benefit. So, we just want to do the best for ourselves and to make our parents proud.

Lilly also says that her family did not have access to college in the Philippines, which was a driving force in her parents' decision to come to the United States. She says that when her parents were still in the Philippines, they would hear stories about America from relatives in the United States, which helped convince them it would be a good idea to go there someday. Lilly's family has an expectation that she will take advantage of the postsecondary opportunities in the United States, like her older sister, and doing so will benefit the entire family. Lilly says that she appreciates their sacrifice and it makes her feel good about her family:

> The only reason why my parents came to America was for us—the kids.
> And, that really makes me smile because they thought about us. Back
> in the Philippines it was really hard to get your studies and to find a job
> because it's poor out there. And they came to America so we could get a
> better education.

Pang says that her family's situation carries a lot of responsibilities for her. Like Lilly, Pang also carries a strong feeling of responsibility and believes that her own success has implications for her immediate and extended family. Pang says that she feels the pressure to strive for an easier and better life for her parents and her in-laws. She says, "My parents always tell me that they don't want me to end up like them, working really hard. They want me to have an easier job, a better life." Simply put, more education leads to more money, which leads to an easier life. Pang describes her pursuit of higher education:

> Well, there are not many Hmong people that are highly educated. And
> just knowing the fact that we are like kind of new to this country I just
> want to try to get a higher education like my family never got.

These stories of sacrifice capture the role that the history of family migration plays in shaping these students' views toward the pursuit of higher education. For Pang, Tony, Trung, and Lilly, the importance of their family's experiences with immigration is paramount in their pursuit of higher education. However, despite the consistency in the role of their parents' immigration histories for their desire to attend college, the likelihood of realizing these goals is far from certain. Factors including differences in language backgrounds, the educational and occupational backgrounds of the parents, and the financial resources available to the family also need to be accounted for. While the dynamics of students' social contexts "are woven into the texture and rhythm of children and parents' daily lives" (Lareau, 2003, p. 236), it is also important to take account of the ways in which different social contexts transmit differential advantages to children and families.

"My Parents Won't Talk with My Teachers"

While Pang has high educational aspirations, driven in large part by the de-sire to achieve a level of education not achieved by anyone else in her family, the ability of her family to provide resources such as information, knowledge, support, and involvement as she progresses through the United States education system has been hindered by some aspects of her parents' backgrounds. Pang says that her parents' experiences as first-generation immigrants have meant many challenges in relation to their language background, in many cases a fac-tor that she recalls has affected them even in their everyday lives. This has meant many things for Pang, who is a fluent English speaker. On the one hand, it meant that she spoke her native Hmong language with her parents and in-laws, which she says has been difficult at times because she "can't remember some of the words." On the other hand, Pang says that her parents and in-laws have often had difficulty communicating effectively in English, which has led to a num-ber of responsibilities for her, including the frequent need for her to translate school documents and handling a lot of translations from English to Hmong and Hmong to English related to daily tasks.

Pang also recalled the times when her parents' poor command of English used to have a negative impact on her when it came to their involvement with her schooling. She says it ultimately prevented them from talking with her teachers or other people at her school: "My parents wouldn't talk with my teachers unless they talked to them." The lack of contact between her parents and her teachers meant that Pang was often caught in the middle, navigating her educational process on her own.

Trung discussed his parents' lack of English skills in relation to his pursuit of college. He says that there isn't any college information in Vietnamese, so even though he has a lot of information, he doesn't share it with his parents "because it's kind of hard for me to translate it into Vietnamese." Ultimately, this means that they don't know what he's grappling with. The impact of language and the need for parents to be involved in the college choice process is also a factor when it comes to keeping track of standardized tests, application deadlines, and other aspects of selective college admissions.

"My Dad Just Says, 'Don't Mess Up'"

Research on the college-choice process has noted that parents' own experi-ence with postsecondary education is one of the strongest predictors for students' aspirations and perceptions of college (Hossler, Braxton, & Coopersmith, 1989; Hossler & Stage, 1992; McDonough, 1997). Tony's parents both had some college experience in the Bay Area, which is where they eventually settled after secondary

migration from the Midwest. Tony says that his parents' knowledge and experience with college has helped him negotiate the college-choice process because they
have experienced the process themselves. Indeed, their many talks about different
majors and fields, coupled with Tony's trips to visit his sister at her college, have
resulted in a high level of college knowledge for Tony. He says that his dad also
"reads magazines and books about college, and talks to his friends and other relatives about college." Tony describes his mother's involvement:

> My mom keeps me on track. She likes to stay on top of all my grades. She
> tells me what I need to do to improve my SAT scores or makes sure I get
> certain grades, stuff like that. She even signed me up for an SAT class.
> She's always ahead of me.

Parents with educational experience in the United States can monitor their
child's educational pursuits by tracking their progress and understanding what
expectations need to be met to pursue specific postsecondary educational goals.
However, this is a sharp contrast to what occurs for Lilly, whose parents did not
attend college in the United States. Although Lilly appreciates her parents' support
and encouragement when it comes to college, she says that it is a rare occasion that
they give her any guidance or share any specific college information or knowledge.
She says, "[My parents] just care about the outcome—not the process. They just
want to know the result, which school I'm going to; they don't even know what the
SAT is. It's hard for them because they didn't go to college in the United States."
Lilly says that her mother is more involved than her father, who works out of state
and is rarely at the family home. So, while her mother has high expectations for
Lilly, she says that her father doesn't seem to take much interest. In talking about
the "agonizing" process of trying to figure out what to do after high school, she
says:

> I think if my dad had pushed for more, like talked to me or someone at
> my school who could help me, then I wouldn't be that messed up right
> now. I'd have something to work toward because he doesn't really guide
> me about school. He just says, "Don't mess up."

How Lilly describes the impact of her parents' educational backgrounds is
similar to the situation of Pang, whose parents and in-laws have almost no formal
education. Pang says she receives very little guidance when it comes to school and
college "because they don't know anything about the United States education system." Pang describes how the lack of experience with education in her family has
created tension between her and her parents and in-laws:

I have a lot of conflict with my parents and in-laws. They sometimes argue with me about staying after school, you know, stuff like that. And sometimes it is kind of hard because you tend to forget that they didn't go to school; they came from a different country and their ways were different. You know, they didn't really have a lot of opportunity to go out and play and stuff. And all the Hmong culture was just strictly gardening, harvesting, and now these days it just seems like they just don't know what's going on. Like they haven't been to school or ever experienced this. So, it's kind of difficult trying to ask your parents stuff about college and stuff. My parents have never stepped foot into college or even school before. And they think that now, if I should go to college, even if I just attend college one day, then I will be successful for the rest of my life. They think that's like a guaranteed fact right there, you know. But then they don't understand why I have to go to college. They don't understand why I have to pay for my education after high school, seeing that it has been free for 12 years.

Pang is left to her own devices to figure out the process of pursuing higher education. She isn't alone when it comes to students pursuing this endeavor with little guidance from family; many of the Hmong, Mien, and Cambodian respondents speak of being "the only one" in their family to pursue higher education. Pang describes the struggle that many Hmong students face when considering the pursuit of higher education:

It is important to me 'cause I'm gonna be the first girl in my family— the first girl or boy—to actually continue on to a higher form of education. Yeah. It's not really that, but I just see how my family's struggling like to make money, and how my brothers are, 'cause they dropped out of high school. And I don't want to go down the same road that they took. In my family, nobody has gone to college. So, I want to be the first to go to college.

Pang says that she turns to her brother-in-law's wife who didn't finish high school, but recently enrolled in a community college. Pang says she talks with her about the college she attends, which makes Pang excited about the possibility for her own future as a college student. Pang says that it is great to see her brother-in-law's wife go to college instead of ending up like her brothers and others in her community, who are "involved in gang activity and not doing anything with themselves." The impact of a lack of formal education and poor command of English among parents, coupled with high poverty among some Asian Americans, is a recipe for tremendous challenges for children.

"I Just Want to Make Money to Help My Family"

The income and wealth gap among Asian Americans is dramatic across ethnic subpopulations. Analysis of data on income by ethnicity among Asian Americans reveals that Chinese ($60,058), Japanese ($70,849), and Asian Indians ($70,708) made two times the median household income of Hmong ($32,384), Cambodians ($35,621), or Laotians ($43,542) in 2000. These data correlate with the wide distribution of Asian Americans across occupational fields. Chinese and Indians were nearly four times as likely to be in managerial or "white collar" positions than Cambodians, Hmong, or Laotians, with the latter group heavily represented in positions that involve manual labor (Reeves & Bennett, 2004). The income and occupation gaps among Asian Americans contribute to wide disparities in workforce participation, unemployment and underemployment, home ownership, and ultimately, poverty, as discussed earlier in this chapter. These differences in income, workforce participation, and poverty have many implications for Asian American students as they think about college.

Trung says that he doesn't have any free time for joining clubs and hanging out with his friends. Rather, he "mostly works," something he says he has been doing since he was very young. He says, "Lately, I feel like all I do is work and help out around my family." He adds,

> There are other things I want to do, but I'm working two jobs now in a restaurant and like a retail business. Thirty hours in one job and a few hours in the other . . . it's stressful, but you got to hang on. At the restaurant, my job title is KCL, which means kitchen crew leader. It's cool because I supervise my other coworkers. I played volleyball for school for one year. But then that's when I didn't work. I wish I could stop working and join some school activity or something. Have a life for once.

Aside from working taking time away from other activities, Trung's two jobs also impact his ability to keep up in school. He says, "I need to get stress off my mind. Yeah, I have a lot of stress." He explains further:

> It's hard to keep up. And my mom tells me, "If you can't keep up you can quit any time." But, that's how I make my money. It's hard for my mom to support me, because what she makes is just enough for the bills and food . . . that's it. Everything else is up to me. What I want is what I have to make. But, working at the restaurant, the work is really hard. When I got home, it's real late, too . . . like at least 11:00 p.m. And then I have like at least two or three hours of homework, you know? I can't finish it all. So like what I do is, I do half of it, and then when I get to school, I do the

other half. And that's a lot of stress. All this stress . . . I tend to fall asleep in class all the time.

Pang says that, like Trung, she and many of her friends, have had to work to help support the family while they are enrolled in school. She connects her drive to work while in school to the impact of poverty on the Hmong community. She says, "I think the hardest thing for Hmong people now is welfare, because most families come to the United States and they first got on welfare. They get dependent on that money, and now that most of the welfare is going away, they get very stressed out."

Since a lack of financial resources at home translates into being overworked and having poorer academic performance for Trung and Pang, it is instructive to broaden the context to examine how the educational aspirations of students are affected by the financial resources that families can put toward their pursuit of college. For many students, the economic backgrounds of their families played a particularly important role in how they perceived the cost of attending college. This is consistent with other research that has found that low-income families often lack information and knowledge about how to finance postsecondary education (McDonough, 1997; Post, 1990). For low-income families, parents' perceptions of cost are often highly exaggerated; in some instances, studies have found that parents think the cost of college is three times its actual cost (Hossler, Schmit, & Vesper, 1999). In addition, many low-SES families believe they are eligible for less financial aid than they actually are.

Tony, despite his parents' long hours at work and lack of time at home, describes himself as being "comfortably middle-class." He says that his parents encourage him to not be concerned about money or working while he is in school. He says, "Somehow my parents will figure out how to handle the cost. My parents just expect me to worry about getting into a good college." He adds, "My parents realize that college is an investment and that only the best is good enough for me." Tony says he wants something different in a college; he wants to attend a private university on the East Coast. He talks more specifically about his father's views on the cost of attending a private university. He said:

My [father] thinks it's worth it to spend more. He says that even though it costs more to go to a private college, he thinks it is still a better education. So he tells me, "Don't look at the prices anymore."

The role that cost plays in Tony's pursuit of college is very different from the role it plays for Trung, who is worried that his family will not be able to afford tuition. He is also worried that, ultimately, paying for college will be a financial burden for his family. Trung's concern about the impact of the cost of college on his family was a common sentiment among Southeast Asians. Trung says he is keeping his options open by keeping community colleges on his list. He says, "I can always go to a community college, work, and pay for my own tuition. I can always transfer later on."

While Trung and many other students are concerned about cost enough to have it be a deciding factor for where they choose to attend college, it is shocking how little students know about the cost of attending college. Most students exaggerate the cost of college, particularly the cost of tuition. While this is true for most students generally, the cost of tuition was exaggerated more among low-income students. Trung, whose mom has told him that he will need to pay for half of his tuition, had an estimate that is exemplary of this point. He said, "to go to a public university in California, it would probably be $100,000 a year. I'm gonna try to apply [for financial aid] to cover my end."

The impact of information, knowledge, and involvement of parents, coupled with students' descriptions of their heavy familial obligations, resulted in many students wanting to attend less selective regional colleges in order to save money on tuition and help with family responsibilities—a trend that was found more among Southeast Asian respondents and low-income Chinese and Filipinos. For these students, alternative strategies were often a part of the conversation about college. Trung says that he even is considering enlisting in the military after he learned that the military will pay for college:

> I might be going into the Marines after high school. But at the same time
> I'm going to be attending college, too. They, they pay for it, you know,
> they advise it. So that will probably be my plan.

Clearly Trung is ambivalent about his plans beyond high school, which is heavily influenced by his fundamental concerns about cost and his ability to finance college.

While the financial stability of the household was a factor in how students perceived cost as a factor in their college choice process, it was also a factor in whether or not students would end up living at home or moving away while going to college. For some students, moving away to attend college is an important part of the college experience; going to college means moving away from home, and gaining "freedom" and "independence." For other students, like Lilly, however, how far college is from home is also a matter of obligations to the family. Lilly's situation where her mother does not want her to move away like her sister did is not uncommon, especially for first-generation students and women. Lilly talked about how her familial obligations shape her postsecondary aspirations:

> If it was up to me, I would really want to attend a UC college. But there's
> like family problems, and I need to support them, too. I guess like right

now there are things going on with my family. I feel that if I go out of town, then my family will go out of control and I want to be in town and be there for my siblings. I want to be there for them.

Indirectly, many low-income, first-generation Asian American students face challenges that require them to play a role in the home. These competing demands on students often predispose them to consider only colleges close to home, so they can commute, work while going to college, or be available to help out at home on a regular basis. Trung says he is having a tough time deciding where he will end up. He says:

Location is a big thing. I want to be close to my family here. But actually I really want to have the experience of going away, too. But then I figure I can do that later on in life. But staying at home, I can also help my parents because we came here about 7 years ago. And right now we are stable. But then they really need help. So I'm trying to stay home, find a job, and help them out with the house and the bills and stuff.

The wide distribution of socioeconomic status and language ability within the Asian American and Pacific Islander population is indicative of how the population is categorically unique compared to other racial groups in the United States. Unfortunately, these distinctions within the population are rarely noted in the broader racial AAPI composite. Acknowledging the demographic distinctions of the population begins to establish how and why AAPI youth who vary by subpopulation differ in their educational and social mobility. Like all Americans, AAPIs with parents who have high educational attainment, higher income levels, and a better command of English are more likely to possess the capital that enables them to succeed educationally. Conversely, AAPI youth living in poverty, with parents who have less educational attainment and little command of English are in a less favorable position for educational mobility in the United States opportunity structure. For AAPI youth, this results in a wide range of postsecondary outcomes because of a wider distribution within the population across these social indicators.

The relationship between socioeconomic indicators and educational mobility is revealed in this chapter. These demographic differences have implications for the quality and the amount of information, guidance, and involvement students receive from their parents. Parents with less command of English and more difficult financial conditions are also in a more difficult position when it comes to their relationship with their child's school and broader educational goals.

This also has implications for the behavior of students. Students with working-class parents with limited command of English are more likely to work to help support the family, translate for their parents, have lower educational aspirations, and be less likely to realize their educational goals. Additionally, differences AAPIs face within the home as adolescents are accentuated by the community context in which they are situated.

The following chapter examines the extent to which the distribution of social and economic capital and language ability is exaggerated by residential patterns of different ethnic populations. In other words, although it is known that AAPIs generally are concentrated in a small number of states, it is often not recognized that the AAPI population is also concentrated residentially, often in ethnic enclaves (Zhou & Bankston, 1998). The characteristics of AAPI communities are discussed in the context of financial, human, and social capital, and their relationship to access to resources conducive to postsecondary preparation and opportunities.

CHAPTER 3

The Community Context

Jay and Katie live in a poor Hmong community in Sacramento that began as a resettlement of refugees in the 1970s. Jay's story helps articulate the boundaries of ethnicity and community in how these aspects of his life circumscribe his own identity and how he interacts with others outside of his community. Jay says that he often feels invisible, which is frustrating because he believes it is important that people recognize the uniqueness of his Hmong community. He says, "People recognizing Hmong is important to me because it was how I was born, it's my culture. Want to respect me? Call me by who I am, not like just identify all the Asians as one group, because we're all different, we're all unique. We're not the same culture." Jay continues, "I hate the question, 'Where are you from?' I feel like telling them, 'Where are you from? From Mars?' It's like walking up to a White person and saying they're Black!"

Karen and Johnny live in a mostly middle-class Chinese American neighborhood in San Francisco that developed as an alternative for Chinatown residents seeking a better situation. Karen talks about her community relative to others by focusing on the pressure to succeed from her parents, extended relatives, and peers. She says, "Within the Chinese community, we have a lot of expectations put upon the children. We have to please our parents. So, there is an underlying thing that pushes us to compete." The competition that exists among Chinese youth is palpable, but can also be found between Chinese and others in the community. Karen describes how she perceives her position relative to people who are more privileged by saying:

> A lot of rich kids have parents with PhDs and Mercedes, who expect their children to get into college. And if their son or daughter is failing a course, they'll have the resources to pay for a tutor. They can afford the $20-an-hour tutor for them to pass their AP Calculus BC course. While our parents are, like, immigrants—they don't know about these tutors because their friends are other immigrants who are struggling just as we are. But, if I work my butt hard enough, then I will be in the same place where they are. So, it's whether or not you can push yourself to where you need to go. So, maybe I don't have tutor, but I have friends and other resources in the community where I can get help. So, I mean, there are other ways to adapt and it's just whether or not I take advantage of it.

51

Jay's and Karen's narratives—and later in the chapter, Katie's and Johnny's—are quite disparate, but all give a glimpse for how important community is for the AAPI population. In this chapter I position the AAPI population within the broader context of how subpopulations are situated as a community, including how the boundaries of community are impacted by structural boundaries like residential patterns. The importance of community cannot be overstated. AAPI communities have been formed and sustained through both geographic and social forces. With regard to communities that are geographic in nature, Huping Ling (2009) describes how AAPI communities are spaces that are both residential and commercial, where new immigrants have found "employment, housing, and cultural comfort, virtually without interacting with the larger society" (p. 3). These immigrant enclaves have served as great potential for upward mobility and opportunity because ethnic solidarity is at the center of their existence (Zhou, 1992). Ling also talks about the importance of "cultural communities," whose significance is not necessarily bound by physical or geographic space, but rather "defined by the common cultural practices and beliefs of its members" (p. 11). These AAPI communities maintain culture and language and are a conduit for social capital for AAPIs who are less connected through ethnic enclaves (Rumbaut, 1997).

PORTRAITS OF AAPI COMMUNITIES

The demography of community is an important starting point to examine the importance of AAPI ethnic enclaves in the shaping of students' educational trajectories. Communities of AAPIs can be found throughout the country. This is particularly true of the West and Northeast, which contain of a number of vibrant ethnic enclaves. Between these two regions of the country, almost every AAPI ethnic population is represented. Yet it is important to recognize that AAPIs can also be found throughout the country, albeit often with less numerical representation. However, it is often the poor numerical and proportional representation of AAPIs and the relatively recent arrival among immigrants in many communities outside of the West and Northeast that create cohesion among AAPIs. Figure 3.1 captures the distribution of AAPIs throughout the United States. The darker regions denote greater proportional representation and indicate a higher level of residential concentration among AAPIs. While there is a high degree of representation in California, Washington, and New York, the Gulf Coast also has a number of communities with Southeast Asians and Filipinos, while pockets of the Midwest have a growing representation of Southeast Asians, South Asians, and East Asians. Thus the residential patterns of AAPIs are a reflection of AAPI ethnic enclaves that are scattered throughout the country.

The AAPI population in these ethnic enclaves has been fueled by the settlement of newly arrived AAPI immigrants as well as the resettlement and migra-

Figure 3.1. Proportional Representation of AAPIs Nationally, 2000

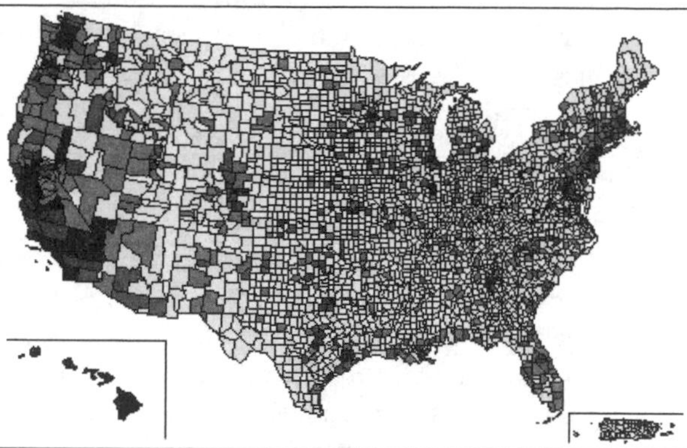

Source. Analysis of data from U.S. Bureau of Census (2000), Summary File 1.

tion of others. These communities are often more distinct because of their specific ethnic makeup, rather than because they are concentrated by AAPIs generally. For Chinese Americans, there are the Chinatown enclaves in San Francisco, Monterey Park, and Alhambra in California, and different pockets in New York City, including Queens, Manhattan, and Brooklyn. South Asians can also be found in large numbers in Queens, New York, DuPage County, Illinois, and Jersey City, New Jersey. Southeast Asian communities can be found in Fresno, Sacramento, Long Beach, and Orange County in California, in addition to Minnesota, Wisconsin, Massachusetts, and in the Gulf Coast region. Some of these communities have assumed names such as "Little Saigon" and "Little Phnom Penh."

Some of these enclaves are more suburban and middle-class, and fit an "uptown" analogy, as described by Vivian Louie (2004). However, many more of these communities are inner-city or rural communities, "downtown" communities that relegate new immigrants to high rates of poverty, few opportunities for upward educational mobility, and non- to limited-English-speaking environments (Fong, 1994; Li, 1999; Louie, 2004). These residential patterns among AAPIs accentuate the effects of the social contexts of family, community, and schools (Fong, 1994; Li, 1999; Massey & Fischer, 1999), which are key factors in mobility and future economic attainment among the children and families that comprise them.

Figure 3.2 provides a portrait of eight ethnic enclaves in 2000: St. Paul, Minnesota; DuPage, Illinois; Wai'anae, Hawaii; Alhambra/Monterey Park, California; Brooklyn, New York; Lowell, Massachusetts; Virginia Beach, Virginia; and New Orleans, Louisiana. Two of the communities, Alhambra/Monterey Park and Brooklyn, are predominately Chinese. Alhambra and Monterey Park, two adjacent communities east of Los Angeles, had some of the highest numbers of Chinese Americans of any city in the country. Nearly three quarters (74.4%) of the 50,000 Chinese Americans in the community were foreign-born and almost half

(45.3%) of the Chinese American adult population had a high school diploma or less. The Alhambra/Monterey Park community is quite different from the Chinese enclave of Sunset Park in Brooklyn. Sunset Park is home to over 120,000 Chinese Americans that comprise two thirds of the AAPI population. More than three quarters (76.8%) of the Chinese American population in Sunset Park is foreign born, with 63.7% of the adult population with an educational attainment of high school or less.

The differences between these communities, although both predominately Chinese, also capture the point made in Vivian Louie's book, *Compelled to Excel* (2004). She examines how class bifurcation, between the Chinese Americans who live in urban Chinatowns and those who live in mainstream suburban America, is a factor in the educational outcomes of the children of these communities. The Chinese American families in these communities, while similar in some ways, live, for the most part, in dramatically polarized worlds, which results in significant differences in the resources and opportunities available for the children of these communities.

Figure 3.2 also offers a portrait of three Southeast Asian communities: St. Paul, Lowell, and New Orleans. These three communities vary with regard to the ethnic group that comprises the population. Hmong from refugee camps of Laos and Thailand began resettlement in the Twin Cities in 1976. In 2000, St. Paul was home to the largest concentration of Hmong outside of Southeast Asia. In this community of nearly 35,000 Hmong residents, 65.4% of the adult population had an educational attainment of "high school or less" (U.S. Census Bureau, 2000) and much of the adult population had limited prior formal work experience that provided them with skills transferable to Minnesota's postindustrial occupational structure (McNall et al., 1994). Coupled with a lack of formal education or relevant job experience are limited English proficiency, difficulty acquiring vocational training, and poor mental and physical health among Hmong adults, which have resulted in a high rate of unemployment and reliance on welfare assistance (Rumbaut, 1995). As a result, the Hmong community has historically faced a high rate of families with children under 18 that live below poverty; at 33.4%, the poverty rate was nearly three times the national average. The disproportionately high household poverty rate is compounded by overcrowding within Hmong households. Hmong in St. Paul had a relatively high proportion (39.1%) of households with six or more persons.

New Orleans has a large Vietnamese population, which makes up 66% of the AAPI population. The first settlement of Vietnamese in New Orleans occurred in 1975 after the fall of Saigon: approximately 1,000 refugees from Vietnam came to the Versailles neighborhood. Through additional secondary migration among Vietnamese immigrants, and a coinciding "White flight" that began sometime in the 1970s (Zhou & Bankston, 1994), Versailles, which is the eastern fringe of New Orleans, went from being about 99% White to 45% Vietnamese in 2000. Versailles

Figure 3.2. Social Indicators for Selected Ethnic Enclaves, 2000

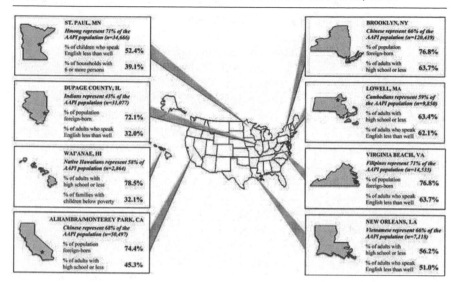

had an abundance of cheap housing for Vietnamese refugees, who initially relied heavily on public assistance. An area characterized as a "rapidly deteriorating
working-class suburb" with "Vietnamese . . . clustered in the poorest part of a poor
area in a poor city in a poor state" (Zhou & Bankston, 1994, p. 828), most of the
Vietnamese in New Orleans are from modest socioeconomic backgrounds. Over
half of the adult population has an educational attainment of high school or less
(56.2%) and most have low occupational status as low-paid, blue-collar employees. The concentration of the Vietnamese population residentially and socioeco-
nomically has also been affected by linguistic isolation with over half the adult
population (51.0%) indicating they do not speak English very well.

About 30 miles outside of Boston, Lowell also has a large Southeast Asian presence. Southeast Asian refugees began arriving there in the mid-1980s; by 2000,
Lowell was home to nearly 10,000 Cambodians, along with a smaller number of
Laotians and Vietnamese. The size of the Cambodian population is significant
considering it is the second largest population of Cambodians in the nation, following Long Beach, California. Together, the Southeast Asians comprised about
20% of Lowell's total population. The Southeast Asian population in Lowell is also
characteristically unique compared to other AAPI communities with nearly two
thirds of the adult population (63.4%) with an educational attainment of high
school or less and a large sector of the adult population (62.1%), which does not
speak English very well. The presence of Southeast Asians has had a significant impact on the community's schools, social services, public housing, and commerce,

including over one hundred privately owned businesses operated by Southeast Asians (Pho & Mulvey, 2003). The sharp increase and large presence of Southeast Asians has been described as a major factor in the school desegregation movement that occurred in the late 1980s, which included a Title IV lawsuit against the city for its treatment of language minorities and unlawful racial segregation.

There are three more ethnic communities depicted in Figure 3.2, comprised of Native Hawaiians, Asian Indians, or Filipinos. Wai'anae, in Oahu, is home to the largest concentration of Native Hawaiians in the United States; it may also be home to one of the longest remaining communities of Native Hawaiians with the loss of land by the Native Hawaiians that began in the mid-nineteenth century. Wai'anae has been described as "a community of one-thousand years of history, where the Native Hawaiian tradition has been handed down . . . " (Chai & De Cambra, 1989). The long history of Wai'anae has faced particular challenges by rapid urbanization and a changing economy, which has conflicted with the Native Hawaiians' traditions of subsistence lifestyle and Wai'anae culture. These conflicts have resulted in a Native Hawaiian community that has faced high poverty and poor educational prospects for the children of the community. Consider that among Native Hawaiians in Wai'anae, 78.5% of the adults had a high school diploma or less as their highest level of education, compared to a national average of 28.6% in 2000. These social conditions have made life in Wai'anae difficult for Native Hawaiians struggling to maintain their own way of life. Kitano and Daniels (1995) said of the migration that has occurred among native populations out of the Pacific Islands that, "Perhaps paradise, as depicted in Hollywood movies, is not sufficient to sustain life, or, more likely, the island image reflects a stereotype, not a reality" (p. 129).

While Wai'anae is symbolic of a long-standing AAPI community struggling to maintain its culture, heritage, and way of life, many other AAPI communities are thriving with a large influx of AAPI immigrants. Illinois is home to a large and growing South Asian population, which is larger numerically than any other AAPI ethnic group in the state. The South Asian population in Illinois doubled between 1990 and 2000 to nearly 150,000 residents. South Asians in Illinois have been described as having a "dual geographic pattern of dispersal" between suburbs and the city, which is not unlike some other AAPI communities. However, what makes South Asians unique in Illinois is that they are three and a half times more likely to be in the suburbs of Chicago as they are in the city itself, with the largest presence in DuPage County, which is adjacent to Cook County and a suburb of Chicago (South Asian American Policy & Research Institute, 2007).[1]

Many South Asians—most of whom are Asian Indian, but there are also Pakistanis, Bangladeshis, and Sri Lankans—end up in DuPage because it is the location of Illinois's technology and research corridor, which has experienced high demand for educated, skilled workers in technology-based industries. The high concentration of managerial and professional jobs in DuPage has resulted in a per capita income that is the highest of any county in Illinois; DuPage is also one of the wealthiest counties in the nation (South Asian American Policy & Research Institute, 2007). However, despite the high educational attainment and per capita income among South Asians generally, the population remains largely foreign-born (72.1%) and has a high proportion of adults who speak English less than very well (32.0%). Additionally, the South Asian population in the Chicago metropolitan area has been found to be quite bifurcated, with Asian Indians experiencing much more favorable outcomes than Pakistanis and Bangladeshis, who have less educational attainment, earn much lower wages, and experience higher levels of poverty.

Virginia Beach is home to one of the largest concentrations of Filipinos along the southeast corridor of the United States. While Virginia Beach has become home to many Filipinos because of the nearby Norfolk Navy Base, which is the central hub for the United States Navy's Atlantic Fleet, it has also been a draw because of its tourist and agricultural industries. Historically, this is not unlike the factors that have driven the settlement of many Filipinos throughout the United States, including Southern California, the San Francisco Bay Area, the New York City region, Seattle, and Honolulu.[2] What makes Virginia Beach unique isn't the size of the Filipino population; it was that Filipinos constitute 71% of the total AAPI population there, which is a much greater representation than can be found in most AAPI communities. This particular community of Filipinos in Virginia Beach is largely foreign-born (76.8%), with a large proportion of the adult population (63.7%) that does not speak English very well.

The residential distribution of AAPIs throughout the United States reflects the complex geography of the population. On the one hand, many AAPIs live in inner-city enclaves for housing, employment, support, and initial settlement upon arrival to America. On the other hand, many AAPIs who have succeeded in these communities often leave for the suburbs. One analogy applied to these dramatically different settlement patterns is inner-city and outer-city. For instance, the inner-city/outer-city analogy has been applied to juxtapose the Chinese Americans in the United States who live in middle-class integrated neighborhoods ("uptown") relative to their counterparts who live in inner-city Chinatown ("downtown") (Kwong, 1987; Louie, 2004; Wong, 1995). While the story of assimilation and moving from cities to suburbs certainly captures what has occurred among some AAPI ethnic communities, the uptown/downtown analogy is certainly not universally applicable.

For many Southeast Asians in the United States, settlement in particular communities is arguably less by choice and more attributable to forced settlement designated by the United States government (Portes & Rumbart, 1996; Zhou, 1992). Concentrations of Southeast Asian ethnic groups—particularly Hmong, Mien,

Cambodians, and Laotians, and to a lesser extent Vietnamese—have resulted in neighborhoods with high concentrations of poverty, high rates of government dependency, low rates of English proficiency, and poor educational resources (Ima & Rumbaut, 1989). The resettlement of Southeast Asian refugees occurred in the Gulf Coast region, the Midwest, the Northeast, and California. AAPI ethnic enclaves throughout the United States are unique demographically and characteristically, which makes it difficult to generalize a single depiction of their residential patterns as a whole. This has resulted in a vicarious position in the research on residential segregation. There are two general assertions made about AAPIs and their residential patterns: first, there is the proposition that, in contrast to their Black, Latino, and Native American counterparts, AAPIs do not have the same levels of racial isolation (Frey & Farley, 1996; Orfield & Glass, 1994; Orfield & Lee, 2005), nor do they experience a level of disadvantage among those who are segregated; second, there is a proposition that when AAPIs are segregated it is by choice as opposed to the result of discriminatory practices like those impacting Blacks (Orfield & Glass, 1994). Some studies argue that when AAPIs are segregated it actually benefits them when it comes to economic and social mobility (Orfield & Lee, 2006).

These propositions are captured succinctly by a *Wall Street Journal* article titled, "The New White Flight" (Hwang, 2005) that proclaimed, "Across the country, Asian-Americans have by and large been successful and accepted into middle- and upper-class communities." The crux of the story was that that high numbers and a greater concentration of AAPIs have caused some schools to be "too competitive" for others causing White students to "flee" two public high schools in the Silicon Valley. The White families were being forced out of their communities by an "Asian Invasion," and had to put their kids in private high schools to escape the intense competition of Asian Americans. Thus, while class is a social mechanism that has brought AAPI and White communities together, race has also been a factor that has kept them apart (Chang, 1999).

While the growth in the educated, white-collar sector of the AAPI population has resulted in a rise in the numbers of AAPIs that live in suburban, middle-class, and mostly White communities, the extent to which this is true for all AAPIs requires further investigation. Even among the AAPI groups that have experienced high rates of integration, for every family that has done so there is another that has not. For Chinese Americans, who have been one of the most integrated AAPI subpopulations, half of the population can be found in suburban America, while the other half can be found in "downtown" Chinatowns in cities like New York, San Francisco, Philadelphia, and Los Angeles. Although forced segregation ended in the 1960s, there remain a number of AAPI communities that consist of residents who continue to self-segregate, including those that can be found in communities within communities, with both residential arrangements resulting in isolation.

The profiles of AAPI communities provided earlier also reveal that the differences across these ethnic enclaves demonstrate that ethnic differences can be further exacerbated by residential patterns and the degree to which subpopulations concentrate residentially. In other words, how ethnic communities concentrate residentially accentuate some of the social conditions faced by AAPI communities. While most scholars of racial segregation would agree that AAPIs, like all racial groups, have unique patterns of residential settlement, it is not clear how extensive segregation is throughout the population, which has implications for the social networks and resources to which they have access. The following section places the different social conditions of AAPIs in a larger context of residential patterns and examines the extent to which the AAPI community is residentially segregated or integrated.

SEGREGATED OR INTEGRATED?

Residential segregation has been one of the most enduring and symbolic representations of the historic vestiges of structural racism in our nation's history. Segregation, which has mainly been defined by the exclusion of Blacks and the isolation of Whites geographically, socially, and economically, intensifies the effects of social conditions that vary by race. In Massey and Denton's (1993) groundbreaking work, *American Apartheid*, they argue, "Segregation is the institutional apparatus that supports other racially discriminatory processes and binds them together into a coherent and uniquely effective system of racial subordination" (p. 8). Because of how residential patterns segregate (and isolate) communities from one another, it is important to take these social boundaries into account when studying mobility. This chapter examines the extent to which this theoretical proposition holds true for AAPIs.

I tested the hypothesis that AAPIs are racially and ethnically integrated by examining two measures of residential segregation, the indices of dissimilarity and exposure, for some of the largest AAPI ethnic enclaves in the United States: San Francisco/Daly City, Los Angeles/Long Beach, and Orange County in California, and Queens, New York. The Index of Dissimilarity measures the difference between the neighborhood population composition of the units of interest and the population composition of the city as a whole (Frey & Farley, 1996; Massey & Denton, 1993). The Exposure Index measures the degree to which one racial/ethnic group is exposed to another racial/ethnic group; that is, the likelihood that somebody from one particular racial group lives in a neighborhood that is comprised by another racial group (Logan, 2001). The Dissimilarity (D) and Exposure (P*) are scores between 0 and 100, where a score above 60 is considered a very high level of segregation; in some of the literature this level of dissimilarity is described as *hypersegregation* (Massey & Denton, 1993).

Figure 3.3. Indices of Dissimilarity for Selected AAPI
Ethnic Enclaves, 2000

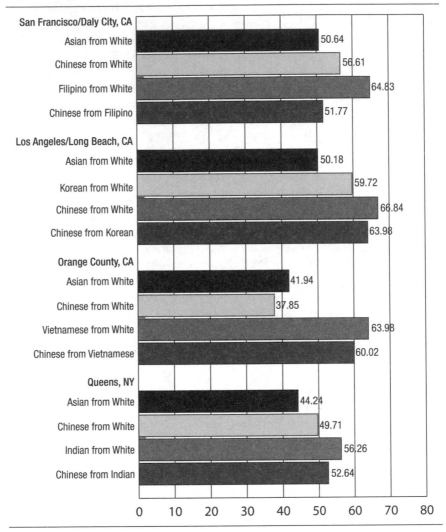

Source. Analysis of data from the U.S. Bureau of Census (2000), Summary File 1.

The following analysis of dissimilarity and exposure are examined comparatively across racial groups, as well as between ethnic groups among AAPIs, with
the hypothesis that the high degree of separation between ethnic enclaves (e.g.,
Vietnamese from Chinese, Chinese from Filipinos) would be a factor in how segregated or integrated the population appears as a whole.

Analysis of Dissimilarity

In the literature, research on racial dissimilarity is typically interested in the gap between Whites and others. As a result, studies that include AAPIs conclude that they are significantly less segregated residentially (Frey & Farley, 1996; Orfield & Glass, 1994; Orfield & Lee, 2006), and the percentage of AAPIs in integrated communities is significantly greater than other racial minority groups (Orfield & Lee, 2005). Thus there is an assumption that AAPIs do not experience segregation at all, and conversely enjoy a high degree of integration (Orfield & Glass, 1994; Orfield & Lee, 2006). However, because the level of segregation and integration are measures relative to Blacks, it is often not recognized that AAPIs do demonstrate medium to high levels of segregation from Whites (Frey & Farley, 1996; Teranishi, 2010). To a certain extent, the measures of segregation impact how we understand the causes and consequences of segregation among AAPIs (Orfield & Glass, 1994; Teranishi, 2010).

In 2000 across four metropolitan areas with high concentrations of AAPIs, Asian Americans experienced moderate to high levels of segregation from Whites (see Figure 3.3). San Francisco/Daly City and Los Angeles/Long Beach had higher dissimilarity scores from Whites (50.64 and 50.18 respectively) than Queens, NY (44.24) and Orange County, CA (41.94). The dissimilarity of Asians from Whites was even greater when factoring in the heterogeneity within the AAPI population. Across all metropolitan areas (with the exception of Chinese in Orange County), AAPI ethnic groups had a higher rate of dissimilarity from Whites than AAPIs as a whole. This result is consistent with other studies that have found that AAPIs have higher dissimilarity rates and a lower exposure rate when measured by ethnicity as opposed to race (Cheng & Yang, 2000; Teranishi & Nguyen, 2009).

In some instances the rate of dissimilarity between AAPI ethnic groups and Whites was substantial and points to a high degree of separation. A high rate of dissimilarity could be found among Filipinos in San Francisco/Daly City (64.83), Chinese in the Los Angeles/Long Beach area (66.84), and Vietnamese in Orange County (63.98). The higher rates of dissimilarity between individual ethnic groups and Whites, as opposed to the population as a whole, are impacted by the diffusion across AAPI subpopulations, which reduce the extent to which the population in the aggregate is concentrated. In each of these communities ethnic populations have significantly greater dissimilarity from each other than from Whites. Thus there is great variation in the extent to which AAPI ethnic subpopulations are segregated from other racial groups, as well as from each other (Teranishi, 2008).

Analysis of Exposure

The patterns of separation between ethnic groups are further supported by an analysis of exposure. Among the four metropolitan areas in Figure 3.4, there

Figure 3.4. Indices of Exposure for Selected AAPI Ethnic Enclaves, 2000

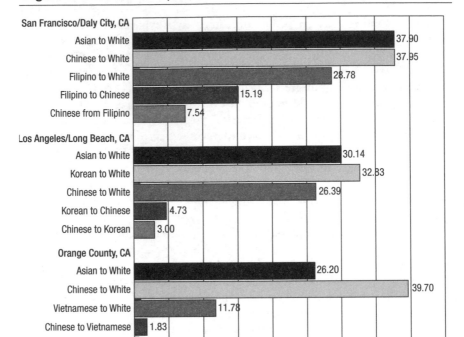

Source. Analysis of data from the U.S. Bureau of Census (2000), Summary File 1.

is great variation in the exposure rate of Asians to Whites. However, consistently among ethnic groups within individual metropolitan areas, there are significant differences in exposure rates. In Orange County, for example, exposure to Whites was much more likely among Chinese (39.70) than it was for Vietnamese (11.78). In addition to differences in exposure between individual AAPI ethnic subpopulations and Whites, it is also important to note the low levels of exposure between AAPI ethnic groups within metropolitan areas, such as the exposure rate of Chinese to Vietnamese (1.83) and Vietnamese to Chinese (0.63) in Orange County.

These data help to make three important points about AAPIs and their residential settlement. First, it demonstrates that AAPIs, when disaggregated by ethnicity, tell a dramatically different story than if they are treated as a whole. Second, the likelihood AAPIs will live near or have access to Whites is dramatically different when examined by ethnicity as opposed to the aggregate. Finally, when the residential patterns of AAPIs are disaggregated by ethnicity, a high degree of dissimilarity and a low degree of exposure between subpopulations are apparent, which is likely a cause for how diffused the population appears in the aggregate. These results are significant for establishing that AAPIs do experience residential isolation and low exposure rates, and these levels of isolation and exposure are mostly occurring at the level of ethnicity, rather than race. Accordingly, these findings demonstrate that the disparities in economic, educational, and cultural barriers can be accentuated by residential patterns, which can have significant implications for the educational experiences and outcomes for different AAPI ethnic communities.

While these quantitative indicators help to establish trends across AAPI ethnic communities, how these social factors play out within communities is better understood through the voices of students as they describe their communities and how their communities impact their educational experiences and postsecondary opportunities. The following section captures how Jay, Katie, Karen, and Johnny describe their communities in the context of a wide range of socioeconomic conditions that influence where individuals and families from different ethnic backgrounds live, the schools the students attend, and the resources and opportunities they have access to as they pursue higher education. The stories help provide a rich, in-depth perspective on various aspects of how their communities impact their lived experiences as they navigate their postsecondary aspirations and life goals.

HMONG AND THE "OUTSIDE WORLD"

Jay and Katie describe their community in a unique way. What is distinctive about their Hmong community in Sacramento begins with their description of their Hmong households. Jay's household, for example, is comprised of his parents, three siblings, and four other relatives, a number that is not unusual among Hmong households, who have the largest number of persons per household of any ethnic or racial group in the United States. Jay says, "It's normal for Hmong to have big families. It's what the Hmong culture is all about." Katie says less about the number of people in her household, and focuses on the tremendous challenges her family faces related to poverty. She says, "Things have been hard financially, we never have enough money, and we live a life that is very poor." She prefaced her description of her household with her parents' unemployment and long-term dependency on public assistance. These circumstances, in themselves, present tremendous challenges for Katie, yet their effect on Hmong children are amplified when repeated among Hmong households throughout their community.

Sacramento contains the third largest Hmong community in the United States and represents a well-established AAPI ethnic enclave. The Hmong community in Sacramento came about in the 1970s following their placement there via refugee resettlement. The arrival of Hmong in Sacramento occurred suddenly and with a great deal of impact to Hmong refugees, as well as the communities in which they settled in large numbers. During the 1990s, three fourths of Hmong were receiving public assistance in Sacramento. Katie says that the people in her community are always struggling and "there are a lot of problems in the neighborhood, like drugs, gangs, and violence, because people here are very poor."

The effects of these conditions may very well be amplified by the isolation that is sought by the Hmong community, which Jay speaks of succinctly; he says the struggle in his community is with the "outside world." It is rooted in a tension that exists within his community around survival and maintaining a Hmong way of life. Jay explains, "My parents have been living here for 20 years, and they haven't adapted to Americanization, yet. They're still like kind of prejudiced against other ethnicities." He goes on to say, "My parents don't talk to other ethnicities in the neighborhood and don't let them into our house." Jay is discouraged from having friends who are not Hmong. "[My parents] don't understand why I even bother to make friends with other races. They think that's totally rude and I'm disrespecting my own culture by bringing someone else in." The prejudice that Jay's parents hold toward others isn't as much a reflection of others as it is of them. In fact, the attitude that Jay's parents hold toward the "outside world" makes a lot of sense when considered in a broader context.

Katie further provides a context to Jay's narrative through her description of her own family's oral history. She says, "Our parents are afraid of us making friends with different races because of the history of what Hmong have gone through during the Vietnam War, you know." She continues, "We were chased out of Vietnam, just like we were chased out of China. From Vietnam, our people moved to Thailand or Laos, and then in those countries we had confrontations too with those people." Katie concludes by saying, "Not trusting people is a part of our history. So I think that's what made us so negative about other cultures." In considering what social forces create a racially or ethnically isolated community, Jay's and Katie's stories provides a glimpse into how the lived histories of the Hmong is one of distinction and isolation.

Jay's and Katie's stories capture how close-knit the Hmong community is in Sacramento. Their stories also demonstrate the extent to which their immediate and extended family is the basic unit of social organization for Hmong. This social organization results in a high degree of isolation outside of the extended family.

According to research that examines how ethnic enclaves operate in unique and powerful ways as sources of opportunities and barriers, this can be both an advantage and disadvantage when it comes to educational mobility and the pursuit of college (Lew, 2004; Louie, 2004). Jay's and Katie's stories are a case in point of this tension. Jay discusses this issue by saying, "My parents are traditional and I'm Americanized. It's difficult to become American while maintaining my culture." He continues by describing how this issue plays out in his multiple worlds of home and school and among his relationships with various social networks:

> I'm Hmong at home. But when I come to school, I'm more like Americanized, you know. I don't speak Hmong at school. I'm not Hmong with my friends at school. You know, when you're at school, you're supposed to be like . . . I act like Americanized. But at home, I'm like Hmong, you know, I got to be myself. So it's like this thing. You gotta like, have two masks. Like at home, I have a Hmong mask, and at school, I have an Americanized mask. So, at home, whenever my parents do stuff, like culture stuff, I'm still with them. I believe whatever they believe. Whatever they believe, I gotta believe 'cause that's my culture, you know. 'Cause if I don't, [my community] is gonna like fade away some day, and I don't want that to happen. But, it's hard because at school, if you act Hmong, you aren't gonna survive. You're not gonna survive in the real world if you act Hmong in America. So you gotta also have American ways, so you can make it through life.

The tension of maintaining a Hmong culture but becoming American is an issue that cuts across cultural practices, language, and religion. Jay adds, "people in my community are afraid. They don't want to lose our language, they don't want to lose our writing, and they don't want to lose our cultural ways." For many students, however, the desire to maintain their culture comes at a price. Jay says that since the Hmong culture "revolves around respect," it makes it difficult to negotiate tension between the two worlds. He says, "They don't want you to question their authority. There's no compromise." This issue comes to a point for women in the family. Pang, who also is Hmong and married when she was 14 years old, talked about her situation in the previous chapter. Katie discusses this issue pointedly, and says of the women in her family:

> For my friends and cousins, it's very sad. They say it's hard. They say that living with their in-laws they feel chained. They don't have enough freedom, and they thought that getting married would be better. But really, it's putting a lot more on them. They can't handle it. They can't balance it with school. In our Hmong culture, people get married really early. We

marry like at 13, 14, 15, in our teens. They become outcasts from society. 'Cause [American] society doesn't do that, so I think most early marriages for Hmong couples is difficult.

Katie says that this type of tension in the community comes down to the conflict between "wanting to maintain culture, but also wanting freedom from culture." For the youth that strongly maintain a culture that is so different from American culture, the implications for life after high school can be difficult to negotiate. Jay also brought up this issue in our conversation by describing his sister's situation:

My parents tell my sister that she has a weak heart, so she cannot be alone. She needs someone to be there for her. She can't go to college because she'll be afraid. If she lives in a dorm, bad people will come. You know, ghosts. So, she can't stay on her own.

While culture is a means for tension in the home for Jay and Katie, they are also aware of the effects of their family histories prior to coming to America, which continue to resonate today within their communities. Katie says, "My family was affected a lot by the war, a lot of families were, and it still affects us today." While AAPIs generally have been found to have higher rates of depressive symptoms than the general United States population (Surgeon General, 1999), mental health indicators among Southeast Asian refugees have been found to be much more severe. Southeast Asian refugees have faced particular challenges associated with traumatic experiences before, during, and after the immigration process to the United States, including high rates of victimization from and exposure to violence in their immediate communities and in their homelands (SEARAC, 2009). A Surgeon General's report (1999) found that nearly 70% of Southeast Asian adults receiving mental health care were diagnosed with post-traumatic stress disorder (PTSD) and 41% suffered from depression, even 10 years after leaving the region (United States Department of Health and Human Services, 1999). A more recent study on a sample of 490 Cambodian adults in Long Beach found that 69% met diagnostic criteria for PTSD, major depression disorder, or alcohol use disorder (Marshall et al., 2006).

Indeed, the psychological effects of fleeing a war-torn country, living in a family with few financial resources, and residing in an impoverished neighborhood have several consequences for the Southeast Asian refugees in the United States. High levels of stress, anxiety, and depression add tremendous challenges when adjusting to a new land (Sack, Clarke, & Seeley, 1996). These mental health conditions are exacerbated by a lack of access to health care and social services that can cater to these particular needs and a high level of poverty throughout the community. For children, this can play out in a way where there are severe negative consequences, including a negative effect on their emotional well-being and a lasting effect on their developmental process (Garbarino, Dubrow, Kostelny, & Pardo, 1992). One study of Khmer refugee adolescents found that 27% either partially or fully met the criteria for PTSD (Sack, Clarke, & Seeley, 1996). Another study of Cambodians in middle school and high school found that half experienced violence directed at them in their communities, while two thirds had witnessed violence (Berthold, 1999).

Jay speaks to the issue of violence in his community: "Sometimes it's hard to be Hmong. There's like many Hmong that do things that make us look bad. You know, gangs and stuff. It's like we're always getting in trouble. It's like, you go somewhere, and then they be like, 'Oh, you're Hmong?' And they think bad about you." Katie also talked about gangs in her community. Her description is also characterized by concern and confusion:

A lot of Hmong are in gangs and they're killing each other, you know. And like, you're asking yourself, "If you have Hmong pride in you, then why are you killing your own people, you know? Why are you like doing this and that, and giving yourself a bad name, and your people? You're not giving other people a bad name, but you're giving yourself and your people a bad name."

What is most concerning about the level of gang activity within the Hmong community is that the violence is mostly occurring between Hmong, rather than between Hmong and some other racial group. Katie says that in her community, the gangs reach "from north side to south side, and from east to west." Jay describes this also, saying "There are a lot of different types of Hmong gangs, starting from the south here all the way to north." He says that Hmong need to be very careful traveling from one side of town to another. "Sometimes in certain areas that you go, you kind of wonder if it's safe. It kind of limits what you can do. You don't want to be mistaken for someone else and end up getting beat up or something like that. And so, to me, it can be very dangerous."

Both Jay and Katie talked about this issue in their community at-large, but also had examples that are much more specific to their own lived experiences. Jay says, "I was mistaken for somebody else, and I was jumped. It's because when I was in elementary, in sixth grade, my friends were like all in gangs. So they thought I was one of them. I'm like, no. And then everybody says, let's jump him. So I ran away. So since that day, I have avoided those guys." Katie says that gangs have also affected her personally. She says, "Some girls wanted to fight me. I told them I'm not in a gang so they backed off. She says that her cousins were not as fortunate as her, and adds that their circumstances are "stupid, disgusting, and such a disgrace." She describes the situation:

One of my cousins was killed a couple of years ago. It was like late at night. Someone pulled up next to the car and just shot him. And he was with his brother, his younger brother. His brother just tried to drive away. But, he went and crashed into another car. My younger cousin ended up in the hospital, but his brother died instantly. I think they caught all of them.

The high rate of gang activity among Hmong in California has resulted in greater exposure to law enforcement. Although AAPI youth in the aggregate have low arrest, adjudication, and incarceration rates compared to other racial groups, significant differences exist within the AAPI population when these data are disaggregated by ethnicity (Arifuku, Peacock, & Glesmann, 2006; Le, Arifuku, Louie, & Krisberg, 2001a, 2001b). Nationally, among males ages 18–39 the incarceration rates of Laotians (which includes Hmong) and Cambodians are six times that of Chinese, Japanese, and Koreans based on analysis of the American Community Survey (U.S. Census Bureau, 2002). Among U.S.-born Laotian (which includes Hmong) men who did not complete high school the incarceration rate was 16.2%, which was greater than the incarceration rate among U.S.-born Blacks (11.8%) or Latinos (6.3%) in the same age group. Katie speaks of these trends relative to her own neighborhood: "Where I live, there's gang task force always coming around. As soon as school gets out, like around 4:00 to 5:00." Jay talks about his own run-ins with the gang task force:

I understand why there are a lot of police [in the neighborhood]. Where I live, it's like a bad place. It's like people do drugs over there. Across the street from us, there was like a drive-by right in front of us. But I also don't like all the police harassing us. They always stop me and my friends and take a picture of everybody. They won't leave you alone unless your parents are right there.

Katie says that she doesn't mind the presence of police in the neighborhood because she feels that the parents aren't able to control what's happening among the children. She says, "The parents, the elders, they are older, and they don't understand what their kids are doing." She says that they have their own problems "and deal with enough in their own daily lives."

The situation faced by Hmong communities has real consequences for youth wanting to pursue college. One major challenge is the lack of social capital that is available in the community relevant to college. In the previous chapter Pang talked about the lack of experience her family members have with the education system in the United States and how neither of her brothers or parents finished high school; the effects are magnified when looking across the community. Jay says that a lack of social networks in his community makes it difficult to convince his parents that he should go to college. He says, "They don't want me to go off to college. Like my parents think that I won't survive on my own. So they think it's better if I just like live with them. Well, I'm ready. They're the ones who are not ready." Jay adds that he tries to give his parents examples of people in the community who have moved away to college, but they often come up with the following counterargument:

> They tell me that I can't survive on my own, and they think that I'll become bad. They say they see other kids that go to big universities or going away home from college who come back being not like when they left. They say, "Those kids are supposed to go there and get an education instead of coming back worse." So, they use that example and then make it seem like we're gonna be the same way.

Jay says that it is difficult to argue against this point because he sees a lot of kids leave for college, but come back without a degree. He says, "They're going to universities, and they're coming back with nothing. Wasting their time I guess, not getting a degree." He adds, "My parents just want me to stay here so they can watch me while I'm going to school."

Katie's discussion of social networks in her community is framed around the need for, but lack of, role models. She says that someone needs to succeed so they can set a foundation for future generations of Hmong in America. She talks about the lack of role models in her community by framing it relative to those who are more privileged:

> It's easier for Whites because they already have people like Albert Einstein to look up to. You know, smart people. But for Hmong people, we don't really have nobody to look up to or whatever. So we got to work our way up to have somebody like that. I just hope that somebody—like me or my friends or somebody—becomes one of those persons that younger Hmong can look up to, you know.

"FOR CHINESE, IT'S SUBLIMINAL: IT'S ALL ABOUT COLLEGE"

Karen and Johnny both live in San Francisco, which is home to the largest population of Chinese Americans in any one city in the United States. Chinese Americans make up about one fifth of the 900,000 residents in San Francisco, which is also the largest concentration of any one ethnic or racial group in this "minority-majority" city. In San Francisco, there are really two enclaves of Chinese Americans. The larger concentration can be found in San Francisco's Chinatown, which has been home to many generations of new Chinese immigrants since the mid-1800s. San Francisco's Chinatown—the oldest and largest Chinatown in the country—has a long history, which is emblematic of Chinese American communities. Chinatown has served as a community where Chinese immigrants have resided, found work, and generally survived and thrived by means of "mutual aid and ethnic networks" (Ling, 2009, p. 2).

San Francisco also has the Richmond District, which is a smaller and relatively newer enclave of Chinese Americans; this is where Karen and Johnny reside. The Richmond District, which fits the analogy of a "satellite Chinatown" (Lin, 1998), is a less densely populated community that has become an outlet for Chinese Americans who seek upward mobility from the densely concentrated immigrant enclave of Chinatown. Johnny lived most of his life in Chinatown, but moved to the Richmond District when he was 14 years old. He speaks of the contrast between the neighborhoods: "Living in Chinatown is different. Yeah, a lot more Chinese people and it's very crowded. It was a big change when I moved here. It's a different area and much quieter." What are also different between the Richmond District and Chinatown are the socioeconomic conditions and language backgrounds of the residents. Analysis of data from the U.S. Census Bureau indicates that the educational attainment rates, household income levels, and use of English in the home among Chinese in the Richmond District were all nearly twice as high as was the case for Chinese in Chinatown in 2000.

Prior to the 1960s the Richmond District was predominately White, but shifted demographically through a large out-migration of these residents to the less densely populated suburbs of the San Francisco Bay Area, coupled with a steady in-migration of Chinese immigrants. Walking through the streets of the Richmond District, one will find a few streets that have Chinese-owned businesses, such as restaurants and retail stores with signage in Chinese languages, but with most of these stores are confined to the major thoroughfares, a sharp contrast to what can be found in San Francisco's Chinatown. Karen describes the Richmond District by saying, "The neighborhood is like a second Chinatown, but it's real different than the real Chinatown. There are not as many newcomers here. People move here after living in Chinatown."

Karen's description of the demography of the Chinese population is observant. There are actually many different Chinese American populations in the Richmond District, which are distinguishable by nativity and immigration backgrounds of the residents. First, there are the Chinese residents who have been in the Richmond District for many decades, even prior to the 1970s. Second, there are families who initially immigrated to Chinatown, then moved to the neighborhood since the 1970s. Finally, there are families that are very recent immigrants who settled directly into the neighborhood upon their arrival to the United States, finding the Richmond District through their family members who are already settled in the community. This cross section of Chinese Americans represents a diverse Chinese American population.

Taken together, the Chinese Americans in the Richmond District are primarily second or third generation, yet new immigration patterns facilitated by family social networks have led to an increasing number of first-generation immigrants. While most of the Chinese households are single families, there are some cases where family reunification has resulted in multiple-family households where recent immigrants live with family who sponsored their immigration. Thus, although the Richmond District has historically been a more established, middle-class neighborhood, it is experiencing an increase of families that are low-income and predominately first generation.

The range of Chinese families that vary by immigration status has meant an interesting mix of children in the neighborhood. Karen and Johnny both describe two major Chinese peer groups: the FOBs—"Fresh Off the Boat"—and the ABCs—"American-Born Chinese." Johnny speaks of the distinction:

> There are some Chinese Americans that are really working hard. These are the most recent ones, the ones who have about 14–15 years of Chinese tradition; these are the "FOBs." They're going to be working harder than average Chinese Americans. They have problems with their English, but they'll work harder than the majority of Chinese Americans who are born here; these are the "ABCs." ABCs tend to be influenced by TV and all the other American styles. They smoke cigarettes and like to hang out. So when it comes to things like education, they just get lazy. They don't really apply themselves.

Karen says the distinction between FOBs and ABCs is a problem because it dichotomizes and polarizes the Chinese youth. She says, "As a Chinese American, it means that I'm either one of the smartest kids or one of the laziest kids. You can't be somewhere in the middle."

Despite the distinctions between FOBs and ABCs, both groups of Chinese youth receive pressure from their parents to pursue college. Karen says of her upbringing, "We are just brought up to think that college is the most important thing, and that you need to get a college degree to get a good job. That's the only way to achieve in life." Karen adds that this is not only true in her family, it is also something that can be found throughout her community. Johnny has a similar description of the push for college. When talking about how driven his peers are when it comes to going to the best college, he says, "When they're young it's like subliminal, it's all about college. It's seems like they just start to worry about it without actually thinking it." He adds, "Eventually the pressure motivates them to work harder. Most of them want to be somewhere, not be someone important, but do something significant."

Johnny says the pressure to succeed is a part of the "Chinese culture" in America. He says, "I know within the Chinese community, we have a lot of expectations put upon our own children. And, then, we have to do what our parents tell us to please them." Johnny describes this pressure as an incentive to try harder in school:

[Chinese] children are brought up to think that college is the most important thing. I learned that you need to get a college degree to get a good job and that's the only way to achieve in life. The pressure motivates me to work harder because I'm afraid of failing. I get stressed out, but I just try harder.

Karen also describes the pressure among children in the community to not let their parents down, but she describes the pressure as debilitating. She says that some of her friends are "worried about being embarrassed if they fail." Karen adds that a big issue is that parents believe that what the kids do reflects on the entire family. So the kids aren't just accountable to the parents, it also to their entire community. She describes how she experiences this firsthand: "It happens all the time, my parents are always comparing me to my relatives or someone else's kid. They say, 'Why can't you do good in school like them?' And if they hear of someone that does something bad, my parents say, 'Don't end up like them.'" Karen says that "this pressure can be overwhelming" as she describes how some of her friends can never seem to please their parents:

> When some of my friends are doing bad in school, if they think they are going to fail, they get stressed out. It's like they are going have a nervous breakdown. I don't know, I think it will be like that for them all the way in life.

Although Chinese parents in the Richmond District had high postsecondary expectations and pressured their children to get into a college, the extent to which they were actually involved in helping their children realize these expectations seemed to be limited. Johnny says that his parents are too busy to be involved:

> My parents have to work hard. And, my mom is self-employed with her own business making clothing. She goes to work about 7 days a week. She works from 8 to like 7, so, 12 hours a day. And at home, she's even working, like while she's watching TV, she's doing something for the work. And my dad, he has a job with the city. So, he has a government job which is steady pay. But, I mean, they don't have time to get involved with my school work.

Johnny says that he and his family rely more on his community, which talks a lot about college. When describing this kind of exchange in the community, he says, "When I'm with my parents we see people on the street and we discuss things like what the kids are doing, and they just talk about the school thing with other adults." He says that his parents also talk about college with his relatives, who also put pressure on him to go to college. He says, "My auntie, my mom's sister, has been living here for quite a while, so they just talk to each other about college."

Accordingly, the importance of family expectations needs to be considered in a broader context of social networks that can help facilitate students' pursuit of college. Studies have found that children are seldom raised and socialized exclusively by their parents; rather they are raised in embedded social networks that extend into a wider range of individuals that constitute family and community kinship (Coleman, 1988; Stanton-Salazar, 1997; Valenzuela & Dornbusch, 1994).

In her network of friends and relatives in the community, Karen says that she can turn to a lot of people to ask about college. She says, "With most of my relatives and friends, education is kind of like a tradition. I come from a long line of high achievers who are well-educated." Therefore, while her parents provide the expectations and encouragement to pursue college, her relatives and friends often provide the information and guidance that will help her realize her aspirations. She explains:

> My parents often tell me to do the best I can in high school and it'll look good when I apply for college. But when it comes to college my parents haven't really experienced it here, so I'll go to my relatives for that kind of stuff. So I really can't get the specifics, like how to go about doing things, from my parents. But I can get it from my cousins directly since they have been through the process.

Karen says of her relatives and friends, "They watch out for me" and "make sure I'm on the right path." So if Karen is feeling lost, confused, or overwhelmed with the options she has or the decisions she needs to make, she can turn to relatives who can help her sustain progress through useful guidance. She adds that she turns to her cousins, in particular, because she can "relate to them."

Johnny says that his relatives are "a major influence" when it comes to college, as opposed to his parents. He says that his immigrant parents have not gone to college in the United States, whereas his friends and relatives "know that kind of stuff." In students' survey responses, more than two thirds (64%) of the participants indicated that their siblings and relatives were their *most* trusted source of information and guidance, compared to only 3% who indicated the same about their parents. Johnny provides the example of his uncle's guidance, which is both comforting and inspiring to him:

> What drives me is something that my uncle said a long time ago. This was when I was young, but it still stays in my head because it really meant a lot. He said, "If you really want to succeed in life, you do something that you really like to do." And my other uncle also encourages me to go to college. I go to them for advice about the college process. I know they try their best to help me out.

Karen says that she would rather turn to her relatives to ask questions about college over the resources that are available at her school. She says, "I trust that my relatives will help me. They keep reminding me what to do." Her extended family has told her about different colleges, the requirements to get in, what college life is like, and how to best strategize for the best experience. Karen adds, "My cousins who are in college are like my role models. I think that's a big part of it, support— as long as you have someone to fall back on. I just follow them and watch what they do." Thus a major theme for Karen is to literally follow the educational path of her relatives who have been successful at pursuing college.

THE NARRATIVES OF Jay, Katie, Karen, and Johnny demonstrate how important their communities are in their lives as they develop and pursue their educational goals. What is consistent between them is the importance of immigration history in their homes and larger communities—the drive to excel educationally and achieve opportunities that were not afforded to their parents. What is also similar is the importance of the social networks that existed in their communities, which mediate access to college information and knowledge. However, the likelihood that students can realize these goals must be understood in a larger context of access to resources and social networks in the community, which varies across different AAPI ethnic enclaves.

At the same time, the role of community forces on the lives of AAPI youth must also be understood within the context of differences in what resources and support they have access to in their homes. In other words, in the context of the previous chapter, some AAPIs have a greater likelihood of having access to parents with higher educational attainment, higher income, and a better command of English than other AAPI subpopulations. Compounding this issue is that groups with higher levels of poverty and living in more difficult community circumstances are also more likely to live in less stable home environments. Ironically, groups that have a higher number of persons per household also are more likely to have children who live in single-parent households. These conditions place even a greater importance on the role of social networks and other resources in the community.

However, while the community context has the potential to provide rich information, knowledge, and guidance for students about college, its role is mediated by the level of firsthand experience possessed by the members of the community. Thus, if a student was situated in a network of individuals who had firsthand experience with college, the information and guidance was quite resourceful; but if a student was not exposed to individuals who had experience with college, the student was typically provided information, guidance, and support that was generally more vague, derived from secondhand sources, or, in some cases, inaccurate or discouraging. Therefore, their communities provided the landscape through which students' networks would shape their social distributions of possibilities.

Jay, Katie, Karen, and Johnny provided descriptions of their communities that supported the earlier portraits of AAPI communities throughout the United States, demonstrating that each AAPI ethnic enclave warrants local treatment as opposed to assumptions based on generalizations that exist about the population as a whole. The resources, opportunities, and social networks of Karen and Johnny's community in San Francisco is different from what may occur in the Chinese enclaves of Brooklyn or Monterey Park/Alhambra, when taking into account the social indicators of immigration backgrounds of the residents, the educational attainment levels of adults, differences in English-usage, and income-levels in the household. Brooklyn is a gateway for new Chinese immigrants, while the Richmond District in San Francisco and Monterey Park/Alhambra in Los Angeles are home to more established Chinese Americans who settled via secondary migration.

The extent to which AAPIs are segregated or integrated has implications for the composition of the schools attended by various AAPI communities. The next chapter considers the implications of these various social characteristics among AAPIs for differential access to quality schools and varying levels of postsecondary preparation. The cumulative effect of community differences and varying levels of access to postsecondary resources result in a wide distribution of eligibility for and access to different sectors of higher education.

CHAPTER 4

Secondary Schools and Postsecondary Opportunities

In previous chapters I have discussed the extent to which AAPI subpopulations are exposed to a variety of social and ecological conditions that impact their postsecondary aspirations. While these factors in themselves can affect the educational mobility of AAPI students, they also need to be examined in the context of how they mediate access to key organizational contexts, such as quality K–12 schooling. In this chapter Eric (Chinese), Jenny (Filipino), and Tommy (Hmong) who describe the ways in which their high school experiences mediate access to college resources and opportunities. Their descriptions of their schools vary quite dramatically and capture the relative differences of high schools throughout the United States.

Eric attends Wilson High School, which is located in San Francisco, California. Predominately comprised of Chinese American students, Wilson High School has a solid reputation for sending their graduates to college. (See Appendix A for description of data collection procedures.) Eric, now in 12th grade, says, "Some parents even move to the neighborhood so their kids can go to this high school." Eric's account of Wilson High includes descriptors like "challenging," "academically rigorous," and "oriented toward college." Eric says that there are better high schools in San Francisco, like Lowell,[1] but they involve a competitive admissions process and most of the students who attend his school weren't admitted if they applied. Nevertheless, Wilson High has an impressive array of Advanced Placement (AP) course offerings in 13 different subject areas, enrolling more than 400 students annually. In 2005 Wilson High sent nearly 400 students to college, which represented more than 75% of the graduates. The majority of these students went to public 4-year colleges, but there were also students who attended 4-year private institutions and public 2-year colleges.

Jenny's description of her school, Hoover High School, is a sharp contrast to how Eric describes his school. Hoover High is located in Vallejo, California, and has a sizeable concentration of Filipino students. Jenny describes Hoover High as a "regular high school." She says that while Hoover High has a solid history of preparing and sending students to college, "it doesn't do as well as some other high schools." She adds, "It's a good high school, but not the best." Jenny says there isn't a big emphasis on college, which is evident by the three AP courses they offer that are only accessible by the seniors. At Hoover High there is a larger emphasis placed on vocational education, which includes 30 courses that are offered each academic year. The subject areas covered include word processing, accounting, home economics, nutrition, woodshop, automotives, and drafting and graphics. A lot of students in their senior year also participate in a robust work experience program, which enables students to work during the school day through arrangements with local merchants. In 2005 slightly more than 60% of the graduates at Hoover High attended college, but nearly 70% of these students enrolled in a public 2-year college.

How Tommy describes his school—Hancock High School in Sacramento, California—is focused more on what it does to get students to graduate than to help students get into college. Delinquency and problems associated with student behavior make for a particularly challenging school environment. Tommy says that his school, which has a sizeable population of Hmong students, "is not known for sending students to college." He adds, "If a student really wants to go to college, they're in the wrong high school." Like Hoover High, Tommy's school also has a sizeable vocational education program. In fact, in 2005 more than half of the seniors were enrolled in at least one of these courses. What is distinctive about Hancock is the high rate of teachers who are new to teaching: In 2005 nearly 40% were in their first two years of teaching, and more than 30% of these teachers were not fully credentialed. Hancock High is not typical for what would be associated with Asian Americans, but it is also important to acknowledge that this association is only true to the extent that one overlooks the reality faced by many Asian American students.

These descriptions of high schools capture the range of experiences in America's neighborhood comprehensive public high schools. Although American public education is open to all students, it has produced differential outcomes despite numerous federal educational reform movements of the 1950s and 1960s (Orfield, 1993). Patricia Gandara (1995) describes in her work how children who live and attend schools in concentrated pockets of inner-city communities are almost exclusively low-income students of color. These patterns of segregation often result in low-income and minority students attending ethnically isolated schools that have poorer funding, fewer resources (such as college preparation courses), teachers with less training and experience, and other conditions that negatively affect student learning. This chapter situates subpopulations of AAPI students in a broader context of their access to disparate school conditions.

RACE, CLASS, AND SCHOOL INEQUALITY

The relationship between K–12 schooling and college enrollment begins with academic preparation, which is the greatest predictor of college aspirations and the likelihood of enrollment in college (Adelman, 2002; Hossler et al., 1999). Access to rigorous college preparatory curricula and qualified teachers are essential components for students' educational pursuits beyond high school. Other organizational practices and policies, such as counseling resources, are important for providing students access to information, knowledge, and guidance during the college choice process. As college admissions become increasingly competitive at the most selective institutions, college preparatory curricula, such as honors courses or Advanced Placement courses, have played an increasingly vital role (Adelman, 1998; Anderson & Hearn, 1992; Astin, 1982, 1985). For example, first-time freshmen enrolling at the University of California–Los Angeles in 2000 had an average of 17 honors and/or Advanced Placement courses during high school, bringing the average high school GPA among this class to a 4.20 (University of California, Office of the President, 2000).

Today, inequalities persist where race and socioeconomic status continue to predict access to quality secondary education and postsecondary opportunities. Different racial groups, as well as students who vary by socioeconomic status, have differential access to college preparatory curricula such as AP courses (Teranishi, Allen, & Solorzano, 2004; Teranishi & Parker, 2010). Top students at an affluent school with a wide range of advanced and college preparatory courses have more of an advantage to attend the most selective colleges than their counterparts at a high-poverty school that offers fewer college preparatory curricula (Oakes, Rogers, McDonough, Solorzano, Mehan, & Noguera, 2000; Wilds & Wilson, 1998). The Chief Justice Earl Warren Institute on Race, Ethnicity and Diversity at University of California–Berkeley released a compelling policy report, *California at the Crossroads: Confronting the Looming Threat to Achievement, Access, and Equity at the University of California and Beyond* (Brown et al., 2006), that found that the University of California (UC) disproportionately serves the state's highest income and best educated families while limiting access for low-income students of color; half of UC's freshmen come from high schools that educate only one fifth of California's public secondary school graduates.

In addition to disparities that exist across schools, there are also within-school variations across race and class that can impact students' preparation and access to higher education (Coleman, 1987). Within-school variations across race and class have been identified as the "school-within-a-school" phenomenon (Horvat, 1996; Oakes et al., 2000). Ability grouping and tracking practices result in disproportionate (and often inappropriate) placement of racial and ethnic minority students in the lowest ability courses. These long-standing practices have had a significant negative effect on these students' opportunity to learn.

Counseling and guidance are also key elements for students' processes of making decisions about college (Alexander & Eckland, 1977; Horvat, 1996; McDonough, 1997; Morrison, 1989). Counseling and guidance inform students of options, provide important information, and help students make decisions that may impact their postsecondary outcomes. Because of the important role of counseling in college choice, high school guidance counselors are gatekeepers to college access (McDonough, 1997) and can play a particularly valuable role as admissions to selective colleges become increasingly complex and competitive. Guidance counselors are often the sole individuals who possess the knowledge and information necessary for students to make the right decisions to prepare for and enroll in college.

Unfortunately, many counselors have little exposure to college planning and are ineffective in helping prepare students and parents for making postsecondary transitions (Boyer, 1987; McDonough, 1994, 1997). Students often lack information about college options and opportunities because of a lack of high school guidance services (McDonough, 1994; Orfield, 1992). In some schools, counselors are not always available to students. One study indicated that the average counselor-to-student ratio at low-income, inner-city schools was 1:740 (Fitzsimmons, 1991). Thus, similar to ability tracking, counselors will often track students by picking those they deem to be "college material" to provide college preparatory curricula or college guidance (McDonough, 1997). This is particularly important considering that low-SES students and students of color, who may not have resources in the home, rely more heavily on counseling and guidance at school (McDonough, 1997). Counselors in low-SES schools often deal with scheduling, discipline, and dropout prevention issues, rather than guiding students with their academic achievement and postsecondary plans.

Perhaps the most important aspect of the educational experience for all students is their access to educators who are knowledgeable, experienced, and caring individuals. These are essential ingredients for providing students with the type of learning environment where they can thrive academically and developmentally. This is important for students' access to higher education because academic achievement, as measured by GPA or performance on standardized tests, is the most important factor in determining the type of postsecondary institution a student attends, or if a student goes to college at all. Unfortunately, teachers in urban schools with high concentrations of students of color or low-income students have been found to have less teaching experience, a higher attrition rate, and lower salaries than teachers working in middle- and upper-class, White communities (Darling-Hammond, 2010; Oakes, 2005). Additionally, many students have to contend with the deplorable conditions, educational practices, and other qualitative features of inner-city schools that are described by Jonathon Kozol (1991) in *Savage Inequalities*.

Despite the vast body of research on the effects of schools on students' postsecondary preparation and outcomes, there is little known about how these factors impact the postsecondary aspirations and outcomes of AAPI students. There are several gaps in the literature when it comes to the AAPI population, including the extent to which their race, ethnicity, or socioeconomic backgrounds impact the

Figure 4.1. Distribution of Students (by Race) Who Attended Schools with 50% or Greater Minority Enrollment, 2005

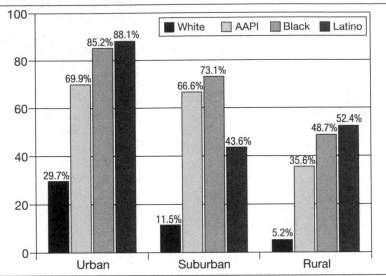

Source: Analysis of data from National Center for Education Statistics (NCES, 2010a).

schools they attend, the extent to which they attend racially segregated schools, or the access they have to college preparatory curricula and other resources, and how that affects their college preparation. The following discussion responds to the gaps in the literature and examines the extent to which AAPIs attend similar or different schools and the extent to which AAPI students have similar or different postsecondary opportunities and outcomes.

ACCESS TO QUALITY SCHOOLING FOR AAPI STUDENTS

Prior to the United States Supreme Court's historic *Brown* decision, racially divided schools not only existed but were sanctioned by law. While some believe that racial segregation was resolved in 1954, many regions of the country in more recent decades are exhibiting resegregation of housing and education across racial and ethnic lines (Orfield & Lee, 2006; Orfield & Yun, 1999). Today, de facto segregation maintains racially isolated public schools throughout America. Nationally, Black and Latino students, on average, attend schools where they represent more than 50% of the student population. White students are even more racially isolated as they are likely to enroll in schools where 78% of the students are also White (Orfield & Lee, 2006).

In the context of school segregation, it is often said that high numbers and a greater concentration of AAPIs are associated with high achievement and academic excellence (Orfield & Lee, 2006). While the growth in the educated, white-collar sector of the AAPI population has resulted in a rise in AAPIs who do live in suburban, middle-class communities (such as the Richmond District discussed in the previous chapter), the extent to which this success story is true for all AAPIs needs further investigation. Similar to previous analyses on residential segregation, the measurement of AAPI school segregation may very well be a factor for how they are positioned in the research. While AAPIs are more likely to attend schools with Whites than Blacks and Latinos are, they also exhibit high rates of attending schools with 50% or greater minority enrollment (Figure 4.1).

In urban schools, where most AAPIs can be found, nearly 70% of AAPIs attended schools that are predominately comprised of minority students. In suburban schools, 67% of AAPIs, compared to 73% of Blacks and 44% of Latinos, attended a predominately minority school. Similar trends can be found in rural schools where 36% of AAPIs attended schools that were predominately comprised by minority students, compared to 52% of Blacks and 49% of Latinos. Thus, while AAPIs do not exhibit levels of segregation that are greater than or equal to Blacks or Latinos, in particular, it does not necessarily mean that they are all attending schools that are predominately White.

Examples of racially and ethnically segregated high schools attended by AAPIs are provided in Table 4.1. These eight schools, all in California, were selected because of their location in distinct AAPI ethnic enclaves. The two schools that were predominately comprised of Hmong students were located in Fresno and Sacramento. The AAPI students, nearly all of whom were Hmong, represented 60.7% of the total enrollment in the Fresno school, and 34.3% of the enrollment in the Sacramento school. Two other schools, one of which was in Westminster and the other in San Jose, had a proportional representation of AAPIs that was between 62.1% and 49.1%. The schools in the Chinese communities had an AAPI enrollment, nearly all of which was comprised of Chinese students, between 70.2% and 71.5% of the total enrollment. Finally, the schools in the Filipino enclaves had an AAPI enrollment that constituted between 44.6% and 57.5% of the total enrollment.

These predominately AAPI schools also enrolled students with a range of social class backgrounds as indicated by the proportion of students eligible for the Free or Reduced Meal (FRM) program and the average parental education levels. In terms of FRM, students in schools that were predominately Chinese or Filipino had a lower rate of eligibility than students in schools that were predominately Hmong or Vietnamese. This pattern was similar to trends in parental education where Chinese schools had a higher average parental education level than Hmong and Vietnamese schools. Schools that were predominately Hmong, Vietnamese, and Chinese also had a larger proportion of their students who were identified as English Language Learners compared to the Filipino schools.

Table 4.1. Characteristics of High Schools in Selected AAPI Ethnic Enclaves, 2000

	Hmong Schools		Vietnamese Schools		Chinese Schools		Filipino Schools	
	Fresno	Sacramento	Westminster	San Jose	San Francisco	Alhambra	Daly City	Vallejo
DEMOGRAPHICS								
Total enrollment	1,015	3,194	1,523	4,341	2,304	2,039	1,669	1,296
Number of AAPIs	616	1,096	946	2,131	1,617	1,458	744	745
Proportion enrollment AAPI	60.7%	34.3%	62.1%	49.1%	70.2%	71.5%	44.6%	57.5%
Free or reduced price meal	49.2%	39.4%	34.2%	30.3%	12.5%	23.2%	14.1%	20.2%
Average parent education*	1.83	2.18	2.39	2.67	2.98	2.83	2.98	2.27
English language learners	30.9%	33.9%	36.7%	28.5%	29.6%	34.4%	13.1%	12.9%
TEACHER EXPERIENCE								
Number of years teaching	15.1	13.1	17.1	15.7	17.2	17.8	13.0	14.8
Teachers with < 2 years experience	12.2%	10.4%	19.7%	17.4%	8.5%	12.1%	31.9%	15.8%
Fully credentialed	89.8%	90.8%	90.4%	86.6%	88.9%	91.2%	85.7%	89.5%
Emergency credentialed	9.5%	8.6%	9.1%	13.0%	8.9%	8.8%	12.1%	9.8%
SAT AND THE AP PROGRAM								
AP exam takers	1	41	106	229	308	256	62	34
AP exams	1	46	134	418	815	463	81	34
AP passing scores	1	3	64	207	536	351	29	9
AP passing rate	100.0%	6.5%	47.8%	49.5%	65.8%	75.8%	35.8%	26.5%
SAT I Takers	38	55	82	371	370	242	144	101
11th/12th grade SAT takers	16.5%	10.6%	34.3%	53.2%	71.0%	51.2%	31.0%	36.6%
SAT I verbal average score	397	420	445	457	451	478	459	434
SAT I math average score	432	474	510	495	521	573	485	435
SAT I total average score	829	894	955	952	972	1051	934	869
AAPI COLLEGE ELIGIBILITY								
A-G courses fulfilled	2.5%	2.8%	18.0%	23.8%	36.5%	41.2%	19.3%	9.0%
A-G, 1100 SAT	0.0%	0.0%	4.3%	7.6%	12.4%	13.8%	3.8%	1.8%
A-G, 1300 SAT	0.0%	0.0%	1.8%	2.7%	4.9%	7.9%	2.3%	0.5%

Note. Data unavailable for outcomes for specific AAPI ethnic groups. However, the majority of AAPI students in each school were predominately of one AAPI ethnic background, which was determined by the school's neighborhood composition.

* Parental education is a scale from 1–5: 1= less than high school; 2= high school completion; 3= some college; 4= bachelor's degree; 5= graduate/professional degree.
Source. Analysis of data from the California Basic Educational Data System (CBEDS).

There are also important differences in teacher experience across the schools. The schools in Vietnamese and Chinese communities had teachers with the greatest number of years teaching, and the schools in Vietnamese and Filipino communities had the largest proportion of teachers with less than 2 years experience (between 15.8% and 31.9%). The schools in Daly City (Filipino school) and San Jose (Vietnamese school) had the lowest proportion of teachers who were fully credentialed and the highest rate of teachers with an emergency credential (12.1% and 13.0% respectively). Varied levels of teacher experience have been found to be correlated with the quality of education in schools, in addition to the availability of certain curricula, such as Advanced Placement and honors courses.

A key representation of the quality of schools and their ability to send students to college can be measured by comparing students' use of the AP program and their test-taking trends. Schools varied widely in the number of students across these schools who took an AP exam. In the two Chinese schools, between 256 and 308 students took at least one AP exam, with students from one school taking a total of 463 exams, and 815 from the other. Students in the San Jose school also had a large number of students who took the AP exam (229), including a high number of exams (418). This is a sharp contrast to the AP participation that occurred in the Filipino and Hmong schools. In these schools, the number of test takers was lower—in the Fresno school, which is predominately Hmong, there was only one test taker—and the number of exams per test taker was also low. The one student who took the exam in Fresno also only did so in one subject. Students from the Filipino school in Vallejo had 34 test takers, with all students taking only one exam.

Similar patterns were evident with regard to the SAT exam. The students attending the Chinese schools and the Vietnamese school in San Jose had a large proportion of 11th and 12th graders who took the SAT I exam (between 51.2% and 71%). Students in the Hmong and Filipino schools had a low of 10.6% of students who took the SAT I exam and a high of 36.6%. Students in the Chinese and Vietnamese schools scored higher on the SAT I, on average, than students in the Filipino and Hmong schools, with the greatest differences found in the math portion of the exam.

Relative to how schools prepared students for college, examining UC "eligibility" is instructive. In California, eligibility for UC is a standardized way to determine access to different sectors of public higher education. Eligibility can be roughly estimated as completing a prescribed set of curricula with at least a "C" grade—often referred to as the A-G requirements because there are seven subject areas. These courses represent the minimum eligibility to attend a public 4-year university in the state.[2] The minimum eligibility along with taking the SAT I exam and scoring a 1050 represents moderate eligibility. Competitive eligibility is measured by the completion of A-G requirements and scoring at least a 1200 on the SAT I (UC Office of the President, 2000). Students in Chinese and Vietnamese schools were more likely to be moderately and competitively eligible to attend a 4-year college than students from the Hmong and Filipino schools. For the schools that were predominately Hmong, no students were considered moderately or competively eligible, which virtually guarantees that they do not have students who can compete for admission to the University of California. This is a sharp contrast to the 7.5% of graduates from the San Jose school and the 13.8% of students in the Alhambra school, both of which were either predominately Vietnamese or Chinese.

These data document the wide distribution of demographic characteristics among AAPIs and how these differences correlate with access to a range of disparate organizational contexts. While there are many AAPIs with access to resources and opportunities that afford them the ability to be competitive for admission to the most selective universities, there are also many AAPIs who are not afforded the same opportunities. Thus the differential access to quality schooling has several implications for the postsecondary academic preparation of AAPI students.

To further this point, it is useful to return to Eric, Jenny, and Tommy, who describe the extent to which their own schools—all of which were profiled in the descriptive quantitative data—facilitate access to postsecondary resources and opportunities. Similar to undertanding how students' relationships with their parents, extended families, and communities facilitate the development of their aspirations, qualitative insights are also useful for gaining perspective on how students navigate relationships with classmates, teachers, adminstrators and other individuals they encounter in their schools. Consider how Mike Rose (2005) in *Lives on the Boundaries* describes his childhood growing up in a working-class immigrant family and the challenges he faced throughout his educational experience, or how Jonathan Kozol (1991) in *Savage Inequalities* provides a portrait of overcrowded, unsanitary, and otherwise deplorable conditions of segregated schools in urban communities. Qualitative information is able to capture individual lives as they are situated within particular school conditions, such as the climate and quality of the school environment, which is diffcult to quantify. Indeed, exploring the qualitative world of schools is important for achieving a richer, in-depth perspective about how students' perceptions of and experiences with their schools facilitates academic performance and college-going behavior.

The foci of these case studies are the narratives of Eric, Jenny, and Tommy as they describe the various resources and opportunities they encounter in their schools pertaining to their postsecondary planning and decision-making processes. I also examine how they describe the disposition of institutional agents with regard to the college information and knowledge that is transmitted to them. Finally, I focus on how Eric, Jenny, and Tommy describe the larger school context that enhances or undermines the ability for institutional agents to provide college information, knowledge, and guidance for students.

WILSON HIGH SCHOOL, SAN FRANCISCO

Eric is well on his way to follow in his two older sisters' footsteps to attend a selective 4-year university. One of his sisters is in her fourth year at UC Davis and the other is in her third year at UC San Diego. Eric proudly boasts of his sisters, "My sisters are great role models for me. I'm really fortunate to have their guidance when it comes to college, because neither of my parents can give me specific advice because they haven't gone to college." Both of his older sisters attended Wilson High, where Eric is currently enrolled. Eric talks about his AP Psychology class and says that he chose to take it because both of his older sisters had taken the class with the same teacher. He says, "My sisters told me he was a cool teacher." There were many teachers in Eric's school who were there when his sisters attended the same school 5 years ago. At the time of Eric's tenure at Wilson High, the faculty had an average of 17 years of teaching, an impressive number for any high school. In the 5 years prior to my discussion with Eric about his high school, there were only seven new faculty hired. Thus, at a time when there had been a teacher shortage throughout California, Wilson High had not experienced problems retaining their faculty or gaining new ones.

Along with a cadre of senior faculty, Wilson High offers a comprehensive curriculum that focused mainly on college preparation, including a robust AP program. Their AP courses in English, history, Spanish, math, biology, chemistry, and physics enroll more than 500 students annually. Evidence of the quality of the AP program at Wilson High can be found in their students' test performance on the AP exam. In 2000, 308 students from Wilson High took 815 AP exams with a passing rate of 65.8%.[3] This passing rate was more than three times greater than the passing rate for California (20.2%) and four times greater than the national average (15.2%) (College Board, 2006).

In addition to his AP Psychology class, Eric is taking three other AP classes this semester: economics, calculus, and physics. Eric says taking so many AP courses at the same time is very demanding academically, but "I take them to get some college credits out of it; it also makes my transcript look good." Speaking of his AP Economics class specifically, he says, "I wanted to try and get some basis for [Economics] because most likely I'm going to be taking that course when I'm in college." Eric's enrollment in four AP courses in one semester was not exceptional for his school. In a survey of students at Wilson High I found that nearly two thirds of the seniors by their fall term had taken five or more AP courses.

Patricia McDonough (1997) describes the ways in which some high schools are in an optimal position to provide their students with the social and institutional contexts through which students can form and realize their postsecondary plans. Wilson High, indeed, had an array of academic resources that were geared toward preparing and sending students to college, including an extensive college preparatory curriculum, a cadre of experienced teachers, and a low turnover rate among teachers. Equally as important, there was a college-going culture at Wilson High, with tangible goals and practices that were conducive to their students' pursuit of postsecondary education. Eric describes how the culture of college was particularly paramount in his AP classes: "My AP teachers have helped me in my college planning. They're the ones that care the most about college." Eric says that teachers in his AP courses give him specific advice about college, such as which institutions he should consider or what he needed to do to get into different types of colleges. He goes on to explain:

> I have an AP teacher that told me, "Do good now so you don't have to take general education classes in college." She also told me special dates and deadlines and helped me with my college essay.

What is evident in Eric's description of his AP teachers is that his teachers care about him and his outcome. He says, "They encouraged me to take those classes; they always tell me how much potential I have." The encouragement, guidance, and support Eric receives is not limited to his experience with his teachers; he also describes the kind of support he receives from the counseling staff at Wilson High. Eric says that he talks with his academic counselor frequently and he likes her because "she allows me to choose my own classes," which he says helps him optimally strategize his course schedules to be the most competitive for college. Eric also uses his meetings with his academic counselor as an opportunity to talk about and get feedback regarding his college plans. He says:

> [My academic counselor] helps me a lot in scheduling my classes, guiding me where I need to go. And, she lets me do basically whatever I want. I practically make my own schedule rather than them scheduling me. I'm also able to talk with her about the colleges I'm thinking about applying to, to see if she can give me some advice about that.

Counseling and guidance are key elements for a student's process of making decisions about college (Alexander & Eckland, 1977; Horvat, 1996; McDonough, 1997; McDonough & Perez, 2000; Morrison, 1989). Counseling and guidance inform students' options, provide important information, and help them make decisions that may impact their postsecondary outcomes. Because of the important role of counseling in college choice, high school guidance counselors are gatekeepers to college access (McDonough, 1997) and can play a particularly valuable role as admissions to selective colleges become increasingly complex and competitive. Guidance counselors are often the sole individuals who possess the knowledge and information necessary for students to make the right decisions to prepare for and enroll in college.

At Wilson High, Eric not only benefits from his many conversations with his guidance counselor about college, he is also fortunate to have access to a college office. The college office at Wilson High is staffed by two part-time college counselors. Both of the college counselors are retired and in their previous work were guidance counselors at the school. One of the college counselors, Ms. Smith, describes the office as a resource to help students find college-specific information and to receive guidance from a counseling staff dedicated to college advising:

> It is a place for students to find a range of college information, including college catalogs, applications for admission, and information about standardized exams and important deadlines. The office is also a place for students to receive both one-on-one and group guidance . . . in some cases with a counselor, but also directly from college representatives. The office also is a place where we house a number of college outreach staff from local colleges and universities. . . . Three days a week, Upward Bound sends a representative to the college office to talk with their program participants at the high school.

Eric describes the college office as an important source of information about college. He says he does everything from "talking to counselors to get advice about college" to "getting college information such as booklets and fee waivers." Eric says that he brings in college information he acquires from other sources, such as family members, friends, or the Internet, so the counselors can provide input, or even help him interpret the information. He says, "I can go to the college counselor and ask questions about the SAT and ACT, and what I should take to better my chances . . . stuff like that. They're helpful." Eric says that he also appreciates how the college counselors are able to facilitate visits by college representatives to talk to students about different college campuses.

Most of all, however, Eric says that he appreciates the one-on-one guidance he is able to get from the college counselors as a discerning college applicant. Eric calls these meetings his "college strategy session." Eric describes how Ms. Smith helped him create a list of possible colleges to consider:

> Ms. Smith already made a list of colleges for me. She says that I don't have to do anything else to get into Riverside, Whitman, UC San Diego, UC Riverside, and UC Santa Cruz. But I'm not sure if I'll get into USC or some of the other ones. I don't remember the other ones, but there were only a few public schools and the rest of them were like private schools.

In talking with Ms. Smith about where the students from Wilson attend college, she proudly boasts about all of the graduates who each year apply to and attend selective public and private colleges, both in state and out of state. She attributes their success, in part, to the office's ability to work with students early on, through frequent meetings to construct a plan for how many and which colleges they should apply to. She doesn't mince words in describing her primary job responsibility at the college office: "My job is to ensure that students can be confident that they will get into the best colleges as long as they keep up their grades." The college counselors do so through building relationships with students and connecting with them frequently throughout their tenure at Wilson High.

Eric describes one other way his school has afforded him a competitive edge when it comes to college admissions: extracurricular activities that keep him quite busy after school. Eric lists the organizations with which he is involved and some of his responsibilities:

> I'm currently the president of the Future Business Leaders of America Club in our school; I have been president for 3 years. I'm in the Math Club. I'm involved with the General Service Society, which is a volunteer group. I'm in the Chinese American Club, where I am on the Board of Directors. Oh, and I'm on the Speech and Debate Team this year. I used to run track and play golf, but I stopped after 2 years.

When asked why he is involved in so many clubs at school, Eric says:

> These extracurricular activities are like brownie points. My teachers and counselors tell me they are important for getting into college. And, with what I have—my classes, my grades, my SAT scores—my sports and extracurricular activities help make me more competitive. I have all these things backing me up. I'll get into some college that I'll probably be happy with.

Eric's description of Wilson High demonstrates the extent to which some high schools can provide their students with the resources and opportunities that are optimal for preparing students for admissions at the most selective colleges. Eric is aware of the advantage that his school affords him, which was evident in how he describes the sharp contrast to the situation that other students are faced with because of the lack of academic preparation they received at other schools. Eric says:

> College is gonna work you hard and you're probably not gonna make it if you're not accustomed to this workload. There's a big difference between college and high school, and if you send a person from school that does not prepare you for college, you're not going to survive when you get there. Well, maybe you can, but you'll have to work 50 times harder than any other person there.

HOOVER HIGH SCHOOL, VALLEJO

Jenny's sister was the first in her family to go to college. After high school, her sister began at a community college which she attended for 3 years and a semester. Jenny's sister recently transferred to a 4-year college in the area. Jenny's sister still lives at home, but Jenny says, "I don't get to see my sister too often because she is always busy with work and school." Jenny's sister attended Hoover High, which is where Jenny is currently enrolled. Hoover High is located in the suburban enclave of Vallejo, about 30 miles west of San Francisco. Vallejo is home to a large and vibrant Filipino community. At Hoover High three out of five students are Filipino, which makes it one of about a dozen high schools throughout the nation that has a sizeable concentration of Filipinos.

Jenny says of Hoover High that "it's a good school, but you need to stay on top of things to be successful." She self-describes herself as being in the "college prep track" at school. Accordingly, she is enrolled in the only two AP courses (English and chemistry) the school offers, which is only accessible by about 5% of students. This puts Jenny in a select group of students who are afforded this privilege. Jenny says that she feels fortunate to be in the college track because that means that she has a couple of teachers she can talk to about college: "These teachers seem to care more about college. And, they like to talk about college." While these teachers give Jenny a good feeling about college, Hoover High students' performance on AP exams indicates a lack of preparation for college-level coursework. Of the 34 students who took an AP exam in 2000, only nine passed, which was a passing rate of only 25%. Compared to Wilson High's passing rate of 66%, Hoover High exam takers performed poorly.

The poor preparation for students to be academically competitive for college had a direct and tangible effect on their chances for being competitive at selective colleges. Nevertheless, Jenny is still fortunate compared to other students in her school. Most students at Hoover High are relegated to the English Language Learner track or the vocational track at her school, where less experienced teachers tend to be concentrated. One in 10 teachers at Hoover High in 2000 were on Emergency Credentials and one in five teachers had been teaching for fewer than 2 years. That sizeable proportion of teachers who were recent hires is a reflection of the high teacher turnover rate at Hoover High. Jenny says that outside of the teachers in her two AP classes, she doesn't have a lot of close contact with other teachers. She talks about her lack of contact with teachers and says that it means that she just needs to be that much more self-motivated in her pursuit of college information and guidance:

> I haven't really developed a real personal relationship with a lot of the teachers. Only some [teachers] I kind of got a little insight into what they're about. At this school, you gotta be a self-starter. You can't rely on

your teachers to give you information or to help you out. They tell you a little bit. You got to go out there and find out more.

Thus, while college preparatory courses offered instructors who provided students with information, guidance, and motivation about college, the students who did not have these classes felt that their teachers were not caring, accessible, or encouraging. For this group of students, the discourse they used to describe their teachers included words like "unavailable," "inaccessible," or "unapproachable."

Jenny's story is not a unique one. Ricardo Stanton-Salazar (1997) has noted that "success within schools has never been simply a matter of learning and competently performing technical skills; rather, and more fundamentally, it has been a matter of learning how to *decode the system*" (italics in original, p. 13). Accordingly, Jenny's success isn't merely a matter of if she can do well in her classes, which she has—her success is also dependent on how she will navigate various relationships with institutional agents in their schools (i.e., teachers, counselors, administrators, and so on). But for Jenny, this means sorting through a lot of vague, conflicting, and sometimes discouraging information and guidance.

Jenny describes an interaction she recently had with one of her teachers about which college she should choose. Her teacher advised her to attend a community college and provided her with the following rationale, "My teacher told me that it's the same thing. You're being taught the same thing you'll get at a 4-year college; it's just that it's the price that's different." This teacher was not the only person to advise Jenny in this direction. She says that her parents also want her to attend the local community college and live at home. Jenny is suspicious of this advice, however, and points to her sister as an example for why she wants to go directly into a 4-year college. She says, "My sister told me that she regrets going to a community college. She says that it is going to take a long time to get her degree and there were a lot of classes that she couldn't get into when she was there." Jenny adds, "Plus, my sister says that I have the grades to go straight to a 4-year college." So the advice that Jenny is getting from her teacher is clearly not providing her with the range of postsecondary options that she should be getting.

When Jenny turns to her counselors, guidance about college is also difficult to come by. One structural factor that adds to the challenge is that Hoover High does not have a college or career center. Jenny says that they are trying to find teachers who can build partnerships with colleges in the area, but the last teacher who did that left a couple of years ago. Jenny recalls that teacher bringing a representative from a community college, but she could not recall any instance when a representative from a 4-year college came for a visit. Thus, despite efforts to create a more concerted focus on college at Hoover High, there continued to be a lack of staff designated specifically for college counseling. Absent a dedicated college counseling regime, the academic counselors were often the source of college advising.

This was a challenge for academic advisors who were also saddled with a range of other responsibilities. Jenny says that counselors visit some of the senior classes, typically just once, to talk with students en masse about different requirements for college, but college is not really their concern:

> Mainly the counselors just focused on graduation requirements, like how many units we needed to graduate. They don't talk to us about anything beyond high school. They don't even talk to us about college, but I wish they did.

Jenny says that she needs to be persistent in asking her counselor about college, although she rarely gets specific feedback that addresses her questions. She says, "I've asked my counselor questions about college, but they don't tell me what I need to know, but I'm gonna keep nagging him to give me information because that's his job—to help out the kids."

How Jenny describes her challenge with getting specific guidance regarding college is not unusual. Unfortunately, many counselors have little exposure to college planning and are ineffective in helping prepare students and parents for making postsecondary transitions (Boyer, 1987; McDonough, 1994, 1997). Like Jenny, there are many students who lack information about college options and opportunities because of a lack of high school guidance services (McDonough, 1994; Orfield, 1992). The difference between schools in quality of guidance regarding college is often a matter of the significantly different types of counseling programs that exist across schools, which affects the accessibility of counselors, as well as the quantity, quality, and type of contact counselors have with students. More specifically, the role of counselors in students' postsecondary aspirations and outcomes was often due to the design of each school's counseling program.

The accessibility of counselors in Jenny's case was also a challenge. She says that if she wants information or guidance about college, it is up to her to take the initiative to talk to her counselor. Jenny explains, "It seems that you need to bring your questions to them because they won't go to you. They won't call you in." Jenny describes the challenge of getting on her counselor's busy calendar by saying:

> Every time I ask for a transcript or something like that because I wanna see how I'm doing, my counselor would say, "Oh, come by after school or come by early in the morning." So, one time, I came by early in the morning, I was there like at 7:15 a.m. And, he didn't come till like 8:10. I'm like, "Come on, dude." I waited almost an hour for him to come. And, then first period came, and he told me to go to class and to come by at lunch. And, when I came by at lunch there was a sign that said, "Office is closed

for lunch." So I went by after school. After school, the office was packed so I was like, "Forget it, there's a line."

When Jenny does get to speak with her academic advisor, she says that her interactions with them are "very brief" and often "impersonal":

> When you're able to meet with a counselor, the meeting is always short or the counselor is always in a rush. They sign your slip and say, "What do you want? A grade change or a class change?" Then they quickly type in your request in the computer, and you're gone. That's it.

Jenny's experiences with her counselor are consistent with other research (Stanton-Salazar, 1997). She says that she does not feel like the counselor takes her seriously or that he cares: "He's not that dependable and I don't really trust him because he's not helping me as much as I need." This makes Jenny wary of the information and guidance she receives from her counselor:

> Sometimes I don't think he is even listening to me. It makes me not want to listen to him. I don't think my counselor cares anyway. I mean how could he? There's too many of us for them to care about each and every one of us. Like I don't think they'd be able to keep up anyway.

The lack of trust that Jenny feels toward her counselor is, in part, driven by his lack of accessibility. This is a persistent problem in many schools where understaffing means that counselors are overworked and have a larger case load than they are able manage effectively (Fitzsimmons, 1991). This is problematic for many students, like Jenny, who have limited access to resources in the home, and must rely more heavily on counseling and guidance at school (McDonough, 1997). But as is evident in Jenny's case, the schools where students need the greatest counseling support tend to be the schools where counselors focus more of their attention on scheduling, discipline, and dropout prevention, rather than guiding students through their postsecondary plans.

Jenny resorts to two other sources to get college information and guidance: her friends and the Internet. In terms of Jenny's use of the Internet, it is often limited because she does not have a computer at home and relies on the accessibility of the computers at school. This isn't always ideal because Jenny needs to wait in line with the rest of the students who rely on the computers at school. She says, "I try to use the computers at school, but most of the time it's just like, 'OK, forget it. I'll try again tomorrow.'" Jenny's other source of college information— her friends—were most readily available, but she can't always rely on them to answer her questions. She says, "A lot of times, they're just as clueless as I am."

HANCOCK HIGH SCHOOL, SACRAMENTO

There are no people in my family to encourage me to go to college. My mom and dad didn't go to college, and they work really hard to get a little bit of money. It's a hard situation for me. But in comparison to other people, you know, I have to look on the bright side. There are a lot of people who have it worse than me. But it's not like I'm going to inherit anything, you know. I have to learn and earn my way into college. So I think that it doesn't matter how many people I have. And it doesn't matter what I don't have. It depends on what decisions I make and what I want to do with my life. If they can do it, I can do it. And what they do, I can do, too.

Although Tommy is keenly aware of the uphill challenge he faces, he is not deterred. The fact that he would be the first in his family to go to college motivates him to try harder in school. He asked one of his older sisters about Hancock High before he started his freshman year there. His sister didn't attend that high school, but she had friends who did. He says, "My sister warned me about this school. She said that she had friends that went here and like, she saw them failing and dropping out." Tommy says he witnesses some of these trends personally as he describes his school: "The atmosphere at this school is just to get students to graduate rather than getting them into college. . . . You hope students will graduate, but half the time it doesn't even work that way because we have a 50% dropout rate." Tommy's concerns about his high school were echoed by the assistant principal, who indicated that the most immediate problem the school was facing was their graduation rate, which was well below the state average. Thus it was evident that Hancock High faced a difficult challenge of creating a means for addressing two persistent problems: retaining and graduating students, on the one hand, and providing college opportunities, on the other.

For those students who do go to college after high school, most attend the local community college. Through conversations with his sister, he knew that outcome was likely for him: "My sister told me that this school didn't have those classes that you need to go to a university." Tommy says that he hasn't been happy with his teachers. He describes a situation in his sophomore year where he didn't even have a teacher for much of the semester: "I got into this algebra class my sophomore year. I was really excited, but only for just one day. My class didn't have a teacher. We eventually got a substitute teacher now, but it's really slow and boring." In his other classes, Tommy says that he doesn't like most of his teachers. Tommy says that he has tried to approach his teachers about college, but "for the most part, teachers are just worried about what they're teaching, like their lesson. Some teachers just don't want to give any good advice. They just basically don't care." Tommy says that his teachers' lack of motivation makes it difficult for him to stay motivated. He says, "In some classes, you're not motivated at all because the teachers don't seem into it."

When asked about his interactions with his counselors, Tommy says, "Honestly, I have never had a chance to talk with her about college. She just gives me the classes I need." Instead, like most students at Hancock High, Tommy turns to Ms. Taylor at the Career Center. Tommy says, "I talk to my counselor, but, well, I don't feel like that close to her. I feel more comfortable talking to the career specialist." The Career Center runs the Regional Opportunity Program (ROP), which is very popular at the school. Tommy says that he is able to explore career pathways through ROP:

> The career center helps me decide which college I should go to based on my interests, my career interests. And we have job training at different job sites. So, I just take the classes that they offer. I'm in a public service class now. Last year, I took a class about automobile engines. So, the best thing you can like learn from school is like learning about these different career pathways. So, they'll send you out to wherever you want to work. If you're into retail, they send you to retail stores, like to Long's Drugs or Styles For Less. And you go and you're a work-study student. You go out and get real world training, you know.

While Tommy is pleased with the different options ROP presents him regarding postsecondary opportunities, the likelihood it will lead to a path to college other than a community college is limited. The other interesting aspect of the Career Center is that it doubles as a college center. Tommy says that there are occasions when colleges come to visit through arrangements by Ms. Taylor. He says, "Last year I was able to talk with a [local community college] representative who usually comes once a year, so that was very convenient." But when Tommy asked about attending a 4-year college, he received some discouraging advice from Ms. Taylor. He says, "I told her that I would like to go to a 4-year college, but Ms. Taylor said, 'If you can't handle high school work, you can't handle college.'" Still, Tommy remains undeterred in his dream of attending a 4-year college right after high school.

These lofty goals, however, are difficult to pursue in a school that emphasizes retention and graduation over college. Moreover, Tommy says that getting students to graduate is only part of the problem at Hancock High. There is also poor attendance and a lot of issues related to delinquency. Tommy describes his school as "hard core" with the toughest gangs in the city. He says that there is some tension between racial groups, but most of the tension is intragroup. Hmong students make up more than one third of the enrollment at Hancock High. Another 30% of the enrollment consists of Black students, and the rest of the students are Latino. Tommy describes the intergroup relations as being "segregated or separated between like Asian students and African American students." Tommy describes how he thinks Hmong are perceived by others in the school:

> I remember back in my freshman year it was really bad. There was like almost 2 full weeks of fighting. It was consecutive days, one day after another. It was all gang related. I tried to avoid all of that. So that's why at lunchtime I always stayed in a classroom. I didn't even go outside. It wasn't safe to go outside at lunchtime. Even in between periods. A lot of people hated Hmong. Like if you're a Hmong, it would be like, OK, no friendship here. Like, "You're dirty. And you're bad. And aren't you the one who got in a fight last week?" There's not much respect here for the Hmong people.

While Tommy is not in a gang and goes out of his way to avoid gang violence, he says that it affects the entire school. He says that there is a lot of peer pressure, which is difficult to deal with. "Being Hmong, you're bound to have like 20 cousins in this school. And, that creates a lot of peer pressure. And sometimes, you never know what you're getting dragged into." It even affects what route Tommy takes to get home after school or if he can visit the local library:

> If my parents don't have the time to come get me, and I need to walk home, I found certain routes where I know are less dangerous. Some routes that you take may have been a bad experience. Sometimes there's just like bad students out there, just waiting to have fun. The gangs hang out in certain areas, like at the library. Sometimes they'll hang around there. So you can't go to the library 'cause they're there, and you don't want to get beat up or anything.

The focus on gangs and violence in the school has resulted in Tommy being mistaken for being a gang member by the school administration. He says, "From what I know, they mix me up with this one guy because we have the same name. And they always call me in, because like that guy has the same name as me. Missing a minute of like a class for me is like missing the whole lesson." Despite explaining this mix-up to the administration on numerous occasions, and even though the other boy is in a different grade level than Tommy, he says that they never seem to get things straightened out. He says that type of incident makes him frustrated with his school. He provides another example of where he has a lack of faith in his school because of tension around strict policies and the punitive measures his school takes when dealing with students:

> Well, the issue is the uniform code that says we're not supposed to wear hats. They let some students slide by if they have a certain type of hat, but

when they see another student with a hat on, they'll take it off. We question authority because there have been 2,400 suspensions within the last two years. And that's 40% of the whole entire school district. You know, "If you guys want to do something, we'll find you under defiance and get you suspended for a week." And, there's no due process. You're supposed to get your warning, and then you get detention, and then suspension. Plus the hearing of why you got suspended, you know. But, that's not how it happens here. My friend Bubu, he got expelled for wearing a hat and not taking it off. He was not given a prior warning, like, "I'm gonna give you detention for it." So, now he's in continuation school. It's kind of like, what do you call it? Like a dictatorship.

Tommy says that the problem is because of a new administration, which includes a principal who has a bad reputation in the district. He says, "Our principal now was the vice principal at another high school in the district. I heard the students didn't like him. There were rumors about him going around calling students, 'niggers.' Some students even threatened to beat him up and stuff." Tommy says that even though he doesn't like the administration, he's been able to steer clear of any major problems at the school. He says, "I'm given detention from time to time, but I haven't been suspended yet. All these things I see at this school pushes me to fight back, to show them that students are not gonna be treated this way."

Talking with Eric, Jenny, and Tommy reveals a rich illustration of how schools play an important role in the development and pursuit of postsecondary aspirations among AAPI youth. One set of factors discussed earlier in this chapter are the ways in which schools unevenly afford students access to postsecondary opportunities and resources, and information and guidance. For more privileged Asian American students, those who lived in suburban, middle-class neighborhoods, schools consisted of an institutional culture that focused on college and dictated the ways in which institutional agents provided resources and opportunities to students who attended these schools. For Asian American students who resided in poor, urban communities, access to resources was not dissimilar to other poor students of color who often lack access to social and cultural capital in the home, and rely more heavily on counseling and guidance at school (McDonough, 1997). Thus, while schools played a critical role for all Asian American students in determining the quantity and quality of information, guidance, and access to opportunities during students' processes of developing and pursuing postsecondary aspirations, it could either promote or diminish their educational trajectory depending on the quality of their school.

Resources are a central aspect for a school's ability to prepare students for college. Unfortunately, the range of college preparatory courses and vocational courses that schools offered was not equally distributed across schools. Some schools have more college preparatory courses through programs like AP, honors, and the Gifted and Talented Education (GATE) program, while other schools in the study were focused on vocational training, such as the Regional Occupational Program, Work Experience, Reserve Officer Training Corp (ROTC), and what some schools called electives (auto shop, woodshop, typing, and so on) (Oakes, 2005).

However, a lack of resources was just one way that some AAPI students are negatively affected by their schools. Many students in poor performing schools felt that their teachers and administrators do not have time for them because they were too busy dealing with issues that were more important to the school. In some cases, this translated into a perception among students that faculty and staff talked down to and treated them as though they were failures, as opposed to recognizing their academic goals and accomplishments. These students often acknowledged the problems in the community and the school, but wanted a chance to prove themselves.

These findings are consistent with other research that has found that because institutional agents play such a key role in determining the information and knowledge that students have access to, they can be considered gatekeepers to college opportunities (Teranishi, Allen, & Solorzano, 2004; Stanton-Salazar, 2001). The social and institutional contexts of schools are instrumental in creating the environments through which students can develop and pursue their postsecondary plans and choices. This, of course, is a tale of two stories in that different institutional contexts can either create or undermine social mobility for students.

Schools played a particularly significant role in providing information and knowledge about college because they often needed to augment a lack of experiential knowledge that was available to students from their families. For better or for worse, students used the guidance from institutional agents to gauge their preparedness and qualifications for college to determine which colleges to aspire to attend. In many cases, students relied on schools as their primary source of information and guidance because these resources were not available at home or in their communities. While families were often students' source of postsecondary aspirations and expectations, schools were where students fulfilled their goals through academic preparation for college and accessing college information and guidance.

CHAPTER 5

Predictors of
College Participation

Returning to Pang, Trung, Tony, and Lilly, who were featured in Chapter 2, this chapter looks again at their college aspirations in light of the circumstances in which they live. Will they reach their stated goals? With what level of certainty can we make that determination based on what we know?

You may recall that a lot of pressure rests on Pang's shoulders. If Pang attends college, she would be the first in her family to do so. In fact, she would be the first to finish high school. But it isn't the pressure to excel academically that she is feeling from her family; rather, the weight on Pang's shoulders is her responsibility to her family—more specifically, her parents, her in-laws, and her husband. The odds are stacked against Pang for reaching her ultimate educational goal of getting a college degree. Pang has two colleges on her wish list: a local, moderately selective 4-year college and a local community college. While Pang has completed all the right courses and received the right grades to get serious consideration by a selective 4-year college, her family situation and the process through which she has been pursuing her aspirations is prohibitive. Pang says, "Oh, God, I don't know if I'm going to [the 4-year college]. I'll be disappointed if I don't, but, you know, I got to do what's best for my family. I can always go to [the community college]."

Tony, on the other hand, is set on his plans to attend a selective private university, "maybe even an Ivy League" he proclaims. Tony plans to one-up his older sister who attends a selective public university in California. He has been told by his father to not be concerned with cost, and he is not setting any geographic boundaries on this college search. Tony describes the applications he is currently putting together for college: "I have nine colleges at this point: Harvard, MIT, Princeton, Cornell, Stanford, USC, and a few UC campuses as a backup." Tony's goals are clear and he has the high school record to substantiate them. He has taken the right courses, received the right grades, and ranks high in his class; he has held leadership positions in student organizations, volunteered in the community, and played sports; and Tony has also scored in the top 5% on the SAT I. Tony exhibits the pedigree of a top-ranked student, which will afford him serious consideration in the high-stakes, top-ranked university admissions process.

Trung also has an exceptional academic record, which he attributes in part to his school, which has a track record for sending a large proportion of its students to 4-year universities each year. Trung's concerns are not if he can be admitted to a selective university, but how he will pay for it once he is admitted. Both of his older sisters who attend 4-year colleges live at home and work part-time jobs. One of his sisters attended a community college after high school as a way to save money on the cost of tuition. Trung's mom has made it clear that he will need to pay for at least half of his college tuition, which is a factor in whether he will enroll in college full-time or part-time. Trung says of his chances, "I'm working as much as possible now to save up money to pay for college. My mom says she'll help out, but that wouldn't be fair to my sisters. Well, there's always another choice . . . I can go to the military." In his high school he has participated in ROTC, which he says will pay for his college, making enlistment a real option.

Lilly is also unsure about her postsecondary plans. She is torn by the competing interests of her mother who wants Lilly to stay home and attend a college nearby, and her desire to leave home to attend a more selective university, like her older sister. Lilly seems to be leaning toward staying close to home, which gives her two options: a community college or a moderately selective 4-year college. When Lilly talks about the colleges she applied to that would require that she move out of the house, she says, "I don't know how I picked these schools. I just kind of picked them. I did it the day the applications were due and I kind of rushed through them. I just think they are too good for me and I'm never gonna make it." Lilly says that a more likely fit for her will be a couple of other options that are closer to home. She says, "It will probably come down to staying close to home and support the family." Lilly says that attending college nearby will please her mother, and it will also mean that she will get a car. She adds in an upbeat tone, "That would be cool."

Up to this point in the book, I have demonstrated that AAPIs pursue college through a unique set of circumstances. Specifically, I have placed their preparation for and trajectory to college in a broader context of societal conditions and organizational settings. Doing so has provided a more complex and nuanced portrait of the wide distribution of opportunities for college. The purpose of this chapter is to examine how social conditions and organizational contexts faced by AAPIs translate into unique patterns of higher education participation for students within the population. More specifically, this chapter situates AAPI participation in higher education within the context of their unique demographic features, the schools that they attend, and the different states and regions in which they reside, and examines how their college participation is distributed by type (community college to 4-year doctorate granting), selectivity (nonselective to highly selective admissions), and control (public and private). The last section of this chapter provides a descriptive and multivariate analysis that examines factors that contribute to how and why demographic features of the AAPI population impact their differential rates of enrollment in the various sectors of U.S. higher education.

TRENDS IN AAPI COLLEGE ENROLLMENT

College participation among AAPIs can be traced as far back as some of the earliest documentation of AAPIs in the United States. Some historians claim that Zeng Laishun, a student of few means came from China to the United States in 1843 and enrolled in Hamilton College in Clinton, New York, in 1846.[1] Laishun left Hamilton after 2 years, thus not claiming the accolade of being the first Asian to receive a degree from an American college, but he has been noted to be China's first college student to study abroad (Rhoads, 2005). The first Asian to receive a degree in the United States may very well have been Yung Wing, who received a bachelor's degree from Yale in 1854 (Worthy, 1965). Yung Wing described his college experience in the United States in an autobiography he published late in his life (Wing, 1909).[2] Aside from Yung Wing and Zeng Laishun, there is little acknowledgement of AAPIs in United States higher education until the turn of the twentieth century when Filipinos accessed United States higher education through the Pensionado program, which was created by the United States government to sponsor several hundred Filipino immigrants to attend American colleges primarily in the Midwest (Kitano & Daniels, 1988; Segal, 2002). There is also evidence of an influx of Asian participation in U.S. higher education during the mid-to-late 1920s, though most did not often stay in the United States after graduation. Takaki (1998) said of these students that many did not stay because of a lack of career opportunities available to them in the United States.

Zeng Laishun, Yung Wing, and the Filipino students of the Pensionado program are just a few examples of Asians in U.S. higher education that can be gleaned from the literature; the historical documentation is limited, as are statistical data. Much of the historical data on race prior to the 1960s was interested in one of two pairings: (1) Blacks and Whites, or (2) Whites and non-Whites. Most states, along with the federal government, did not collect data for Asian Americans or Pacific Islanders until the mid-1970s, which is an appropriate place to begin a discussion of the contemporary enrollment of AAPIs in college, because it coincides with the rise in their population generally in the United States.

In 1975, AAPIs constituted 1.6% of the more than 11 million students enrolled in United States higher education. Figure 5.1 shows that by 1990, AAPI enrollment more than tripled to 578,000, and nearly doubled again over the next decade and a half. In 2005, there were more than one million AAPIs participating in United States higher education. While the number of AAPIs enrolled in college between 1975 and 2005 increased at a staggering pace, AAPI enrollment is projected to continue a sharp increase by another half million between 2005 and 2020.

While the growth in AAPI participation has been dramatic—a fivefold increase over a 30-year period—it needs to be examined in a larger context. First, while the gains in enrollment among AAPIs may seem like a feat fit only for a "super minority," the reality is that these gains are perceptively deceiving. Consider AAPI

Figure 5.1. Total AAPI Enrollment in U.S. Higher Education, 1980–2005

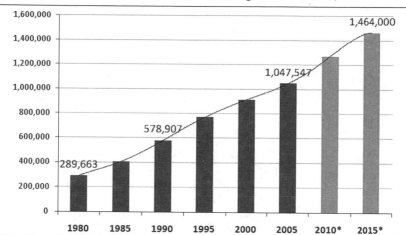

Note: Data through 1990 are for institutions of higher education, while later data are for Title IV, degree-granting institutions.

*Data for 2010 and 2015 are "middle alternative forecasts."

Source: Analysis of data from the National Center for Education Statistics (NCES, 2010b).

enrollment gains relative to their demographic changes overall during the same time period: The sheer size and growth of the AAPI population since the 1970s has created a larger pool from which AAPI college students could be drawn. Thus the rise in college participation among AAPIs coincides with dramatic shifts in population growth overall, as well as in K–12 enrollment.

It is also important to note how other organizational contexts were factors in the increase in AAPI college participation. The population changes among AAPIs coincided with the tail end of a great expansion in U.S. higher education. While in 1975 U.S. higher education had a total enrollment of over 11 million students, the number of students in 2005 increased to 17.5 million. Therefore, U.S. colleges were enrolling approximately 6.5 million more students in 2005 than they did in 1975, with much of the gains coming from groups that were just beginning to gain access to college. Generally, during this era of great expansion in U.S. higher education, the growth of AAPI total enrollment is actually quite similar to the pace of the growth among African Americans and Latinos (see Figure 5.2). This similar rate of growth (as represented by the slope of the curves) is telling for AAPIs as well as Blacks and Latinos. What is surprising about this rate of growth for Blacks is that prior to 1975, Black enrollment had already begun a dramatic increase following the end of legal segregation and the advent of the civil rights era. Therefore, the exponential growth of Black enrollment after 1975 reflects the expansion of

Figure 5.2. Total Enrollment in U.S. Higher Education for Blacks, Latinos, and AAPIs, 1976–2005

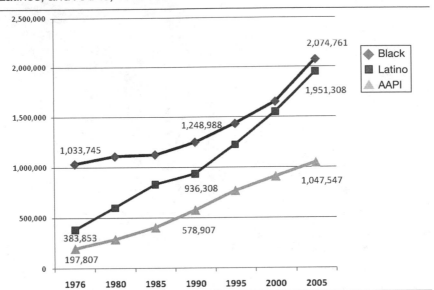

Note: Data through 1990 are for institutions of higher education, while later data are for Title IV, degree-granting institutions.

Source: Analysis of data from the National Center for Education Statistics, Integrated Postsecondary Education Data System (IPEDS) (NCES, 2010b).

opportunity that began decades earlier. For Latinos, the growth is also surprising, but for different reasons. Despite being over 6% of the U.S. population in 1975, Latinos only comprised only 3% of college students. Since 1975, Latino enrollment has increased dramatically. In the 15 years between 1990 and 2005, Latino enrollment increased by 108%, compared to an 81% growth among AAPIs and a 66% increase by Blacks.

While all minority groups experienced dramatic gains numerically and proportionally from 1975 to 2005, the proportional representation of Whites during this same time period decreased from 83% to 66%. While this seems quite significant, the shifting racial composition hasn't come at the expense of Whites. Numerically, over this same time period White enrollment increased by over three million students. Nonetheless, the gains by Whites, Blacks, Latinos, and AAPIs represent considerable changes in United States higher education policies and practices that have led to greater capacity and opportunities for many students who had previously been denied access. The GI Bill in the 1950s increased the availability of financial aid. Affirmative action led to concerted efforts to recruit and enroll women and minorities. Together, concerted policy efforts have played an important role in opening up the doors to college for millions of students who otherwise did not have opportunities.

Social conditions and organizational contexts played a key role in the unique patterns of college participation among AAPIs. It has resulted in AAPI participation that can be traced back to our earliest accounts of AAPIs living in the United States, and that tremendous growth in the AAPI population overall, amidst a general expansion of higher education for all students, has coincided with a massive increase in AAPI college participation from 1975 to 2005. The next sections of this chapter examine AAPI college participation within an organizational context, considering access to higher education for AAPIs in the context of a complex system of institutions that vary by region, type (2-year versus 4-year), control (public versus private), and selectivity (nonselective versus selective).

AAPI Participation by Region, Type, Control, and Selectivity

While there has been tremendous growth in AAPI participation in U.S. higher education overall, it is important to consider the distribution of AAPI enrollment in different regions of the country. Colleges and universities in the United States are distributed unevenly with some states and regions having larger student enrollment than others. The disparate distribution of student populations across different states and regions is often correlated with the variations in the distribution of the general populations throughout the country. Similar to the residential distribution of AAPIs nationally, the regional distribution of AAPIs in U.S. higher education is also unique. AAPI college enrollment is highly concentrated in a small number of states. In 2005 nearly two thirds of all AAPI college students attended college in 8 states. Nearly half (49%) of all AAPI college enrollment nationally was found in just two states: California and New York. California alone enrolled over 368,000 college students, which represented more than 40% of all AAPI college students nationally.

While the distribution of AAPI college students in 2005 is quite concentrated in a small number of states, it was actually more dispersed than had been the case in the past. In 1980, nearly two thirds of all AAPI college students attended college in two states (California and Hawaii), compared to six states in 2005 (California, New York, Texas, Illinois, Hawaii, and Washington). This shift in AAPI student demographics represents the increasing dispersion of AAPI students out of the few states that have been home to most AAPIs in past decades, such as California, Hawaii, and New York, to institutions in other regions of the country where the AAPI population has been on the rise in recent decades.

The dispersion of the AAPI student population from certain states to others is partially a reflection of a regional shift in AAPI residents. While the largest share of the national AAPI student population has historically been concentrated in the

West and Northeast, the greatest growth in AAPI college participation has been occurring in the South and Midwest between 1995 and 2005.[3] Analysis of data from the National Center for Education Statistics indicates that during this 10-year period, AAPI total enrollment increased by 105.8% in the South and 75.2% in the Midwest, compared to a 65.6% increase in the Northeast and a 56.3% increase in the West. The South and Midwest have historically had a very small AAPI population overall and very few AAPIs enrolled in higher education. However, in recent decades these regions have experienced an increase in their AAPI population caused by immigration settlement directly to these regions along with migration and resettlement among AAPIs looking for better occupational opportunities and a lower cost of living (see Teranishi, 2004).

The tremendous growth in the AAPI student population in the South and Midwest is caused by a number of states in these regions that have historically had very few AAPI students enrolled. Twenty-five states doubled their AAPI enrollment between 1980 and 2005, with five states increasing their enrollment threefold. For example, Georgia had fewer than 900 AAPIs enrolled in college in 1980, compared to 13,100 in 2005. This trend is also true for other regions of the country. During the same time period, AAPI student enrollment in Nevada, for instance, increased from 708 to nearly 10,000 (NCES, 2005). These state trends reflect an increasing AAPI enrollment in states that have historically had very few AAPI students.

The regional concentration of AAPI college enrollment is also representative of a large concentration of AAPI student enrollment in a small number of institutions. In 2005 two thirds of all AAPI college students nationally were concentrated in 200 institutions. These institutions represented less than 5% of the 4,500 degree-granting colleges and universities in the United States. Three quarters of all AAPI college students nationally were concentrated in less than 300 institutions. The distribution of AAPIs across a small number of institutions is nearly always overlooked in research and policy considerations. Also overlooked is the extent to which the demography of the population generally has been a key factor in the concentration of AAPIs in certain states.

In addition to regional concentration, there are also important trends in AAPI college participation by institutional type that can be traced to their unique social demography. One of the stories told about AAPI college students over the years has been that AAPIs are taking over the most selective colleges and universities in the nation (Abboud & Kim, 2006). For example, there was a news story about the Asian "invaders" in UC Berkeley's alumni association magazine, *California*, "Facing the Asian Invasion" (Ling, 1998). In fact, the enrollment of AAPIs in a number of highly selective universities throughout the United States is notable: In 2005, AAPIs consistently comprised between 11.1 and 13.8% of total enrollment at Ivy League institutions (NCES, 2005).

While this is certainly one story that needs to be known about AAPI college participation, this story does not represent all AAPIs. Actually, Ivy League universities enrolled only a small fraction—less than 1%—of all AAPI students enrolled in U.S. higher education in 2005. America's interest in our most selective institutions is not new—in fact, it has been the focus of, and the driving force behind, higher education for centuries (McDonough & Antonio, 1997). This, however, has changed with the rise of the public 4-year sector and the advent of the community college. There has been a shift in consciousness toward a broader, more complex understanding of American higher education. For AAPIs, however, this shift in consciousness has apparently not transpired. So, while it is easily understood that the 120,000 students enrolled in the Ivy League do not represent the story of the nearly 12 million college students (NCES, 2005), AAPIs are treated as though one percent of their enrollment can tell the story for the rest of the 99% of the college-going population. As is quite evident, whether or not these AAPI students are representative of all AAPIs should not be the question, because clearly they represent a small fraction of AAPI college students. Thus, adding to the discussion of the complex heterogeneity of AAPI college participation, including trends in the overall AAPI college participation rate and their changing regional representation, it is also important to consider the distribution of AAPI students in colleges and universities that vary by a number of institutional characteristics.

U.S. higher education, in an organizational context, is diverse and highly stratified; postsecondary institutions range in type (2-year and 4-year), selectivity (selective and nonselective), and control (public and private). When total AAPI enrollment in United States higher education is disaggregated by institutional type and control, there is evidence of a wide distribution of AAPI participation. In 2005 there were 358,889 AAPI undergraduates enrolled in public 4-year institutions, representing 39.7% of all AAPI undergraduate college students in the United States (NCES, 2005). Another 136,099 AAPIs attended private 4-year institutions, 85% of whom were enrolled in not-for-profit institutions. Most surprising is that 389,641 AAPI college students enrolled in public 2-year institutions, representing the largest concentration of AAPIs in any one sector of United States higher education. Another 10,500 AAPIs are enrolled in private (for-profit and not-for-profit) 2-year institutions.

There are other important trends in AAPI participation by institutional type that should be noted. In addition to enrolling the highest number of AAPI college students, the community college sector is where there has been the greatest proportional change in AAPI enrollment during the 25-year period between 1980 and 2005, as well as the 15 year period between 1990 and 2005 (see Table 5.1). While total AAPI participation between 1980 and 2005 increased in all sectors of U.S. higher education, AAPI community college enrollment increased by 370% between 1980 and 2005, and 88% between 1990 and 2005.

The rise in AAPI community college enrollment, at a faster pace than the rise in AAPI enrollment in other sectors of higher education, represents a steady shift over the 25-year period between 1980 and 2005 from AAPIs being more repre-

Table 5.1. AAPI Enrollment in U.S. Higher Education by Institutional Type, 1980–2005

	1980	1990	2005	Change 1980–2005	Change 1990–2005
4-Year Public	94,973	213,446	356,448	275.3%	67.0%
4-Year Private	29,173	71,101	114,893	293.8%	61.6%
2-Year Public	84,773	211,920	398,384	369.9%	88.0%

Note. Does not include 4-year private for-profit institutions or 2-year private not-for-profit institutions. Data for 1980 are for institutions of higher education, while data for 1990 and 2005 are for Title IV, degree-granting institutions.

Source. Analysis of data from the National Center for Education Statistics, Integrated Postsecondary Education Data System (IPEDS) (NCES, 2010b).

sented in the 4-year public sector to the 2-year sector (see Figure 5.3). During this period, enrollment of AAPIs in the private sector (2-year and 4-year, public and private) has remained fairly stable in terms of overall distribution. The trends in AAPI community college enrollment are almost never discussed relative to the educational achievement of AAPIs despite their growth and representation in this sector.

In some states large proportions of AAPI college students attend community colleges, including some states with overall high AAPI total enrollment (e.g., California, Texas, Hawaii, and Illinois). In 2005 California alone enrolled over 220,000 AAPIs in 2-year colleges, which was 59% of the AAPI college enrollment in the state. Other states that have a much smaller number of AAPIs enrolled in college also have a large share of their total AAPI enrollment in the community college sector. In 2005 Wyoming had 7,014 AAPI students enrolled in 2-year colleges, but that small number represents 67% of AAPI total enrollment in the state.

In almost all states AAPI participation in the 2-year sector is increasing at a faster rate than in the 4-year sector. This trend is particularly pronounced in the South and Midwest, regions in the United States that are experiencing the fastest overall growth in AAPI residents. During the 10-year period between 1995 and 2005, Georgia and Louisiana experienced significant gains (130.1% and 48.2% respectively) in AAPI 2-year enrollment. The increases in community college enrollment in these states during this 10-year period were greater than the increases that occurred in 4-year enrollment over the same time period. In the Midwest during the same time period, Minnesota (76.4%) and Wisconsin (64.8%) also experienced significant gains in the 2-year sector at a faster pace than in the 4-year sector.

While the West and East did not post gains in community college participation at the same rates, the gains were still quite impressive. Consider that in California

Figure 5.3. Change in AAPI Total Enrollment by Institutional Type, 1980–2005

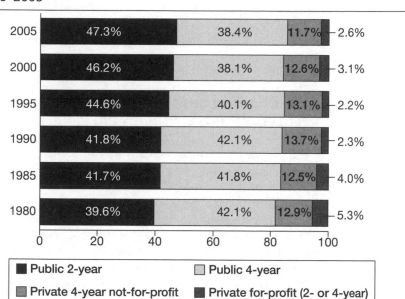

Note. Data through 1980 are for institutions of higher education, while data for 1990 and 2005 are for Title IV, degree-granting institutions.

Source. Analysis of data from the National Center for Education Statistics, Integrated Postsecondary Education Data System (IPEDS) (NCES, 2010b).

alone there were nearly a quarter million AAPIs enrolled in the 2-year sector in 2005. This number is 40% greater than in the decade prior and represents a greater increase than in the 4-year sector. On the East Coast, New York (47.6%), New Jersey (56.1%), and Massachusetts (39.6%) all had significant gains in AAPI community college enrollment during the same time period. The gains in the 2-year public sector were all substantially greater than in the 4-year sector in these three states at 22.6% combined. State policies that sort students into different institutional types by design (e.g., California Master Plan for Higher Education) may have contributed to these trends, but the trends also need to be considered in the context of state capacity and other demographic factors.

These descriptive trend data demonstrate the wide distribution of AAPI college participation by institutional type. While AAPIs have very unique enrollment patterns throughout the system of United States higher education, it is important to consider the extent to which specific demographic characteristics found within the population are factors in this outcome. These trends speak to the relationship between disparities in social conditions, school resources and opportunities, and the ability for AAPI students to be prepared and on the right track for different sectors of higher education. The following section examines these trends through descriptive and multivariate statistical analyses that control for the relative effects of ethnicity, social class, and school effects on the selectivity of institutions attended by AAPI students.

BEYOND A SINGLE STORY:
AAPI PRECOLLEGE POSTSECONDARY PREPARATION

While patterns of educational achievement and attainment have been found to vary by ethnicity, social class, or immigration status, few studies have examined the relationship between these demographic characteristics relative to educational outcomes. Jamie Lew (2004a), in her book, *Asian Americans in Class: Charting the Achievement Gap Among Korean American Youth*, examines the relationships between ethnicity and social class relative to social capital among Korean high school students. She found that low-SES Korean students had limited social capital and weaker ethnic ties than their high-SES Korean counterparts. Louie (2004) had similar results in her comparison of Chinese Americans who lived in mainstream communities and urban ethnic enclaves. Upper-middle-class Chinese families had access to information, resources, and other forms of capital that were not available to low-income Chinese families. In my own research, I have found that social class operates differently among ethnic groups, which has implications for the educational mobility for different AAPI subpopulations (Teranishi, 2003, 2004).

One indicator that should be considered in students' ability to attend college is whether or not they finished high school, an issue that was first raised in Chapter 4. In research on college participation, this aspect of the education pipeline is often overlooked. Consider how most measures of college participation have high school graduates in the denominator. Accordingly, of the 3.2 million youth who graduated from high school in 2007, 2.2 million (68.6%) enrolled in college (U.S. Bureau of Labor Statistics, 2009). This measure of college participation, however, does not take into account the high number of students in the United States that do not finish high school. The percentage of ninth graders who graduated high school in 4 years was 53.4% for Black students, 49.3% for American Indian and Alaska Native students, and 57.8% for Latino students in 2004 (Editorial Projects in Education Research Center, 2007). Taking these trends into account when calculating college participation provides a different perspective on the pipeline to college. For states with some of the largest minority populations, the likelihood of any student enrolling in college by age 19 was 36.3% for California, 35.4% for Texas, 44.4% for New York, 32.4% for Florida, and 45.4% for Illinois (Briscoe, 2009).

AAPIs are often considered to have the greatest likelihood of completing high school. For example, in 2000 the high school completion rate among all U.S. adults, ages 18–65, was 80.4%, which was equal to the rate for Asian Americans and slightly better than is the rate for Pacific Islanders (see Figure 5.4). However, the high school completion rates vary widely for AAPI subgroups, a trend that is often not recognized by education researchers, policy makers, or school administrators. The proportion of Southeast Asian adults who have not completed high school is two and a half to three times greater than the national average. Some Pacific Islander groups also exhibit high rates of having not completed high school. At the same time, some East Asian and South Asian subpopulations have high rates of high school completion or greater. Thus, while the dropout rate for AAPIs as a whole is lower than is the case for other racial groups, there are differences across ethnic subgroups that are often hidden among aggregated data.

The high school completion rates also play out differently in local school districts in notable ways. While the 4-year dropout rate for Asian Americans in the Oakland Unified School District in California was similar to the statewide average in the 2006–07 academic year (Figure 5.5), Pacific Islanders and Filipinos were nearly twice as likely to drop out compared to Asian Americans as a whole. The gaps between men and women were also greater among Pacific Islanders and Filipinos compared to all of the Asian Americans in the same district and compared to the statewide average. Anecdotal evidence of dramatic differences in high school graduation rates across AAPI subpopulations can be heard elsewhere, but disaggregated data to examine these trends are not available (National Commission on Asian American and Pacific Islander Research in Education, 2008), which is also the case for national datasets.

These indicators point to the distribution of educational outcomes among AAPIs that can be captured through empirical research that acknowledges the heterogeneity within the AAPI population. They also demonstrate that AAPIs are not easily comparable to other racial groups because the population represents such a wide range of subgroups. To further this point, I provide analyses on how AAPIs are distributed across standardized admission test scores, which are also typically overlooked because of a focus only on average AAPI test scores. Consequently, there is a lack of attention to the scores within larger categories, which conceals many hidden indictors associated with college preparation and access that are not known to scholars and the public alike.

It is not widely known that AAPIs have a great deal of variation in standardized test scores. In fact, the distribution of Asian and AAPI test scores from the mean score is often overlooked even though Asian and AAPI test scores actually have the widest standard deviation for any racial group.[4] In other words, among Asians and AAPIs, there are higher numbers of scores that distribute from the mean score than is true for other racial groups. One study found that AAPIs were six times overrepresented in top scores, but also five times overrepresented at the

Figure 5.4. Proportion of AAPI Adults Without a High School Diploma or Equivalent by Ethnicity, 2000

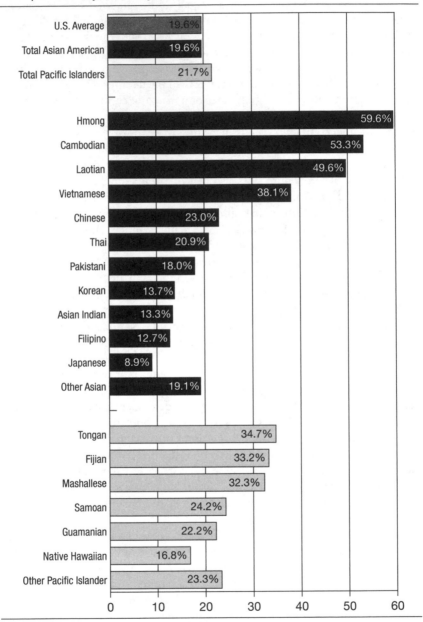

Note. Data is for adults, ages 18 to 64.

Source. Analysis of data from the U.S. Census Bureau (2000), Summary File 3.

Figure 5.5. Four-Year High School Dropout Rate Statewide in California and for AAPI Students in Oakland Unified School District, 2006–2007

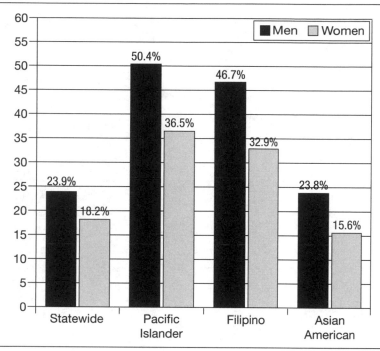

Source. Analysis of data from the California Basic Educational Data System (CBEDS).

bottom. This is likely driven by the wider distribution of demographic characteristics among AAPIs that is not necessarily found among other racial groups. These demographic differences have implications for the wide distribution of scores that are found among AAPIs. For example, among Asian and AAPI students who took the SAT Verbal in 2004, whose parents had less than a high school diploma, the average score was 411, compared to an average score of 562 for Asian and AAPI students with parents with a graduate level education. Similar trends in test scores are evident when looking at parental income. Students with parental income above $100,000 a year score over 120 points higher on the SAT verbal than students with parents with income below $30,000 a year (Figure 5.6).

English language proficiency is also a barrier to performance on standardized tests. The average SAT Verbal score for AAPI test takers whose primary language is English is 525 compared to 473 for AAPI test takers whose primary language is not English. The variation in scores, which is systematically linked to many social conditions among the population, is particularly troublesome for the AAPI population in college admissions. The eventual consequence of a wide range of test scores

Figure 5.6. Asian and AAPI SAT Verbal Scores by Parental Education and Parental Income, 2004

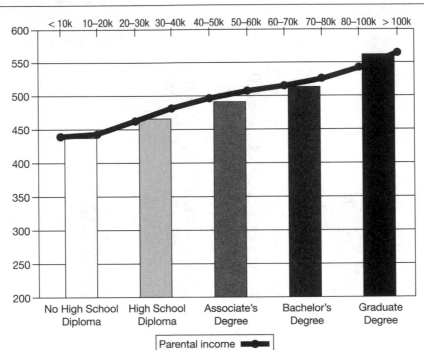

Source. Analysis of data from the College Board (2006).

among the AAPI population is a wide range in eligibility and competitiveness for institutions that range by selectivity.

Adding to the challenge of understanding the distribution of scores that contribute to the mean SAT score for AAPIs, there are many international students who attend selective institutions in the United States and are required to take the SAT—thus their scores are being conflated with the scores of domestic AAPI students. Consider that 582,984 international students enrolled in U.S. higher education in 2006, many of whom were from Asia. In fact, 278,324 international students in 2006 were from just five Asian countries: India, China, Korea, Japan, and Taiwan (Open Doors, 2007). Since the College Board's categorization for AAPIs is actually inclusive of "Asians, Asian Americans, or Pacific Islanders" there is a confounding of scores that includes Asian international students. The scores for Asians, Asian Americans, or Pacific Islanders that attended high school outside the United States are higher than for Asians, Asian Americans, or Pacific Islanders in

Figure 5.7. The Distribution of Asian and AAPI SAT I Math Scores, 2004

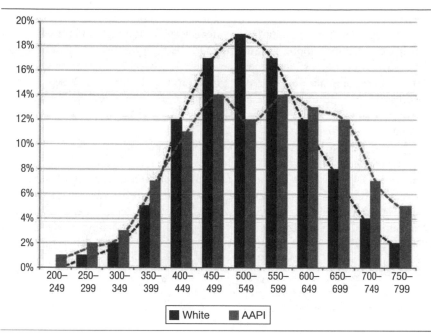

White ■ AAPI

Source. Analysis of data from the College Board (2006).

the United States, indicating a conflating of international and domestic student performance and outcomes. For the Math portion of the test, students who attended high school outside the United States scored 90 points higher, on average, than students who attended a high school in the United States. For the Verbal portion of the exam, students who attended high school outside the United States also scored higher than their counterparts who attended high school in the United States, with a difference of 33 points on average.

The gaps in scores for various subpopulations among AAPIs results in a bimodal distribution of scores rather than the smooth distribution from the mean which can be found among all test takers. The score distribution of the Math section of the SAT I for AAPIs and White students shows a very different distribution of scores (see Figure 5.7). The pattern of score distribution among AAPIs is yet another way that AAPIs are categorically different from other racial groups relative to college access and participation. Thus for AAPIs it is important to consider which student characteristics are correlated with the scores at the top of the curve, as well as at the bottom. Together, the wide range of scores that are unevenly distributed across AAPI students that vary by ethnicity, social class, language background, and other factors create an average score that is not necessarily representative of either end of the spectrum.

The bimodal distribution of AAPI scores on standardized tests again points to the ways in which the population is categorically unique. These indicators also mirror trends found among graduation rates that vary across AAPI subgroups. The distributions in these outcomes are representative of the dangers of using the mean score to generalize to the entire population. In fact, no single score across any measure can capture the heterogeneity within the population. Rather, the only constant when looking across the population is the extent to which there are more differences than similarities.

The vast range of demographic characteristics among AAPIs has several important, and often unrecognized, implications for their educational experiences. In many ways, the AAPI population is truly unique and is comprised of subpopulations with very different lived experiences, relative to other student populations in the United States. At the same time, there are some sectors of the population who share similar experiences as other groups. In either case, both stories are lost in the generalizations that exist about the population as a whole. This reality cannot be understated, and it commands a more comprehensive perspective on what accounts for the postsecondary preparation and mobility for AAPI students. The impact of these disparate outcomes on college participation among AAPIs is examined in the following analyses.

AAPI COLLEGE ENROLLMENT DISAGGREGATED

The following analysis looks more closely at trends in the factors that impact the postsecondary outcomes of AAPIs through an examination of the intersection between the demographic characteristics and organizational contexts of AAPIs and its relationship to different patterns of college participation. The data source for this analysis consists of a national sample of 18,106 AAPI college students who attended 469 colleges and universities across the United States in 1997.[5] This rich dataset examines college choice variables for this sample of students, taking into account differences by ethnicity and social class backgrounds among AAPIs.

The results indicate that the type of college AAPI students attended varied significantly when examined across different AAPI subpopulations. First, there were distinct differences between AAPI ethnic groups with regard to the type of institutions attended. Korean Americans (38.1%) and Chinese Americans (34.6%) had larger proportions of students who attended selective colleges compared to Filipino Americans (18.5%) and Southeast Asian Americans (24.6%) (see Table 5.2). Chinese Americans, Japanese Americans, and Korean Americans were more likely to attend private institutions, while Filipino Americans and Southeast Asian Americans were more likely to attend public 2-year colleges and moderately selective public 4-year colleges.

Table 5.2. Distribution of Selected Institutional Characteristics by Ethnicity

	Percentage Among				
	Chinese Americans	Filipino Americans	Japanese Americans	Korean Americans	Southeast Asians
Low selectivity	65.4	81.5	74.0	62.0	75.4
High selectivity	34.6	18.5	26.0	38.1	24.6
4-year public college	26.7	43.6	30.5	27.3	32.0
4-year private college	14.8	15.9	29.8	19.0	15.9
4-year public univ.	35.8	27.8	21.4	36.5	38.4
4-year private univ.	22.7	12.7	18.3	17.2	13.7

Note. Weighted N = 66,561. Percentage sign (%) has been eliminated.

Source. Analysis of data from the Cooperative Institutional Research Program (CIRP, 2010).

Even among a sample of low-SES AAPIs (parental income less than $25k per year), Chinese Americans (24.5%) and Korean Americans (29.5%) had greater representation in highly selective institutions compared to Japanese Americans (19.4%) and Southeast Asian Americans (15.2%) from the same income levels (Table 5.2). Most of the low-SES Chinese Americans and Korean Americans attending selective institutions were able to do so by attending public universities (36.5% and 38.3% respectively). Among the highest income bracket, Filipino Americans (31.4%) and Southeast Asian Americans (41.5%) had lower representation in highly selective public universities, compared to Japanese Americans (52.2%) and Chinese Americans (51.3%).

In terms of differences in college choice behavior, it is important to examine students' use of information and guidance resources, the influence of cost and financial aid, and the influence of the prestige and reputation of postsecondary institutions. These factors have been found to be associated with attending different types of institutions (e.g., public, private, selective, nonselective). Filipino Americans (23%) and Southeast Asian Americans (23.6%) had higher rates of being influenced by relatives and wanting to live near home than their Japanese American (12.8%) and Korean American (12.6%) counterparts (see Table 5.3). Filipino Americans and Southeast Asian Americans from the lowest income bracket were most likely to choose a college because it was close to home. "Living near home" is an important variable to examine since attending a more selective college often involves moving away from home, living on campus, and being a full-time student. Chinese Americans (44.3%) and Korean Americans (52.4%) had the highest rates of taking SAT preparation courses, with those from the highest income

Table 5.3. Ethnic Differences in College Decision-Making Factors

	Percentage Among				
	Chinese Americans	Filipino Americans	Japanese Americans	Korean Americans	Southeast Asians
INFORMATION AND GUIDANCE					
Relative's wish	8.2	11.5	9.5	9.1	12.6
Wanted to live near home	15.4	23.1	12.8	12.6	23.6
Teacher	4.4	4.8	5.9	3.7	6.7
High school counselor	7.3	9.1	8.3	7.7	11.3
Private counselor	2.6	3.5	2.8	2.4	2.8
SAT preparation course	44.3	38.8	35.1	52.4	34.1
INFLUENCES OF COST AND AID					
Major financial concerns	17.5	21.0	16.3	17.2	28.5
Offered financial aid	31.2	34.7	30.0	34.8	43.2
Low tuition	26.0	33.3	22.7	29.0	29.5
INFLUENCE OF PRESTIGE/REPUTATION					
Academic reputation	58.0	59.5	55.6	56.2	58.0
Social reputation	22.4	27.1	26.0	21.2	24.5
Grads get good jobs	53.3	57.0	44.6	50.6	55.5
Grads go to top grad schools	37.8	37.6	30.7	38.9	40.5
Ranking in national magazine	19.6	14.7	12.2	17.5	16.5
COLLEGE APPLICATIONS AND CHOICES					
Applied to only one school	11.8	17.4	18.7	12.5	22.3
Applied to 5 or more schools	54.6	37.3	40.9	50.2	30.7

Note. Weighted N = 66,561. Percentage sign (%) has been eliminated.

Source. Analysis of data from the Cooperative Institutional Research Program (CIRP, 2010).

bracket with the greatest likelihood of taking these courses; in the competitive environment of admissions to the most selective campuses, students who take these courses often carry an advantage in the admissions process if the courses improve their scores.

In terms of the role of perceptions, three important factors were influential to students' college choice process: college affordability, students' perception of institutional prestige, and students' perceptions of whether or not an institution will help a student get a job or be admitted to graduate school. Measures of affordability included the cost of tuition and living expenses, as well as the amount of financial aid that a student received. Southeast Asian Americans and Filipino Americans—especially from the lowest income bracket—were most likely to indicate that they had major financial concerns about college. Filipino Americans (33.3%) and Southeast Asian Americans (29.5%) were also most likely to choose a college because of low tuition, a trend that was true across all income levels among these groups. Filipino Americans, Southeast Asian Americans, and Korean Americans were most likely to select colleges based on the amount of financial aid that was offered to them. In terms of students' perceptions of institutional prestige, Chinese Americans, Filipino Americans, and Korean Americans had slightly higher rates of indication that rankings were important in their decisions. Across all ethnic groups, students also felt that being able to get a good job or admission to a good graduate program were also important to consider when selecting a college.

Recent studies on college choice have also examined the rate by which students submit applications for admissions to college (Hurtado, Inkelas, Briggs, & Rhee, 1995; McDonough, 1997). These studies have found that applying to more colleges was associated with pursuing and attending more selective institutions. In addition, submitting more applications broadened students' options. Filipino Americans (17.4%), Japanese Americans (18.7%) and Southeast Asian Americans (22.3%) were nearly twice as likely to apply to only one campus compared to Chinese Americans (11.8%) or Korean Americans (12.5%). Conversely, a large proportion of Chinese Americans (54.6%) and Korean Americans (50.2%) applied to five or more campuses during their college application process.

Multivariate analysis confirmed the findings from the cross-tabulations.[6] With regard to the role of background characteristics on college destination among all AAPIs, being either Chinese American or Korean American was positively associated with attending a more selective institution, after controlling for all other variables in the equation (see Table 5.4). Conversely, being Filipino American or Japanese American was negatively associated with attending a more selective institution at the final step. The impact of being Southeast Asian American was not a significant predictor of attending a more selective institution after controlling for all other variables in the equation.

Among all AAPI students in the full sample, parental income and parental educational levels were significant positive predictors for attending more selective colleges. Father's education level was a slightly higher predictor than mother's education level. Whether students were native English speakers was insignificant in the model; however, being a United States citizen or permanent resident was negatively associated with attending a more selective college. These findings suggest that, indeed, the influence of background characteristics on college destination varies among the AAPI student population as demonstrated earlier in the cross-tabulations.

High school achievement and experiences played a significant role in determining attendance at a more selective college. High school GPA was also a very strong factor associated with attending a selective college. This can be attributed

Table 5.4. Predicting Attendance at Selective Institutions Among AAPIs

Variable	b	β	
BACKGROUND CHARACTERISTICS			
Chinese American	29.27	10	***
Filipino American	-34.11	-09	***
Japanese American	-11.64	-02	***
Korean American	29.09	08	***
Southeast Asian American	0.45	01	
Parental income	3.20	09	***
Father's education level	2.83	05	***
Mother's education level	3.39	06	***
U.S. citizen/perm. resident	-11.43	-02	**
Native English speaker	3.05	01	
HIGH SCHOOL EXPERIENCES			
High school GPA	23.19	25	***
Took SAT preparation course	-4.94	-02	**
More time spent on homework	2.62	03	***
High degree aspirations	15.01	09	***
COLLEGE CHOICE FACTORS			
Relative's wish	1.32	01	
Teacher's advice	1.14	01	
Academic reputation	25.87	11	***
Low tuition	-40.80	-25	***
High school counselor's advice	6.45	03	***
Private counselor's advice	-3.75	-01	
Wanted to live near home	-21.24	-12	***
Friend's advice	-5.90	-03	***
Grads go to top grad schools	4.88	03	***
Rankings in national magazines	28.64	17	***
(Adjusted R^2)		**(41)**	

Note. * $p<.05$; ** $p<.01$; *** $p<.001$ at the final step. Percent signs (%) have been eliminated. N=17,835.

Source. Analysis of data from the Cooperative Institutional Research Program (CIRP, 2010).

to the high correlation between GPA and SAT scores, which are often the primary criteria for admitting students at the most selective colleges. Interestingly, students who utilized resources, such as SAT preparation courses, were less likely to attend more selective institutions. Previous college choice research found that these activities during high school were positively associated with attending selective colleges. Students who pursued college to make more money or to get a better job were less likely to attend selective institutions. These students may be more inclined to pursue a technical rather than a liberal arts education, the latter of which is more closely associated with highly selective colleges.

Among factors that determined the type of college a student attended, the academic reputation of the institutions was very important among those who attended more selective colleges, while students' financial concerns and desire to live near home were associated more with students who attended less selective colleges. In terms of the influence of social networks, the influence of counselors or teachers was insignificant in predicting attendance at a more prestigious college; however, taking advice from friends was associated more with attending a less selective college.

Among the regression results for the separate ethnic groups (Table 5.5), there were distinct factors that impacted the college destinations with regard to selectivity. These regressions accounted for between 32% of the variance in the dependent variable (for Filipino Americans) and 41% (for Chinese Americans). With regard to the role of background characteristics, parental income was a stronger predictor for attending a selective college among Filipino Americans and Southeast Asian Americans. The role of father's education level had the most influence for Korean Americans, Filipino Americans, and Japanese Americans while mother's education level was only significant among Chinese Americans. These findings suggest that different social class factors impacted the separate ethnic groups differently.

In terms of citizenship and residency, Japanese American United States citizens or permanent residents were more likely to attend a selective college as opposed to Southeast Asian Americans citizens or permanent residents who were more likely to attend less selective colleges. In terms of the role of language ability, being a native English speaker was only a significant positive predictor for Filipinos and Southeast Asians, and a negative predictor for Japanese Americans.

With regard to students' high school achievement and experiences, academic performance had the greatest impact among Korean, Chinese, and Filipino Americans and less of an impact among Southeast Asians. Interestingly, Korean students' use of resources such as SAT preparation courses was a significant and positive predictor of attending a selective college, whereas for all other groups, it was either negative or insignificant. This finding demonstrates that students from different ethnic groups may have either had differential access to these types of resources or had utilized these services for different reasons. Along the same lines, Filipino

Table 5.5. Predicting Attendance at Selective Institutions Across AAPI Subpopulations

Variable	Chinese Americans (n=5,016) b	β	Filipino Americans (n=2,549) b	β	Japanese Americans (n=1,527) b	β	Korean Americans (n=2,906) b	β	Southeast Asians (n=1,934) b	β
Background characteristics										
Parental income	2.22	06***	4.36	11***	4.00	08**	1.72	04*	4.04	12***
Father's education level	2.30	04*	5.82	09***	8.07	10***	5.28	08***	2.62	05
Mother's education level	3.44	06**	-1.69	-02	-1.84	-02	1.29	02	1.74	03
U.S. citizen/perm. resident	-0.72	-01	-9.21	-01	39.30	10**	9.85	02	-59.57	-13***
Native English speaker	-2.99	-01	15.87	06**	-44.88	-14***	-8.05	-03	19.11	07**
(R² Change)		(09)		(06)		(07)		(05)		(16)
(Adjusted R²)		(09)		(06)		(07)		(05)		(16)
High school experiences										
High school GPA	24.67	26***	21.10	26***	22.83	24***	27.76	30***	15.11	17***
Took SAT preparation course	-6.17	-02*	-4.91	-02	-22.42	-08**	8.12	03*	-12.39	-05*
More time spent on homework	2.79	04**	0.98	01	4.35	06*	1.78	02	0.46	01
High degree aspirations	17.02	10***	10.91	08***	21.38	13***	15.50	09***	20.02	13***
(R² Change)		(17)		(14)		(16)		(19)		(10)
(Adjusted R²)		(26)		(20)		(23)		(24)		(26)
College choice factors										
Relative's wish	4.60	02*	-1.77	-01	0.10	00	3.77	02*	-0.44	-01
Teacher's advice	-0.27	-01	12.96	07**	0.24	00	-3.72	-02	5.71	03
Academic reputation	23.23	10***	19.64	10***	33.02	14***	23.21	11***	29.19	13***
Low tuition	-44.97	-28***	-27.15	-19***	-46.96	-25***	-40.32	-25***	-27.38	-18***
High school counselor's advice	11.62	06***	0.40	00	7.43	03	6.92	03	-3.34	-02
Private counselor's advice	-5.77	-02	-17.18	-06**	-10.43	-03	12.99	04*	-2.60	-01
Wanted to live near home	-28.71	-16***	-18.52	-13***	-25.90	-13***	-15.99	-09***	-16.76	-10***
Friend's advice	-8.25	-04**	-7.76	-05*	-9.75	-04	-6.31	-03*	-14.95	-08**
Grads go to top grad schools	5.10	03*	4.89	03	5.14	03	8.86	05**	-2.61	-02
Rankings in national magazines	27.28	15***	28.71	19***	28.21	15***	23.74	14***	36.39	22***

Note. * $p<.05$; ** $p<.01$; *** $p<.001$ at the final step. Percent signs (%) have been eliminated.

Source. Analysis of data from the Cooperative Institutional Research Program (CIRP, 2010).

Americans and Japanese Americans—and not other groups—were more influenced to attend a selective college if they spent more time on homework.

Among other differences between ethnic groups in their college-choice processes, Chinese Americans and Korean Americans were more likely to attend more selective colleges because the colleges had graduates who attended top graduate schools. However, Chinese Americans, Japanese Americans, and Korean Americans who had greater concerns about the cost of tuition were most likely to be attending less selective colleges. Only Chinese Americans and Korean Americans had a positive association between the influence of their relatives and attending more selective colleges, whereas Filipino Americans who attended more selective colleges were more likely to be influenced by teachers. Chinese American students were the only group to be positively influenced by a high school counselor's advice. In terms of attending more selective colleges, Chinese Americans, Japanese Americans, and Southeast Asian Americans were more likely to be adversely affected by wanting to live near home or being influenced by close friends than Filipino Americans or Korean Americans.

These analyses document the effects of ethnicity, social class, and school effects on the selectivity of the colleges attended by AAPI students and confirm the patterns of enrollment that were described in the descriptive data earlier in the chapter. Together, these data demonstrate the ways in which AAPI subpopulations experience unique social conditions and organizational contexts that translate into unique patterns of higher education participation. More specifically, disparities in social conditions and school effects, which varies for different AAPI subgroups, results in a wide distribution of participation in United States higher education that varies by institutional type.

This chapter provides much needed new data on the distribution of postsecondary opportunities available for AAPIs across a range of institutional types. The data highlights how and why trends in participation are showing signs of enrollment growth in 2-year colleges and less selective or nonselective institutions. Colleges and universities need to be aware of these trends and plan accordingly for these diverse populations of AAPI students, as well as the projected growth of AAPI students in certain sectors of higher education. This is particularly important because many of these institutions have historically not had a presence of AAPI students.

The ways in which AAPIs are affected by the stratification of higher education tell a unique and important story about their college participation. These data confirm what has been pointed to in previous chapters by demonstrating how and why AAPIs end up with this particular distribution of enrollment in different sectors of higher education.

CHAPTER 6

AAPI Degree Attainment and Field Representation

This chapter returns to Eric, Jenny, and Tommy, who described their individual high school experiences in Chapter 4. The focus of their narratives in this chapter is on the likelihood they will earn a college degree and how they describe their preferred college majors and career aspirations. Eric lives in San Francisco and describes his high school as a competitive environment that has prepared him well for college. He has a good outlook for attending a selective university after high school. He says that the curriculum has been particularly informative for his career outlook. If Eric attends a selective university, his likelihood of completing college is very high.

Eric speaks of his probable major choice and the factors that contribute to his decision: "The major I like is business. Well, it's between business and engineering, but I'm more closer to business. Both of these fields make lots of money, I think that's a priority." Currently enrolled in AP economics, Eric says it has been preparing him well for college-level courses in that field. His aspiration related to money are his parents' doing; they are relying on him to do well financially to take care of them when they are older.

Jenny is pretty much set on living at home and working while she attends college. Accordingly, she has committed herself to attending a local community college or a moderately selective 4-year commuter college. If Jenny enrolls in a community college after high school, however, her likelihood of transferring to a 4-year college is low. Nationally, the transfer rate of first-time community college students has been less than one in five (Bryant, 2001; Dougherty, 2001). This in itself will severely decrease the likelihood that she will earn a bachelor's degree. If Jenny attends the local 4-year college after high school, the likelihood of obtaining a bachelor's degree increases somewhat, but is still a 50-50 proposition, based on the 6-year graduation rate at the institution.

Jenny is also less sure about her major choice when she goes to college. She has not had much guidance during high school and she is torn between pursuing a career that makes a lot of money and working with kids, which she enjoys. Jenny says, "I'm thinking about majoring in computer science, computer engineering, or business administration, which is where the money is. But I also want to go into liberal studies to get a teaching credential. My job now is working with little kids."

Her parents would rather see her pursue the more tangible and lucrative fields, but her sister, who is in college now, tells her to pursue what she enjoys. Jenny says that she is not too worried about making a commitment to a major at this point. She says, "Besides, like, I heard that people change their jobs five to seven times, and it's like, if I need to change my major, then that's what I'll do."

Tommy says that he is excited about going to college. He says, "[The day I go to college] will be a great day because I will be the first in my family to do this." His parents are proud just to see him graduate from high school, which is certainly commendable considering that half of the students who begin at his high school will not finish with a diploma. Tommy will likely attend a local community college after high school, live at home, and commute, like Jenny. They will be among the 85% of college students nationally who attend nonresidential colleges, attend part-time, and commute to school (Horn & Berktold, 1999). In Tommy's case, his matriculation at the local community college is following a common pattern among students who graduate from his high school and attend college. This cadre of students at the local community college represents most of the people in college with whom he has contact. Unfortunately, like Jenny, his chances of obtaining a bachelor's degree are slim, but Tommy intends to beat the odds just as he has done to earn his diploma at his high school.

Like Eric and Jenny, Tommy is interested in a tangible career trajectory. He is influenced less by his parents or his school and more by what he sees in his community. He describes his career goals by saying, "I really want to become a police officer. Yeah, 'cause I've grown up seeing my brothers get locked up, and other people in my neighborhood. You know, I want to stop the violence and help my community." When asked what he would major in during college, he says, "I heard that I can become a police officer just by finishing community college." Tommy's plan is to attend the local community college after high school, and by doing so, he will bring pride to his community. He says, "You don't see a lot of Hmong students planning to go to college. You know, I want to be the one that goes to college and graduates. I want to be way up there and prove to everybody that the Hmong people can do it." Becoming a police officer also will bring pride to Tommy's community and is a job where people will look up to him.

Similar to the lack of inclusion of AAPIs in discussions about racial equity in higher education participation, there is very little known about the AAPI college experience, including the likelihood AAPI subgroups will navigate through higher education to earn a degree. Eric, Jenny, and Tommy's narratives speak to differences in AAPI students' college plans and postcollege aspirations. Their stories demonstrate that enrolling in college will only be part of the story of their likelihood of succeeding after high school. Accordingly, the purpose of this chapter is to consider AAPI students' persistence and completion rates, the major fields that they pursue, and how their degree attainment has implications for the representation of different populations in different fields of occupation.

This chapter examines how, why, and how much AAPI students differ in their degree attainment, the major fields they pursue, and the implications of these trends for representation of different subpopulations in different fields of occupations. I begin with a discussion of the differences in degree attainment rates for AAPIs, move to an examination of AAPI field representation, and finally, focus intently on the representation and career trajectory of AAPIs in one particular field—education—as a way to demonstrate the importance of including the AAPI population in broader discussions about the importance of diversity in concerns of U.S. workforce development.

DEGREE ATTAINMENT AMONG AAPIs

For college students there are various factors that influence degree attainment, including the type of institution they attend, their experiences with the academic and social environment, and their psychosocial adjustment (Allen, 1992; Fleming, 1984). These factors are important for all students, not just AAPIs. It is also imperative that the success of students in college is considered beyond access given the trend of declining degree production of U.S. colleges and universities: While enrollment in higher education among high school graduates increased from 51% in 1970 to 67% in 1999, degree attainment rate remained flat at around 40% (Turner, 2004).

Indeed, the focus on participation in higher education policy needs to be considered in the context of the ability of colleges to help students persist and eventually earn a postsecondary credential, particularly for students who enter college with this goal in mind.[1] For example, research consistently demonstrates that students who enter a 2-year college are much less likely to obtain a bachelor's degree than students who begin in a 4-year college (Brint & Karabel, 1989; Dougherty, 1992). The AAPI population is no exception to this trend. AAPI students who attend less selective or nonselective institutions after high school are less likely to complete college. Because the college participation of AAPIs is within a wide range of colleges that vary by type (2-year and 4-year), control (public and private), and selectivity (nonselective, moderately selective, and highly selective), it is not surprising that degree attainment also varies for different AAPI subpopulations. Put another way, AAPIs are not unlike others when it comes to degree attainment rates. For AAPI first-time freshmen in public 4-year institutions, only 6 out of 10 received their bachelor's degree based on a cohort of students in 1999.[2] In public 2-year institutions, the degree attainment rate was much worse, with only one quarter (25.2%) of AAPIs receiving their associate's degree, based on a cohort of students in 2002.

Examining levels of educational attainment among AAPI adults in the United States among those who have attended college is revealing (see Figure 6.1). The data reveal that some ethnic groups have a high likelihood of having a bachelor's

Figure 6.1. Degree Attainment Among Asian American College Attendees, 2000

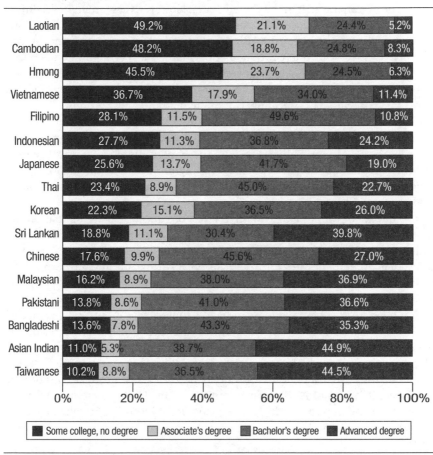

Note. Data reported for adults, ages 25 or over.

Source. Analysis of data from the U.S. Census Bureau (2000), Summary File 4.

degree or advanced degree, as opposed to an associate's degree or some college with no degree. This is particularly true among South Asians (Asian Indian, Bangladeshi, and Pakistani) and East Asians (Chinese, Taiwanese, Korean, Japanese). Then there is another sector of the AAPI population that has attended college that has a small proportion that has not completed a bachelor's degree or more. Rather, they are far more likely to have attended some college but not have a degree, and are more likely to only have earned an associate's degree as their highest level of degree attainment.

These results are counterintuitive to popular belief about the educational attainment of AAPIs, who are routinely lauded as the population with the highest levels of degree attainment in the United States. However, these trends tell a different story when the data are disaggregated by ethnicity, which shows the tremendous variation within the aggregated AAPI category. Disaggregated data demonstrates that there is a sector of the AAPI population that has a very high rate of college degree attainment, which skews the data for the population in the aggregate. Even the data for these groups also must be contextualized in order to understand the factors that contribute to educational attainment among these groups.

One revealing perspective on these high rates of educational attainment is that they do not necessarily reflect the extent to which AAPIs are earning degrees in the U.S. educational system. Rather, the high rate of educational attainment reflects the restrictive immigration policies that favor highly educated individuals when it comes to immigration from certain countries of origin, in particular China, India, and Korea (see Chapter 2).

The impact of immigrants with high levels of educational attainment on the educational attainment rates for AAPIs generally is evident when a comparison is made between American-born and foreign-born AAPI adults.[3] Table 6.1 compares educational attainment rates for American-born AAPIs and foreign-born AAPIs (who arrived after the age of 25), by ethnicity. For the foreign-born AAPI population, there are two trends that are evident. First, a very high proportion of some foreign-born AAPI subpopulations (Indians, Chinese, Taiwanese, Sri Lankan, and Bangladeshi) have an educational attainment of either a bachelor's degree or advanced degree. But, at the same time, there are also foreign-born AAPIs from some subgroups that have a high rate of attending college, but not earning a degree (Cambodians, Laotians, Hmong, and Vietnamese). This is mostly a reflection of how different groups of AAPIs gain admittance to the United States (see Chapter 2), where some groups have a high proportion of new immigrants who arrive via employment preferences, while other groups are admitted via refugee or asylee status.

Table 6.1 also contains data on American-born AAPIs, which is more indicative of the educational attainment that is occurring within the United States higher education system for AAPIs. The data reveal that the high educational attainment among foreign-born adults is also a trend that can be found among American-born AAPIs for some subgroups (Chinese, Japanese, Indian, and Taiwanese). But the data also reveal that there are dramatic differences between subpopulations of American-born AAPIs with regard to the proportion of students who enroll in college but never earn a degree. Among American-born Southeast Asians, the likelihood of attending college but not completing it is especially high, with 30 to 50% of American-born Hmong, Laotians, and Cambodians attending college but not earning a degree. Similar trends are true for American-born Filipinos and Thai, who both have a higher rate of not completing college than their foreign-born counterparts.

Table 6.1. Degree Attainment Among Asian American College Attendees by Nativity Status, 2000

	Some College, No Degree		Associate's Degree		Bachelor's Degree		Advanced Degree	
	U.S.- Born	Immigrated After Age 25	U.S.- Born	Immigrated After Age 25	U.S.- Born	Immigrated After Age 25	U.S.- Born	Immigrated After Age 25
Asian Indian	16.0	9.7	6.4	4.9	38.3	39.4	39.4	46.0
Bangladeshi	n/a	10.2	n/a	7.2	n/a	36.7	n/a	45.8
Cambodian	56.7	49.2	12.2	21.7	31.2	20.1	n/a	9.0
Chinese	16.3	14.0	8.4	8.9	46.7	33.3	28.6	43.8
Filipino	35.6	20.5	15.6	7.7	38.6	60.0	10.3	11.8
Hmong	31.3	53.8	14.1	22.7	48.1	16.1	6.5	7.5
Indonesian	39.9	27.1	13.1	9.0	32.1	35.3	14.8	28.6
Japanese	26.2	16.8	12.5	15.2	42.1	46.9	19.1	21.1
Korean	20.9	19.7	6.9	8.8	41.4	48.1	30.8	23.4
Laotian	37.9	51.2	13.6	22.9	26.0	17.9	22.5	8.0
Malaysian	32.9	21.4	11.4	13.2	19.7	33.2	36.0	32.2
Pakistani	14.3	12.0	11.6	5.9	49.3	41.6	24.8	40.5
Sri Lankan	14.7	21.8	7.7	11.4	68.6	24.6	9.0	42.3
Taiwanese	7.4	10.6	6.1	10.6	49.4	35.6	37.0	43.3
Thai	37.1	18.3	5.9	17.9	36.2	37.3	20.8	26.5
Vietnamese	40.0	44.6	11.2	20.4	34.0	24.6	14.9	10.4

Note. Data is for adults, ages 25 to 64; "n/a" indicates sample sizes that are unreliable. Percent signs (%) have been eliminated.

Source Analysis of data from the U.S. Census Bureau (2000), Summary File 4.

Although a large and growing body of research has examined how degree attainment is impacted by race, class, and generational status, very few studies have considered the causes specifically for AAPI college students. Why does such a large sector of AAPI students start college but not finish with a degree, and are the reasons similar to or different from others students'? Responding to this question must begin with recognizing that AAPIs have a unique experience with the interpersonal and group dynamics that comprise the college experience (Edgert, 1994).

Research has found that AAPIs have a distinct experience with their identity development during college (Chae, 2000; Ortiz, 1997), which varies for different ethnic groups (Besnard, 2003; Joshi, 2001; Kawaguchi, 2003; Park, 2001). AAPIs have also exhibited unique challenges associated with the psychological climate (Kim, 1993) including higher levels of stress, depression, and psychological distress, (Louie, 2003), lower self-esteem (Tang, 1996), and lower levels of satisfaction during college (Suzuki, 2002; Villalpando, 1994). The persistence and degree attainment of AAPI students needs to be considered in the context of these unique psychosocial factors, particularly as it pertains to the varied experiences and outcomes of students who differ by ethnicity, social class, and institutional setting.

AAPI subgroups with the lowest rates of degree attainment also exhibit the highest rates of poverty, low educational attainment among parents, and high unemployment. These socioeconomic conditions often translate to a lack of access to various instruments that can assist in students' preparation for higher education, including tutoring, extracurricular training, and counseling, not to mention access to comfortable housing, good nutrition, and physical and mental health care (Massey, 2003). Additionally, parental education has also been found to be linked to *cultural capital*—the norms, values, and practices that are comprised by cultural knowledge.

AAPI subgroups with the lowest rates of degree attainment are also attending institutions that are in the worst position to help their students successfully earn a college degree, including 2-year colleges and nonselective 4-year colleges. AAPI students at these institutions are more likely to begin college with less academic preparation, more likely to attend part-time, and have fewer resources and support systems to help them succeed. They are also less likely to have parents with college degrees and are more likely to work more than 20 hours per week while taking courses. All told, AAPI students in 2-year and nonselective 4-year institutions carry many of the risk factors that predict college dropout.

In addition to differences within the AAPI population with regard to their likelihood of earning a degree, there are also important distinctions among AAPI college students when it comes to the field in which they pursue their degrees. The next section examines trends in major and field choices among AAPIs and the following section discusses the education field more specifically.

"WE'RE NOT ALL SCIENCE MAJORS"

Often using the analogy of a pipeline, a number of efforts exist to improve opportunities in fields and disciplines where there are wide discrepancies in the representation of minorities and women. These efforts are often focused on the ways in which underrepresented groups are encouraged, motivated, and supported in their goals. Unfortunately, AAPIs have been mostly excluded from efforts to improve the pipeline in a number of areas that are of concern for other groups: science, technology, engineering, and math (STEM); teacher education; nursing. For example, when it comes to the STEM fields, a common perception is that AAPI students are overrepresented. While there are certainly a large number of AAPIs

Figure 6.2. Percentage of Bachelor's Degrees Awarded in Non-STEM Fields for Blacks, Hispanics, and AAPIs, 1985–2005

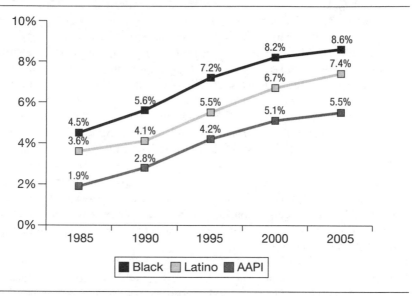

Note. Data through 1990 are for institutions of higher education, while later data are for Title IV, degree-granting institutions.

Source. Analysis of data from the National Center for Education Statistics (NCES, 2010b).

who do pursue STEM fields, trends also show that a large proportion of AAPI students enroll in and obtain degrees in the social sciences and humanities: In 2005, less than one third (30.6%) of bachelor's degrees awarded to AAPIs were in STEM fields.

It is also important to note that the proportion of bachelor's degrees awarded to AAPIs in the STEM fields in 2005 was actually less than prior years. This is quite a unique trend compared to other racial groups. Among bachelor's degrees awarded between 1995 and 2005, all groups (except for Whites) had a greater proportional increase than AAPIs (Blacks, 47.3%; Hispanics, 64.8%; Native American, 47.1%; AAPIs, 45.9%). Conversely, the proportion of AAPI degrees awarded in non-STEM fields increased from 63.4% in 1995 to 69.4% in 2005. The rate of increase in bachelor's degrees awarded in non-STEM fields among AAPIs was greater than any other racial group at 67.3% between 1995 and 2005. This resulted in an increase in AAPI representation among bachelor's degrees awarded in non-STEM fields between 1985 and 2005 (see Figure 6.2). In 1985, AAPIs were only 1.9% of bachelor's degrees in 1985, compared to 5.5% in 2005. The gains in representation among these degrees were at a similar rate as Blacks and Latinos.

Gains in graduate degrees in non-STEM fields show similar trends, with their representation increasing from 3.3% of non-STEM master's degrees in 1995 to 4.6% in 2005. Among doctorates awarded, AAPIs represented 3.7% in 1995, and increased to 4.3% in 2005. A convoluting factor in the perception of AAPIs being only in STEM fields is a high number of international students that attend college in the United States to pursue specialized training in these fields. International students are often confused with AAPI students, not only in perception but also how they are treated in practice and policy. For example, whereas data from the *Eighteenth Annual Status Report for Minorities in Higher Education* show that 32% of doctorates conferred in the United States were to "Asians," 86% of these degrees were actually conferred to international students from Asia, rather than "AAPIs" (Harvey, 2001). A recent National Science Foundation (2006) publication reported that in the same time period, doctoral degrees awarded to Asians who were U.S. citizens accounted for a mere 2% of all doctoral degrees awarded. It is essential for research, policy, and practice to transcend the single story of AAPIs "taking over" the STEM fields and to consider the majority of AAPI students, in all levels of higher education (bachelor's, master's, and doctoral), who are pursuing degrees in non-STEM fields.

Policy makers need to be aware of misguided assumptions about AAPIs. Through empirical evidence, this chapter challenges the notion that educational attainment tells a full story about AAPI access to and participation in U.S. higher education. Educational attainment relative to and from the perspective of others should not be the only perspective that guides the treatment of AAPIs. Most notably, this chapter is a step toward problematizing the idea that "universal success" is an accurate characterization of the AAPI population. This stereotype is often driven by false assumptions of AAPI overrepresentation in higher education as a whole, which is often predicated by the idea that there is an "Asian Invasion" in U.S. higher education. These assumptions are further challenged in an analysis of the implications of the lack of presence of AAPIs in the education sector.

Placing a focus on AAPI educators and administrators throughout America's education system is important and necessary given the research that has found that diversity among these professionals is an essential asset for achieving many desired outcomes within America's vast education system (Darling-Hammond & Berry, 1999; Quiocho & Rios, 2000). In addition to the need for responding to America's increasingly diverse student body, a diverse education workforce can increase opportunities for all students to learn about different cultures, perspectives, and identities. The importance of diversity among educators and administrators is only magnified by our increasingly globalized society that requires specialized knowledge, skills, and experience related to culture and language.

AAPIs IN THE EDUCATION SECTOR

Similar to the lack of inclusion of AAPI students, there is very little attention given to AAPI educators and administrators, both in K–12 schools and higher education. Research on the pipeline to the careers in education tends to either consider minorities in the aggregate under the rubric of "people of color" or focus on Blacks and Latinos as "minorities" (Rong & Preissle, 1997). Little attention has been given to the representation and recruitment of AAPI K–12 teachers and school leaders, or AAPI faculty and administrators, even in major reports specifically focused on diversity issues within the field of the education (Rong & Preissle, 1997). This section responds to issues of diversity and equality among educators and administrators first in the K–12 sector and then in the higher education sector, with a particular focus on AAPIs who serve a critical role in America's system of education.

AAPI Educators and Administrators in the K–12 Sector

For all students—including AAPI students—diversity among educators is an essential asset for achieving many desired outcomes within America's vast education system (Beardsley & Teitel, 2004; Darling-Hammond & Berry, 1999; Quiocho & Rios, 2000). It has been found that teachers of color see themselves in their students and have an orientation toward teaching as a way to give back to the communities in which they teach (Ladson-Billings, 1994; National Collaborative on Diversity in the Teaching Force, 2004). Unfortunately, according to data from the National Center for Education Statistics (NCES, 2008) *Schools and Staffing Survey*, the teaching pool in America's public schools remained overwhelmingly White at 83% in 2004. Among teachers of color, Blacks had the greatest representation at 7.9%, followed by Latinos at 6.2%. That same year, there were 40,385 AAPI teachers nationwide, which constituted a mere 1.5% of America's K–12 teachers. This level of representation among AAPIs had been consistent since the mid-1990s despite efforts to increase diversity among teachers of color in America's K–12 schools. As a result, the disparity between the representation of AAPI students and AAPI teachers increased dramatically when AAPI student enrollment experienced tremendous growth over the past few decades.

While this representation of AAPI teachers is poor, it might even be worse than what is represented by this data. Data provided by NCES does not separate out the approximately 10,000 to 15,000 teachers recruited from outside the United States who are working with temporary visas, many of whom are from Asian countries, according to data from the Center for Economic Organizing (Barber, 2003). India and the Philippines are the top countries of origin of foreign teachers in the United States. Because the U.S. Department of Education does not collect data on foreign teachers, these estimates are drawn from visa applications and through information from international teacher recruiting companies in the United States, many of whom serve as sponsors for the foreign teachers. Temporary employment of international teachers from Asia may be a factor in the lower retention rates among "Asian" teachers.

The prevalence of these "Asian" teachers who are not citizens or permanent residents in the U.S. education system isn't particularly a problem, especially given the projected two million teacher vacancies over the next decade (National Collaborative on Diversity in the Teaching Force, 2004). What the trend speaks to, however, is an inflation of already low numbers of AAPI teachers, and a poor pipeline into the teaching field for AAPIs. Consider that the recruitment of teachers from outside the United States is mostly occurring in rural regions of the country, particularly to fill positions in the South and Midwest in schools that are predominately White. This raises questions about the extent to which the few Asian and AAPI teachers who are the in the field are even working in schools that enroll AAPI students.

In addition to poor representation within the K–12 teacher workforce, AAPIs also tended to have fewer years teaching, compared to other teachers. When looking at the distribution of public school teachers according to years of teaching experience in 2000, all teachers (regardless of race) in K–12 schools have an average of 14.8 years of teaching experience in 2000, while AAPIs average only 12.1 (see Table 6.2). This number of years of experience was similar to that of Latinos at 11.0. A large number of AAPI teachers had 3 or fewer years teaching experience (21.6%), or 4 to 5 years of teaching experience (13.9%). Thus more than one third (35.5%) of AAPI teachers had 5 or fewer years of teaching, which was 10% more than was the case for all teachers overall. This data points to the need to understand not only the factors that impact the recruitment of AAPI teachers, but also the retention of them.

Maybe not so surprising, the low representation of AAPIs in the K–12 sector has yet to set off alarms for improving retention of AAPI teachers or for recruiting others. Unfortunately, there is evidence that suggests many AAPI teachers must contend with issues of "standing out," which has several consequences for the experience and retention of AAPIs in the field (Sheets & Chew, 2002), with many AAPI individuals in the K–12 sector indicating that they are the "only one" in their schools. With more than 8 out of 10 teachers being White, many AAPI teachers are encouraged to assimilate, or adopt, a mainstream identity (Ramanathan, 2006), forcing many to relegate their racial and ethnic identities to the background. Some research has found that this is a factor in the retention of AAPIs and other minority teachers. Those who perceive schools to be insensitive to diversity may choose other professions altogether (Hassan, 1987; Wei, 1986). Other studies have argued that the low number of AAPIs in the teaching force is explained by a tendency to gravitate toward technical careers that less frequently challenge one's backgrounds and beliefs (Gordon, 2002; Rong & Preissle, 1997; Wei, 1986). Gordon (2002) ar-

Table 6.2. Average Number of Years Teaching Among Public School Teachers by Race, 2000

	Average Experience (in years)	Number of Years Experience		
		3 or fewer years	4–5 years	More than 5 years
AAPI	12.1	21.6%	13.9%	64.5%
Black	14.6	18.9%	10.3%	70.8%
White	15.1	14.9%	8.7%	76.4%
Latino	11.0	26.0%	11.8%	62.2%
All Teachers	14.8	16.0%	9.1%	75.0%

Source. Analysis of data from the National Center for Education Statistics (NCES, 2010c).

gues that parents, professors, and community members do not support their students' choosing a career in teaching. In her interviews Gordon found parents who were concerned with status and low salary and professors who told their students that they can do better than "just teaching." This is certainly an issue that needs closer attention.

Examining data from the NCES (2008) *Schools and Staffing Survey* provides some additional insight. Among AAPI teachers who left their teaching position in 2004–05, 45% did so to pursue a career outside of teaching (see Figure 6.3). This was a much higher rate than among Latinos (31%), Blacks (25%), and Whites (25%). While many teachers left their positions to return to graduate school, AAPI teachers were much more likely than other racial groups to pursue studies outside the field of education, and the least likely to return to school within the field of education. Thus many AAPIs seem to be leaving the field of education altogether, as opposed to leaving teaching to pursue another position within the field.

The trends in diversity and retention among AAPI teachers are disturbing, considering the unique educational needs of AAPI students. According to Peter Kiang (2006) there is a pressing need for AAPI teachers, administrators, and policy leaders who are sensitive to the differences among ethnic groups, especially Southeast Asians, South Asians, Native Hawaiians, and Pacific Islanders. There are significant gaps in the representation of different AAPI ethnic groups among teachers, which result in gaps in language and cultural resources for subpopulations of AAPI students. In other words, Chinese Americans in San Francisco may have very different educational experiences and needs from Vietnamese Americans in New Orleans, or Hmong Americans in northern Wisconsin (Root, Rudawski, Taylor, & Rochon, 2003; Sheets & Chew, 2002). This issue has been particularly problematic when it comes to the diverse language backgrounds of AAPI children.

Figure 6.3. Reasons Why Public School Teachers Left Their Positions, 2004–05

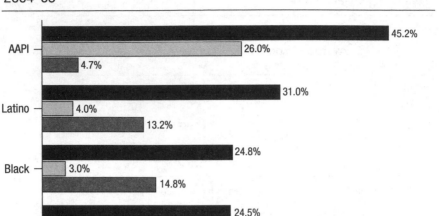

Note. Chart indicates those that reported "Very Important" or "Extremely Important."

Source. Analysis of data from the National Center for Education Statistics (NCES, 2010c).

With over 70% of the AAPI population comprised of new immigrants, and a rate of growth among the population that is greater than any other racial group, there is a large sector of the AAPI student population that has particularly significant needs associated with language and cultural conflict in their schools. AAPI teachers with bilingual or multilingual backgrounds are needed in schools and districts that serve large percentages of recent AAPI immigrants (Rong & Preissle, 1997). As I discussed in Chapter 2, nearly one out of four (24%) AAPI children and youth (ages 5–18), was an English Language Learner in 2000 (AALDEF, 2008). In just five states (California, New York, Texas, Minnesota, and Washington), the ELL population totals more than 250,000. Among certain AAPI ethnic groups, the ELL rate among children and youth is significant. Hmong Americans (52%), Vietnamese Americans (39%), and Cambodian Americans (33%) exhibit particularly high levels of ELL children and youth. Some ethnic groups have a high number of ELL children and youth nationally (e.g., Chinese 115,000, Vietnamese Americans

95,000, Korean Americans 51,000), even though the number might not consti-tute a high proportion among the 5–18-year-old population. Clearly, the ELL rate across AAPI subpopulations is quite disparate, and is affected by ethnicity, timing of immigration, and the language(s) spoken in the country of origin among im-migrants. Thus, while the representation of AAPI teachers is poor overall, its effect on particular subpopulations of AAPIs is important to consider.

The diverse needs of AAPI students in New York City alone underscore this point. Since September 11, 2001, the Indian ethnic group of Sikhs have been sin-gled out as "terrorists" as a result of recurring media images and negative por-trayals of men in turbans. A 2007 survey of 208 Sikhs attending school in New York City—6 years after 9/11—documented a persistent pattern of harassment, violence, and bias toward Sikh youth in New York City schools (Sikh Coalition, 2007). In Queens, New York, more than three quarters (77.5%) of Sikh boys re-ported being teased, physically abused, or verbally harassed on account of their Sikh identity. Among the students that reported complaining to school personnel, nearly one third indicated that they never received any help.

In another incident that involved Lafayette High School in the Bensonhurst neighborhood of Brooklyn, New York, harassment of AAPI students, along with a coinciding "lack of diversity of awareness," was so severe that the U.S. Depart-ment of Justice implemented a consent decree to oversee the school between 2004 and 2007 based on evidence of "severe and pervasive peer-on-peer harassment of Asian students" (AALDEF, 2008). The situation faced by these two populations of AAPI youth in New York City schools underscore the need for teachers and school personnel who are in a position to educate the broader school community and respond to the diverse and unique needs of the AAPI student population. Both of these cases, which are emblematic of problems faced by many AAPI communities throughout the nation,[4] underscore how schools must be a place where issues of difference and tolerance are dealt with.

AAPI teachers are also an important asset for providing valuable insight to subject matter material, including cultural competence in the classrooms. In her book *The Dreamkeepers*, Gloria Ladson-Billings (1994) tells of the importance of culturally relevant classrooms, which have the power to improve the lives of not just African American students, but all children. She found that teachers with the ability to teach with culturally relevant practices can see their place as a part of the community, and that teaching is a way to give something back to the commu-nity. In doing so, students learn to make connections between their community, national, and global identities. Given these findings, it could be hypothesized that AAPI educators can play an important role in the U.S. education system by pro-viding a unique culturally relevant educational context for AAPI students and all students. This is important for increasing awareness about our country, and its relationship to the world, which is important for all students regardless of their racial or ethnic backgrounds. However, in a study of Chinese American teachers enrolled in a bilingual teacher education program, Sheets and Chew (2002) found that the curriculum and pedagogy was often Eurocentric, with almost no sensitivity to the Asian diaspora, and its impact on the United States or the world. The study found that AAPI teachers and students were often silenced through exclusion in the curriculum.

Recognizing the unique needs of AAPI educators is important for educational leaders in the K–12 sector. Unfortunately, while AAPIs are largely absent from the classroom as teachers, their representation among principals was less than half that of their representation among teachers. According to data from the NCES (2008) *Schools and Staffing Survey*, 82.4% of principals were White, 10.6% were Black, and 5.3% were Latino in 2004. That same year, there were only 487 AAPI principals in public elementary and secondary schools nationwide, which was equal to six tenths of one percent. Unfortunately, while AAPI administrators have the potential to bring greater awareness about and leadership to the wide range of needs of AAPI students, teachers, and the broader community, they are too few in number and not in the decision-making positions of most institutions. There is a dire need for more research and a concerted effort by the education field to respond to these hidden problems.

AAPI Educators and Administrators in the Higher Education Sector

Research suggests that within colleges and universities, efforts to diversify the academic workforce may be lagging behind efforts to diversify the student population (Jackson & Phelps, 2004). In other words, there is a lack of faculty and administrators of color in higher education despite the fact that the number of doctoral degrees awarded to students of color, particularly in the field of education, has increased significantly over the past 3 decades (Allen et al., 2000). This discrepancy is particularly pronounced in the nation's most selective universities, which continue to make very little progress in the quest for racial parity (Allen et al., 2000; Delgado Bernal & Villalpando, 2002; Kulis, Shaw, & Chong, 2000). The lack of faculty of color is easily seen just by looking at the proportional representation of White faculty. In 2005, White faculty made up 77.0% of the faculty in public 4-year institutions, 79.7% in the private 4-year sector, and 81.0% in the community college sector (see Table 6.3). This level of representation is often overlooked during discussions about faculty of color, especially with regard to AAPI faculty (Lee, 2002).

Looking at the distribution of faculty by race in the aggregate (without taking into account rank and tenure status), it would appear that AAPIs have good representation relative to other faculty of color. In 2005 there were 42,858 AAPI faculty, which represented 7.2% of the total. Among AAPI faculty, there was a high proportion working in the public 4-year sector (60.8%) compared to the proportion of AAPI faculty working in the public 2-year sector (24.5%). This trend was not

Table 6.3. Number and Distribution of Full-Time Faculty by Race and Institutional Type, 2005

(Percent Reads Across)	White	Black	Latino	AAPI	Native American	Total
ALL INSTITUTIONS[A]	469,610	31,572	26,654	42,858	2,801	599,124
% of total across race	78.4%	5.3%	4.4%	7.2%	0.5%	100.0%
PUBLIC 4-YEAR	239,838	15,511	13,696	26,043	1,559	311,646
% of total across race	77.0%	5.0%	4.4%	8.4%	0.5%	100.0%
% of total within race	51.1%	49.1%	51.4%	60.8%	55.7%	52.0%
PRIVATE 4-YEAR[B]	147,843	8,597	7,215	12,563	451	185,467
% of total across race	79.7%	4.6%	3.9%	6.8%	0.2%	100.0%
% of total within race	31.5%	27.2%	27.1%	29.3%	16.1%	31.0%
PUBLIC 2-YEAR	69,210	5,943	4,675	3,570	686	85,496
% of total across race	81.0%	7.0%	5.5%	4.2%	0.8%	100.0%
% of total within race	18.8%	17.5%	8.3%	24.5%	12.0%	18.8%

Note. Includes all faculty and all ranks (tenured and untenured, and on and off tenure track).

[A] Title IV Degree Granting Institutions. [B] Private not-for-profit only.

Source. Analysis of data from National Center for Education Statistics (NCES, 2010b).

dissimilar to other racial groups. While this is the data that is typically cited when looking at the distribution of faculty in U.S. higher education, it does not reveal the ways in which AAPIs are unique. A closer look at faculty by rank and tenure provides a more revealing portrait of AAPI faculty representation.

Research has found large disparities in promotion rates by race, with White faculty being twice as likely as Asian faculty to be promoted to the rank of associate or full professor (Palepu, Carr, Friedman, Amos, Ash, & Moskowitz, 1995). National data on faculty appear to confirm these trends. Similar to other faculty of color, AAPIs had a lower proportion of faculty with tenure (36.3%), compared to Whites (45.9%) (see Table 6.4). However, there was a larger proportion of AAPI faculty who were on the tenure track, but not tenured (25.4%), compared to other racial groups.[5] There is a need for research that can examine the discrepancy between the proportion of AAPI faculty on the tenure track and the proportion of AAPI faculty who are tenured.

What is also quite notable in Table 6.4 is the high proportion of AAPI faculty who were not on the tenure track; a trend that was most prevalent in the 4-year sector. In public 4-year institutions, 20.6% of the AAPI faculty were not on the tenure track, compared to 13.1% of all faculty. In the private 4-year sector, a higher proportion of the AAPI faculty were not on the tenure track at 26.8%, but that number was also greater among all faculty at 23.9%. The public 4-year sector is

Table 6.4. Distribution of Full-Time Faculty by Tenure Status, Rank, Institutional Type, and Race, 2005

(Percent Reads Down)	White	Black	Latino	AAPI	Native American	Total
ALL INSTITUTIONS[A]						
Tenured[B]	45.9%	34.5%	39.7%	36.3%	32.3%	43.2%
Tenure track, not tenured	17.4%	22.1%	18.4%	25.4%	19.3%	19.3%
Not on tenure track	16.1%	15.7%	14.4%	20.9%	12.2%	16.4%
Instructor or lecturer[C]	20.7%	27.7%	27.6%	17.4%	36.2%	21.2%
All ranks	100.0%	100.0%	100.0%	100.0%	100.0%	100.0%
PUBLIC 4-YEAR						
Tenured	54.2%	44.6%	51.3%	45.1%	43.7%	51.1%
Tenure track, not tenured	19.4%	27.3%	22.3%	24.6%	26.2%	21.9%
Not on tenure track	12.5%	12.4%	9.9%	20.6%	10.9%	13.1%
Instructor or lecturer	13.9%	15.7%	16.5%	9.6%	19.1%	13.8%
All ranks	100.0%	100.0%	100.0%	100.0%	100.0%	100.0%
PRIVATE 4-YEAR[D]						
Tenured	45.9%	30.1%	36.3%	33.3%	30.2%	42.4%
Tenure track, not tenured	20.8%	27.1%	21.9%	28.6%	23.5%	22.5%
Not on tenure track	23.3%	26.5%	27.0%	26.8%	23.5%	23.9%
Instructor or lecturer	10.0%	16.2%	14.8%	11.3%	22.8%	11.2%
All ranks	100.0%	100.0%	100.0%	100.0%	100.0%	100.0%
PUBLIC 2-YEAR						
Tenured	25.0%	23.2%	17.4%	19.8%	12.7%	24.0%
Tenure track, not tenured	6.1%	6.8%	5.6%	6.4%	3.6%	6.1%
Not on tenure track	13.6%	10.5%	6.5%	9.9%	9.5%	12.6%
Instructor or lecturer	55.3%	59.5%	70.4%	63.9%	74.2%	57.3%
All ranks	100.0%	100.0%	100.0%	100.0%	100.0%	100.0%

[A]Title IV Degree Granting Institutions only. [B]Any Rank. [C]Tenured and Not Tenured. [D]Private not-for-profit only.

Source. Analysis of data from the National Center for Education Statistics (NCES, 2010b).

where AAPIs had their greatest numbers and proportional representation. In the 2-year sector, AAPI faculty had a similar share of their faculty who were not on the tenure track (9.9%), which was lower than it was in the sector generally. This was a similar trend to other faculty of color. However, in the 2-year sector, AAPI had a greater proportion of their faculty who were instructors and lecturers (63.9%) than the total faculty overall (57.3%), which was also a similar trend among all faculty of color. This contrasts with the number of AAPI instructors and lecturers that could be found in the 4-year sector. In the public 4-year sector only 9.6% of AAPI faculty were instructors or lecturers, compared to 19.1% of Native Americans, 16.5% of Latinos, 15.7% of Blacks, and 13.9% of Whites. Rather, AAPIs exhibited a similar distribution of faculty within ranks as international scholars (i.e., "nonresident aliens").

What we know about AAPI faculty is severely limited by the dearth of research, coupled with how researchers report on aggregated faculty data. Consider that when AAPIs are included in many reports, it is difficult to differentiate international scholars with Asian origins from AAPIs. This is particularly problematic for AAPIs for at least two reasons. First, international scholars from Asia make up a large portion of all international scholars. According to the Institute for International Education, there were 98,239 international scholars who were teaching and/or conducting research at United States campuses in 2006 (Open Doors, 2007). Nearly half of these international scholars (45,948) came from just five Asian countries (China, Korea, India, Japan, and Taiwan). Second, mixing just a small proportion of international scholars with the counting of domestic faculty disproportionately impacts the relatively small number of AAPI faculty in U.S. higher education at 42,858. These two problems alone or in combination can have a large impact on the number of AAPI faculty we count in U.S. higher education, as well as what we know about their proportional representation relative to other racial groups.

Having accurate and nuanced information about the representation of faculty of color is critically important. Throughout the ranks of all disciplines and fields, the importance of faculty of color has been underscored in a number of important studies. Antonio (2002) found that faculty of color were 75% more likely than White faculty to choose a career in academia because they saw a connection between the professoriate and the ability to affect change in society. He also found that faculty of color dedicated more time to conducting research and were more inclined to value the experiential knowledge students brought with them from outside of the classroom. Faculty of color have also been found to be effective in pushing the boundaries of their disciplines and fields, often to develop theoretical perspectives and epistemologies that capture the perspectives and experiences of communities of color (Delgado Bernal, 1998; Delgado Bernal & Villalpando, 2002). Ethnic studies and Asian American studies have been found to be a par-

Table 6.5. Higher Education Administrators by Race, Gender, and Institutional Type, 2005

Percent Reads Across	White	Black	Latino	AAPI	Native American	Total
All institutions[A]	159,494	18,353	8,420	5,493	1,120	196,324
% of total within race	81.2%	9.3%	4.3%	2.8%	0.6%	100.0%
Public 4-Year	60,236	7,443	2,972	2,146	449	74,241
% of total within race	81.1%	10.0%	4.0%	2.9%	0.6%	100.0%
Private 4-Year[B]	74,318	7,611	3,564	2,618	285	90,415
% of total within race	82.2%	8.4%	3.9%	2.9%	0.3%	100.0%
Public 2-Year	21,293	2,713	1,488	622	314	26,770
% of total within race	79.5%	10.1%	5.6%	2.3%	1.2%	100.0%

[A]Title IV Degree Granting Institutions only. [B]Private not-for-profit only.

Note. Administrators include executive, administrative, and managerial staff.

Source. Analysis of data from the National Center for Education Statistics (NCES, 2010b).

ticularly prevalent gateway through which AAPI students cross on their way to becoming teachers.

Unfortunately, the knowledge and perspective of faculty of color, including AAPIs, have been found to be systemically devalued by White faculty (Delgado Bernal & Villalpando, 2002; Moody, 2004). Climbing the ranks of the academy for faculty of color means overcoming presumptions that they are incompetent by White male faculty, being marginalized through isolation, overcoming a lack of mentoring and being excluded from valuable connections and networks, and hypervisibility because they are looked upon to represent their entire group (Moody, 2004). Thus many faculty of color continue to experience systems of subordination and marginalization within academia which result in poor representation at the top of the academic hierarchy (Allen et al., 2000; Delgado Bernal & Villalpando, 2002). Turner (2003) explains, "The potential for expansion for scholarship in all fields depends on the ability of institutions to recruit scholars with different perspectives and racial/ethnic backgrounds who . . . have the power and independence to influence the direction of research" (p. 118). This sentiment was echoed by Ben Baez (2000) who describes the unique contributions of faculty of color, including their mentorship to students and service to their institutions; he calls for the academy to reimagine service and move beyond its relegation to the margins.

Table 6.6. College Presidents by Race, Sex, and Institutional Type, 2003

Percent Reads Across	2-Year Institutions			4-Year Institutions			All Institutions		
	Men	Women	Total	Men	Women	Total	Men	Women	Total
White	749	262	1,011	1,461	309	1,770	2,210	571	2,781
	89.0%	85.4%	87.5%	88.6%	84.2%	87.8%	88.7%	83.8%	87.7%
Black	45	31	76	106	31	137	151	62	213
	5.3%	9.7%	6.5%	6.4%	8.4%	6.8%	6.0%	9.0%	6.7%
Latino	42	18	60	60	25	85	102	43	145
	4.9%	5.7%	5.1%	3.6%	6.8%	4.2%	4.1%	6.3%	4.5%
AAPI	6	3	9	22	2	24	28	5	33
	0.7%	0.9%	0.8%	1.3%	0.5%	1.2%	1.1%	0.7%	1.0%
Native American	8	4	12	4	3	7	12	7	19
	0.9%	1.3%	1.0%	0.2%	0.8%	0.3%	0.5%	1.0%	0.6%

Note. Figures include presidents of Title IV, degree-granting institutions in the United States and Puerto Rico. Data were compiled March 2003.

Source. American Council on Education, (2005).

AAPI representation among higher education leadership positions is also quite revealing. A survey of higher education institutions reveals that the number of AAPI administrators overall was quite low (see Table 6.5). In 2005 there were only 5,493 AAPI professional executive, administrative, and managerial staff, which was 2.8% of the total. Their representation in public 4-year and private 4-year institutions was equal at 2.9%, and their representation in public 2-year institutions was lower at 2.3%. Analysis by sex among AAPIs did not reveal differences between male and female representation.

The poor representation among AAPIs in positions of leadership in higher education was particularly pronounced among college presidents. In 2003, AAPIs made up a mere 1.0% of college presidents (of any institutional type) (see Table 6.6). AAPIs had a slightly higher representation among presidents in the 4-year sector (1.2%) than in the 2-year sector (0.8%). While the proportional representation is quite glaring, it is also important to consider the actual numbers. Throughout all United States colleges and universities, there were only 33 AAPI college presidents. In the community college sector, the number was only nine—three of whom were women. At a recent meeting of scholars seeking to address the educational needs of AAPI students, participants joked that two thirds of the AAPI community college presidents were in the room. Jokes aside, AAPIs by far have very poor representation among college presidents.

The poor representation among AAPI presidents results in a threefold problem that needs closer attention. First, consider the many colleges and universities with high concentrations of AAPI students in states like California, Hawaii, and New York: in these institutions, there is a lack of AAPIs among institutional leaders, which diminishes the likelihood AAPI students "see themselves" as leaders in their institutions. Second, there is a growing AAPI student population over the past decade in the South and Midwest regions of the country, as well as a growing presence in the community college sector. In these institutions the implications of a lack of AAPI representation among leadership presents problems for raising awareness to and solutions for these rapidly changing demographic trends among AAPIs. This leads to a third problem: A lack of AAPI high-level administrators often means fewer opportunities for bringing attention to the institutional challenges that are associated with the AAPI student population, especially among networks of high-level administrators who discuss institutional priorities and how to respond to emerging trends in higher education overall.

AAPI leadership in higher education is also essential for the leadership, insights, and skills to both globalize collegiate studies and help the United States understand diversity and nuance in the vast regions of Asia and the Pacific. We must begin with the talent that can be found among the few AAPI students, faculty, and administrators who are able and willing to take up such leadership positions. This is particularly important because the problems with representation are systemic, with reports that suggest there are very few AAPI graduate students working toward advanced degrees that might lead to positions in student affairs or higher education administration. As such, improving the educational and career pipelines for AAPIs into leadership positions in higher education requires more awareness of the issues that impact AAPI students, which can be a catalyst for bringing more AAPI educators and policy makers into such positions of leadership (Committee of 100, 2005; Ong, 2008).

STRATEGIES TO IMPROVE THE AAPI EDUCATION PIPELINE

There are a number of strategies that can be employed to respond to the poor representation of AAPIs in the education and academic pipelines. The first strategy would be to improve the inclusiveness of AAPIs in existing programs that are focused on increasing the representation of underrepresented students in certain fields and disciplines (Spellman, 1988). Well-established programs, such as the Mellon Mays Undergraduate Fellowship Program and the Institute for Recruitment of Teachers,[6] have a proven track record for addressing these issues for other minority groups, but overlook—or, in some cases, overtly exclude—AAPIs as a target population (Sheets & Chew, 2002). There is a need for greater recognition of how the AAPI pipeline in the education field can benefit from and contribute to these programs.

Another avenue to provide support for AAPI students, faculty, and administrators—particularly for those institutions with a critical mass of AAPIs—is through the U.S. Department of Education's Minority-Serving Institution programs. In 2007 Congress created the Asian American and Native American Pacific Islander-Serving Institution (AANAPISI) program to allocate federal funding to institutions that disproportionately serve AAPI students and low-income students. Initially funded under the College Cost Reduction and Access Act of 2007, the AANAPISI program was reauthorized in 2008 under the Higher Education Opportunity Act (HEOA) joining similar programs that fund Minority-Serving Institutions (MSIs). The AANAPISI legislation is significant for the AAPI community because it acknowledges the unique challenges facing AAPI students in college access and completion, and represents a significant commitment of much-needed resources to address these issues for the population. The rationale for the program structure is simple: In order to maximize limited federal resources, funding should be allocated among those institutions enrolling a critical mass of AAPI and low-income students.

This policy strategy is particularly effective for reaching AAPI students for at least three reasons. First, the AAPI undergraduate student population is highly concentrated in a small number of postsecondary institutions; as of 2006 two thirds of AAPI students were concentrated in 200 institutions. Second, AAPI students are unique in their demographic backgrounds and educational needs; a large sector of AAPI students are immigrants and the first in their families to attend college, face unique challenges because of their language backgrounds, arrive on campus underprepared for college-level work, and are from low-income backgrounds and struggle to secure the financial resources to support themselves while in school. Finally, AAPI students have a particularly high growth rate at public 2-year institutions, a sector of higher education with the fewest resources, yet enroll students with some of the greatest needs.

The first cohort of AANAPISI campuses was created in 2008, which included six institutions. In 2009 another computer yielded two additional campuses. With the exception of two institutions, all awardees were public 2-year colleges, and all were geographically dispersed across five states and the unincorporated territory of Guam. As a group, these institutions are quite remarkable; nearly 1 in 10 AAPI students nationally attends one of these AANAPISI campuses, and together these campuses enrolled nearly 60,000 AAPI undergraduates and awarded over 5,000 associate's and bachelor's degrees to AAPI students in 2006–07. Individually, each campus also has a unique portrait of success and challenge. At De Anza College (in Cupertino, California), which has one of the largest enrollments of any community college in the nation, 42% of the students were AAPIs. As described by campus administrators, most of the AAPI students are not prepared for college-level work and account for nearly 50% of students enrolled in remediation and basic skills classes. Indeed, AANAPISIs represent important organizational settings for addressing the needs of low-income, high-need AAPI college students.

AANAPISI campuses create programs that support students in their transition from high school to college, and create intervention strategies that improve the retention of AAPI students. AANAPISIs are also a policy strategy for improving the teacher pipeline for AAPI students. South Seattle Community College, an AANAPISI campus in the 2008 cohort, developed a program to "Strengthen Pathways for AAPI Students to Become Teachers" through a partnership with a 4-year institutions, Heritage University (in Toppenish, Washington), which has a track record of producing teachers who earn a teaching credential and work in the local community. There are two aspects of the partner institution that are interesting to note: First, the partner institution has historically had very few AAPI students enrolled overall (<1%) and only a couple of AAPI students each year in their education program. Second, the partner institution is also a Hispanic-Serving Institution (HSI), showing that partnerships can be formed between institutions that serve different student populations with regard to race, but similarities in terms of the needs of their students and the ways in which institutions can respond to them. The AANAPISI program, in conclusion, is an effective policy mechanism for helping increase AAPI participation, degree attainment, and representation in fields and disciplines where they are underrepresented. The students, their institutions, and the communities in which they are geographically situated gain access to resources and opportunities that recognize their unique needs and challenges.

INCLUSIVENESS OF AAPI educators and administrators throughout America's education system is an essential ingredient for responding to broader problems that impact the participation, experience, and outcomes of AAPI students. This is because the presence of AAPI educators and administrators in K–12 and higher education is a key factor for dispelling and replacing the myths about Asian American and Pacific Islander students so that our education system and society as a whole can fully develop and engage these students; they play a central role in the development of a renewed public vision for implementing policies and practices based on facts about AAPIs. Greater representation among AAPI educators and administrators will lead to the changes needed to better serve AAPI students and the educational system as a whole.

CONCLUSION

Beyond a Single Story

The "model minority" is an enduring concept that has become deeply entrenched in America's ethos. The stereotype has several implications for Asian Americans and Pacific Islanders. First, it affects how AAPIs are perceived and treated by others because oversimplified generalizations prevent people from acknowledging the complexity of individuals or subgroups within the population. Second, stereotypes about AAPIs have led to racism, prejudice, and discrimination on both interpersonal and structural levels.[1] Finally, stereotypes affect how AAPIs, as individuals and as a group, view themselves (Steele & Aronson, 1995). Stacey Lee (1996), author of *Unraveling the Model Minority Stereotype: Listening to Asian American Youth*, found that AAPI students internalize the myth and assess themselves according to this image, which is problematic because the image of the "model minority" is often unattainable in reality.

While the model minority myth is very different from other stereotypes that are ascribed to racial minorities, it is important to recognize the ways in which it is similar. It is tied to the idea that race is correlated with and even a predictor for achievement and mobility. This assertion is not a new concept and historically has led to a number of problematic explanations for the relationship between race, educational achievement, and social mobility.[2] There is a pressing need for more and better research that can inform our understanding of how race operates in American society, particularly as it pertains to groups that represent "wildcards" in the Black/White paradigm that has framed our understanding of race in American society.

This research cannot be reactionary; nor should it challenge claims using the same theoretical and conceptual framing that guided the existing assertions in the first place. It must be based on alternative perspectives that capture the uniqueness of the population. In the following concluding remarks I provide some examples of how research can transcend the conceptual blockages that have severely limited the knowledge that exists about AAPIs and their education and social mobility in America.

TRANSCENDING CATEGORIES AND BOUNDARIES

Relative to educational mobility and postsecondary opportunities, the inclusion of AAPIs needs to be considered in the context of categorical inequality. This framework reminds us that AAPIs are positioned within and affected by the same categories that serve as the boundaries of opportunity for all racial groups. The empirical research presented in this book demonstrates that AAPI students, like all students, are a part of the same systemic institutional and social realities that privilege some, while simultaneously disadvantaging others. Similar to countless other Americans, some AAPIs are vulnerable to the realities of poverty, poor English language ability, low educational attainment, and poor access to other forms of capital. At the same time, other AAPIs have high educational attainment, wealth, and many other forms of capital that translate easily into educational and social mobility. Also similar to Americans as a whole, AAPIs have a wide distribution of postsecondary outcomes, with some students attending the most selective institutions in the United States, some attending institutions that are nonselective or moderately selective, and a large sector of students who do not attend college at all.

Among AAPIs who do attend college, they are not unlike others when it comes to degree attainment rates. For AAPI first-time freshmen in public 4-year institutions, only 6 out of 10 received their bachelor's degrees, based on a cohort of students in 1999.[3] In public 2-year institutions, the degree attainment rate was much worse, with only one quarter (25.2%) of AAPIs who received their associate's degree, based on a cohort of students in 2002. Indeed, the focus on participation in higher education policy has led to decreased attention to the success of institutions in helping students successfully leave higher education.

A large and growing body of research has examined how degree attainment is impacted by race, class, and generational status; however, very few studies have focused specifically on the AAPI student population. Specifically, why do so many AAPI students start college but not finish with a degree, and are the reasons similar to or different from others? Responding to this question must begin with recognizing that AAPIs have a unique experience with the interpersonal and group dynamics that comprise the college experience (Edgert, 1994). Research has found that AAPIs have a distinct experience with their identity development during college (Chae, 2000; Ortiz, 1997), which varies for different ethnic groups (Besnard, 2003; Joshi, 2001; Kawaguchi, 2003; Kou, 2001; Park, 2001). AAPIs have also exhibited unique challenges associated with the psychological climate (Kim, 1997) including higher levels of stress, depression, and psychological distress, (Louie, 2003), lower self-esteem (Tang, 1996), and lower levels of satisfaction during college (Suzuki, 2002; Villalpando, 1994). The persistence and degree attainment of AAPI students needs to be considered in the context of these unique psychosocial factors, particularly as it pertains to the varied experiences and outcomes of students who differ by ethnicity, social class, and within different institutional settings.

These distinctions within the AAPI population, similar to the unique set of indicators and outcomes associated with their college access and participation, are important to perspectives for positioning AAPIs along the race continuum in social science research. The wide distribution in demographic characteristics within the population means that a single story cannot represent the unique American experience of the many AAPI subpopulations that comprise the population in the aggregate. More specific to educational achievement and mobility, the mean score for all AAPIs when it comes to grades, test scores, or college-going rates cannot accurately reflect the wide distribution of subgroups from the mean. Thus, while AAPIs are similar to many groups, there are also ways that they are quite unique and misplaced within the categorical model of race. Said another way, even when the demography of AAPIs is characteristically similar to others with regard to heterogeneity, the ways in which particular characteristics contribute to differences within the AAPI population is quite unique relative to other groups.

The boundaries of race need to be problematized and transcended, which is not easily accomplished. Charles Tilly (1998) describes bounded categories (race being one of them), which are classifications of stratification. He says, "boundaries do crucial organizational work" (p. 6) of separating the powerful from the powerless, the exploiter from the exploited, and are reinforced through institutionalization. I argue that transcending the boundaries of race toward a more nuanced approach has relevance for many other groups. While most of this book has been focused on how AAPIs are different from other racial groups in nearly all measurable ways, ironically, it may be highlighting something that they share in common with other groups: The idea that race, by itself, "predicts," is "associated with," or "reveals" anything about educational or social disparities leads to problematic generalizations about groups.

The basis for these claims often leads to a deficit perspective that informs practice and policy. In a society that is increasingly globalized financially and culturally, we need to transcend the idea that one way can represent the right way, if we are to be productive citizens in the global community. The globalization of industry and communications has created the need for greater competencies in cultural and linguistic knowledge beyond what America's education system has traditionally offered students. In addition to the value of such knowledge for the marketplace, the strength of U.S. national security is predicated upon the availability of competent intelligence officers who have been sufficiently trained in languages and cultures originating in a variety of international settings, including Asia and the Pacific. Recognizing and appreciating the assets that different groups bring to the table are an essential first step toward this goal. A greater understanding of histories and customs of Asian nations and peoples will substantially enhance the education of students who will both want and perhaps need to pursue future employment opportunities in a global workforce. Thus, while immigrant and foreign students and communities certainly need to learn about U.S. culture and history, all Americans should also better understand the cultures and histories of Asians, Asian Americans, and Pacific Islanders.

THE NEED FOR MORE AND BETTER RESEARCH

Moving toward practice and policy that values the peripheries of the mainstream requires research that can address the severe knowledge gaps in understanding the educational experiences, opportunities, and outcomes of AAPIs, and other minority populations. For AAPIs, there is a need for more and better research that examines their unique population demography and how it is characteristically similar to or unique from other populations in America. There is very little that is known about how AAPIs vary in their educational experiences and mobility given their wide distribution of where they live and go to school. Neither of these issues has been connected well to their status and mobility in American society. In terms of the American education system, there is very little that we know about the AAPI student, faculty, and administrator experience. These are just some baseline issues that require much more attention.

In addition to a need for more research, the problems that have driven the existing research have often been narrowly defined, often focusing on the gaps between groups. This scholarship has often led to generalizations about groups instead of an understanding of the unique experiences that exist within groups. Scholars of race, social status, and educational mobility need to conduct research that demonstrates that generalizations, assumptions, and stereotypes as the basis for practice or policy will not lead us to a better understanding of the problem, and cannot lead us to any viable solutions. Research that is driven by narrow understandings of race only perpetuates the use of stereotypes and generalizations. This is simply unacceptable. These conceptual blockages can be overcome by deliberately incorporating interdisciplinary perspectives, such as critical race theory.

In addition to reconceptualized research, it is equally important for scholars and policy makers to collect and report data in a way that allows for further deconstruction of the variation within racial categories (by ethnicity, nationality, immigration history, and language background). This data would tell us more about the vast diversity among all students in our schools and colleges. For AAPIs, this is a first step toward a deeper understanding of their educational experiences and outcomes, which are difficult to pinpoint with existing data. Consider the impact of the 280,000 international students and 45,948 international scholars in U.S. higher education from just five Asian countries (China, Korea, India, Japan, and Taiwan) in 2006. The presence of these students and scholars affects the perception of AAPI presence on college campuses and can also affect practice and policy based on data if even a small proportion of them are inadvertently counted as AAPI students or faculty. There were only about one million AAPI students and 45,000 AAPI faculty in all of United States higher education in 2006. More and better data also means the use of a wide range of research methodologies, including qualitative analyses of focus groups, individual interviews, and observations, in addition to survey-based quantitative techniques.

More and better research must also be central to practice and policy decision making in education. This means that research, practice, and policy making should not occur in a vacuum, and research should be a collaborative process that directly engages communities, institutions, and the policy arena. This process will bring to the table divergent vantage points and constituents with different types of experience and expertise. Together, a collaborative research process can collectively engage the process of inquiry, deciding as a group how to frame problems and how to address them empirically. This process is imperative at all stages of the research process, including setting goals, identifying and understanding problems that inhibit goals, and creating solutions to address them.

AN ESSENTIAL MISSING LINK

This book also points to the imperative of hiring and retaining more AAPI educators and leaders in K–12 and higher education. These individuals will hire more school counselors who will be trained to recognize the unique needs of Asian American and Pacific Islander students for whom they are responsible, resulting in targeted support for at-risk students as well as meaningful involvement and participation by parents with little or no formal United States education. This includes equitable support for AAPI students who may have unique needs and concerns that may be overlooked under existing paradigms of what constitutes a problem. Consider the need for more attention to the unique mental health needs of AAPI students, including effective approaches for those students who are affected by trauma associated with their transitions as immigrants in a new country, as well as supporting those students who face pressure to succeed from their parents.

AAPI leadership in K–12 and higher education will also lead to an increase in the participation of Asian Americans and Pacific Islanders in civic roles because more AAPI role models will be visible in positions of leadership. AAPI students will be encouraged to pursue careers as educators and administrators in both K–12 and higher education through an increase in the number of mentors and role models for AAPI youth. Role models will also lead to improvements in retention rates of AAPI students in high school and college through healthy and supportive interactions and meaningful relationships.

AAPI teachers and administrators can identify and guide work in education at every level, on behalf of all groups, including AAPIs. These AAPI educators and professionals can also serve as subject matter experts for policy development. This will move our education system beyond a deficit model when it comes to dealing with language and cultural differences in our schools, and modify our desired learning outcomes to include curricula that reflect AAPI history, art, literature, and culture. This change will benefit all students in our increasingly globalized society where multicultural competence is imperative.

In terms of the capacity of our education systems, policies, and practices, AAPI leadership can bring improvements to the collection and reporting of data in a way that allows for further deconstruction of the variation within broad racial categories. This data, coupled with insight from AAPI educators and administrators, will tell us more about the vast diversity among all students in our schools and colleges. A critical mass of AAPI professionals in the K–12 and higher education sectors will also lead to greater capacity to connect with AAPI community leaders and organizations to enhance the cultural capacity of our institutions and improve student outcomes. In the K–12 sector, these collaborations would result in a better connection between school professionals and AAPI parents, and improvements to curricula and language policy. In higher education, these collaborations will improve admissions, outreach, and financial aid practices, change the way we approach student services, and result in new institutional initiatives in the local community.

MORE SO TODAY than at any other point in America's history, we are in the position to move toward such a model. A new alternative perspective on race and racial minorities can dispel harmful generalizations and assumptions and lead higher education and society to fully develop and engage marginalized students who have much to contribute to our schools, communities, and country as a whole. Indeed, a change in our collective orientation toward AAPIs can open our eyes to many exciting possibilities.

APPENDIX A

Data Sources
and Methodology

In order to examine the linkages between the demography of AAPIs and their educational mobility, I analyzed data from a number of sources. Quantitative data are utilized to capture the conditions and educational outcomes that exist among AAPIs. These include descriptive statistics that capture status indicators related to individuals, communities, and institutions, as well as multivariate analyses of how various social conditions among AAPIs are factors in their educational mobility. While the use of numbers present one set of opportunities, they also have their limitations. Thus qualitative methods are also utilized to give voice to the lived experiences of AAPI students as they develop and pursue their educational aspirations.

In terms of units of analysis, one major focus is the demography of and social conditions among AAPI students, families, and communities. Thus I place AAPI students' experiences and outcomes within a broader context of varying social conditions that exist for different AAPI subpopulations. Additionally, I examine the AAPI experience within the context of various educational institutions enabling a more thorough and thoughtful understanding of AAPI access to and participation in higher education. The institutions and contexts, which are the focus of this work, include secondary schools that vary demographically and in terms of resources, and colleges that vary in terms of type (2-year and 4-year), selectivity (highly, moderately, and nonselective), and control (public, private-nonprofit, and private-for-profit). These multiple layers of data offer an interrogation that is rich with comprehensiveness and complexity, offering both depth and breadth of analysis.

U.S. Census Bureau

To examine demographic trends, I analyzed data from the U.S. Census Bureau 100 percent file and 5-percent PUMS (Public Use Microdata Sample). This data reports on the demography of the AAPI population, including size, geographic distribution, and characteristics of the population. It is also used to examine the processes of population change, including patterns of residential settlement and migration.

Office of Immigration Statistics

Data from the Office of Immigration Statistics, U.S. Department of Homeland Security, were used to complement demographic data. Coupled with the census data, this information served as the context within which the educational participation and outcomes of AAPIs can be better understood.

National Center for Education Statistics (NCES)

For information on higher education, I examined data from the National Center for Education Statistics (NCES), U.S. Department of Education. Data were drawn from the Intersegmental Postsecondary Education Data System (IPEDS), which is the core postsecondary education data collection program for NCES. Data for IPEDS are collected from all primary providers of postsecondary education in the country in areas including enrollments, program completions, graduation rates, faculty, staff, finances, institutional prices, and student financial aid. These data were used to analyze and track trends in higher education participation and attainment. For analysis of participation and completion rates, this study limits its focus to degree-granting postsecondary institutions with Title IV status. Title IV of the Higher Education Act of 1965 (as amended) establishes federal financial aid programs (e.g., Pell Grants and Stafford Loans) for students attending postsecondary institutions.

Data from NCES also include information from the Common Core Database (CCD), which tracks information on K–12 public schools in the United States These data were used to track information on enrollment patterns and characteristics of schools attended by AAPI students. Finally, data from NCES include information from the *Schools and Staffing Survey*, which helps to examine the representation and experiences of K–12 teachers and administrators. From the survey, data were drawn from the Public School Teacher Data File and the Public School Principal Data File.

Cooperative Institutional Research Program (CIRP)

I also utilized data from the Higher Education Research Institute (HERI) at the University of California–Los Angeles. The data were drawn from the Cooperative Institutional Research Program (CIRP), which administers a Survey of College Freshmen. The specific data consist of a national representative sample of AAPI first-time freshmen in 1997. The data collected during this particular year was the only year the Cooperative Institutional Research Program collected demographic data that disaggregated the Asian American category into distinct ethnic subcategories. This dataset represents the only large, national dataset that links AAPI subpopulations and their college choice behavior to specific college destinations. AAPI students consisted of 10% of all respondents in the 1997 freshman survey. The subsample of AAPIs included 18,106 first-time, full-time AAPI freshmen (5,089 Chinese Americans; 2,580 Filipino Americans; 1,559 Japanese Americans; 2,937 Korean Americans; 1,975 Southeast Asian Americans; and 5,139 students who identified as "Other Asian") who attended 469 colleges and universities across the United States.[1]

In addition to descriptive analyses, regression analyses were conducted in three stages in order to examine the relationship between specific high school experiences, reasons for going to college, key socioeconomic factors, and the prestige of the college attended. First, exploratory regression analyses utilizing a broad array of 45 independent variables from the Freshmen Survey were conducted on the entire AAPI student population to examine the effects of ethnicity and other key socioeconomic factors on attending a selective institution.

Second, exploratory regressions were conducted separately for each of the five AAPI ethnic groups to examine how attendance at selective institutions might be influenced differently for each group. Based on the results of these exploratory regressions, a final set of regression analyses was conducted using only those independent variables that added significantly to the prediction of attending a selective institution for at least one AAPI ethnic group. For purposes of making comparisons across the five samples, these analyses included identical blocks of independent variables that were force-entered into the regression equations for each group.

The multivariate analysis was regressed using institutional selectivity as a dependent variable. The selectivity of institutions that different students attend is a sufficient indicator of differential access to higher education opportunities (Astin, 1985; Bowen, 1977). The selectivity of the college was operationalized as the average freshman class Scholastic Aptitude Test (SAT) scores reported by the institutions attended by the respondents. Independent variables were divided into three blocks (see Table A.1). All of the variables described below were significant for at least one of the five ethnic groups in a preliminary regression analysis and were therefore included in final analyses.

The first block includes six student demographic characteristics (ethnicity, parental income, highest level of father's and mother's education, student citizenship status, and whether the student is a native English speaker). The second block includes four variables measuring high school experiences and activities (high school GPA, whether or not a student took an SAT preparation course, hours per week spent studying, students' self-reported degree aspirations). The third block includes 10 variables measuring students' reasons for going to college (relative's wish, teacher's advice, high school counselor's advice, friend's advice, private counselor's advice, academic reputation of college, college has low tuition, wanted to live near home, college rankings in national magazines, and the belief that graduates go to top graduate schools).

Unstandardized and standardized regression coefficients are provided to facilitate comparison across and within groups. In most cases, discussion of results is limited to findings significant at the .001 level because of differences in sample size. The full regression model accounts for 41% of the variance in the dependent measure for all AAPI students. Standardized regression coefficients were examined to discuss the impact of ethnicity and other demographic background characteristics, high school achievement and activities, and college choice factors on predicting college attendance at selective institutions.

CHOICES: Access, Equity and Diversity in Higher Education

I examined the college decision-making process of AAPI high school seniors in 10 comprehensive public high schools in California. The criteria for selecting the 10 high schools were primarily based on the racial and social-class composition of the student body. Students were selected from schools that were located in ethnic enclaves throughout California. These communities represent some of the highest concentrations of AAPI ethnic groups of any communities in the nation, including Monterey Park, San Francisco, Vallejo, Daly City, Fresno, Westminster, San Jose, Sacramento, and Oakland (Teranishi, 2003, 2004). The schools were selected based on a high concentration of AAPI subgroups within these communities. In addition, I also took into consideration the location of the schools (South-

Table A.1. Description of Variables in Multivariate Analysis

Block	Variable	Description
Dependent Variables	Institutional Prestige	Institutional selectivity is a measure of the average combined SAT scores of the incoming freshman. The range is 400–1600.
Block 1	Ethnicity	Five dummy variables indicating ethnicity of students (Chinese American, Filipino American, Korean American, Southeast Asian American, and Japanese American); coded 1=no; 2=yes.
	Parental income	Parent's income is measured on a 14-point scale from less than $6,000 to $200,000 or more.
	Father's education	This variable is measured on an 8-point scale from grammar school or less to graduate degree.
	Mother's education	This variable is measured on an 8-point scale from grammar school or less to graduate degree.
	Citizenship status	Citizenship status; 1=not U.S. citizen; 2=U.S. citizen.
	Native English speaker	English is native language: 1=no; 2=yes.
Block 2 High school experiences	GPA	High school grade point average measured on an 8-point scale.
	Took SAT prep. course	Dummy variable indicating whether or not student had previously taken an SAT preparatory course: 1=no; 2=yes.
	Time spent on homework	Hours per week spent on homework measured on an 8-point scale.
	Degree aspirations	Degree aspirations are measured on a 10-point scale from none to other.
Block 3 College choice factors: Reasons for going to college	Relative's wish	Reason for going to college measured on a 3-point scale: 1=not important; 2=somewhat important; 3=very important.
	Teacher's advice	Reason for going to college measured on a 3-point scale; 1=not important;.2=somewhat important; 3=very important.
	Private counselor's advice	Reason for going to college measured on a 3-point scale; 1=not important;.2=somewhat important; 3=very important.
	Wanted to live near home	Reason for going to college measured on a 3-point scale; 1=not important;.2=somewhat important; 3=very important.
	Academic reputation	Reason for going to college measured on a 3-point scale; 1=not important;.2=somewhat important; 3=very important.
	High school counselor's advice	Reason for going to college measured on a 3-point scale; 1=not important;.2=somewhat important; 3=very important.
	Friend's advice	Reason for going to college measured on a 3-point scale; 1=not important;.2=somewhat important; 3=very important.
	Low tuition	Reason for going to college measured on a 3-point scale; 1=not important;.2=somewhat important; 3=very important.
	Graduates go to top graduate schools	Reason for going to college measured on a 3-point scale; 1=not important;.2=somewhat important; 3=very important.
	Rankings in national magazines	Reason for going to college measured on a 3-point scale; 1=not important;.2=somewhat important; 3=very important.

Table A.2. Interview Respondents by School Locale

School Locale	Predominant Ethnic Group	Female Respondents	Male Respondents	Total
Monterey Park	Chinese	20	20	40
San Francisco	Chinese	20	20	40
Vallejo	Filipino	20	20	40
Daly City	Filipino	20	20	40
Fresno	Hmong	16	13	29
Sacramento	Hmong	11	17	28
Westminster	Vietnamese	15	14	29
San Jose	Vietnamese	16	14	30
Sacramento	Mien	7	8	15
Oakland	Laotian; Thai	17	11	28
Total	—	162	157	319

ern California and the Bay Area), the different types of neighborhoods that surround the schools (suburban and urban), and college enrollment rates. As a result, I was able to narrow down more than 800 comprehensive public high schools in California to the 10 in this study.

There were two key criteria that were used to systematically select interview participants for this study. First, I identified all seniors that were of the same ethnicity as the school where they were being interviewed. For example, I would focus on a sample of Chinese American seniors in the schools that were selected to study Chinese American students. Second, I wanted to target students who were college bound or at least considering college as a postsecondary option. This was done in a number of ways depending on the willingness of the key informants in each school to divulge different types of information about their students. College-bound students were often identifiable through the following indicators: advanced placement or honors course enrollment; being enrolled in courses that satisfied admissions criteria for 4-year colleges, such as advanced math (trigonometry or calculus) or science courses (chemistry or physics) in their senior year; or class rank, usually compiled by their overall GPA, which is often used to identify the valedictorian candidates or students eligible for the UC system under the Eligibility in the Local Context (ELC) Policy. What I found to be crucial in selecting students that met the criteria described above was the great deal of input and willingness to participate among the key informants at each high school in the study.

I ended up with a purposeful sample of high-achieving, college-bound AAPI high school students in California. This dataset includes 319 respondents from different ethnic backgrounds (Table A.2). Among ethnic groups, respondents also varied by socioeconomic backgrounds, generational status, and language backgrounds.

The interviews were conducted by students and faculty from UCLA, University of Pennsylvania, and New York University. Most interviews lasted between an hour and an hour and a half and were guided by a loosely structured protocol. In addition to the interviews, background information was gathered from the students through a short questionnaire. The analysis was designed to capture the aspirations, information sources, and postsecondary decisions of AAPI ethnic subpopulations from different social-class backgrounds. The research designed involved administering a survey to and conducting individual and group interviews. Together, the interview and questionnaire data provide useful insights into the college-choice process for Chinese, Filipino, Hmong, Mien, Cambodian, and Vietnamese students. Having the participants express in their own words their understanding of pursuing college allowed for a deeper understanding of these students' educational challenges and experiences (Bogdan & Biklen, 1998). These stories are valuable because they allow the students to describe their experiences in pursuing higher education within the context of the socioeconomic situation of their families and communities.

Other Analyses and Data Sources

Additional data to examine indicators of college access were drawn from state databases, such as the California Basic Education Data System (CBEDS). Data was also acquired from the College Board, which provided information on the demographic characteristics of SAT test takers and test scores.

Data Instruments: Individual and Group Interview Protocol

POSTSECONDARY ASPIRATIONS

What are your college plans?
    Probe: Types of colleges (UC, CSU, CC, out of state, private, and so on)

How did you decide on these colleges?
    Probe: Reputation of campus, academic preparedness of student
    Probe: Proximity to home; public, private; 2-year, 4-year; costs

ACADEMIC/SCHOOL-RELATED STRATEGIES

How do you decide on what courses to take at school?
    Probe: Honors/AP courses, tracking, use of counselors, teachers, advisors, role models, friends

What kinds of things are you involved in outside of class?
    Probe: School-sponsored events or activities, clubs, sports

SOCIAL NETWORKS AND INFORMATION SOURCES

How have your parents or other family members influenced your decisions about college?
    Probe: Pressure/expectations versus support/guidance
    Probe: Educational experience, work commitments, congruency

How have teachers, counselors, programs, or other people who work in your school influenced you?
    Probe: College office, academic counseling, college culture of school, tracking

How have friends influenced your decisions about college?
    Probe: Friends at school versus friends at home (similarities/differences); significant other
    Probe: Racial/ethnic makeup of friends
    Probe: Competition

Are there resources in the community that have helped you with your decisions about college?
>   *Probe*: Church, Saturday language schools, prayer groups

Is there anyone or anything else informing your process to go to college?
>   *Probe*: Books, rankings in magazines, TV, Internet, CD-ROMS, SAT preparation course(s)

RACE/ETHNICITY

Do you think that being Asian will limit your chances of getting into college?
>   *Probe*: Why?
>   *Probe*: Advantages/disadvantages in terms of getting into different types of colleges?

Do you think Asians are treated differently than students from another racial group?
>   *Probe*: Versus other AAPIs and/or other racial groups
>   *Probe*: Social context versus academic context
>   *Probe*: Model minority, affirmative action

Do you think you would feel welcome at a UC campus?
>   *Probe*: Stereotypes, campus racial climate, Prop 209, Affirmative Action

GENDER

Are there any expectations of you by parents or other people because you are a male/female?
>   *Probe*: Ethnic culture, values, beliefs, and so on
>   *Probe*: Are your parents traditional, religious?
>   *Probe*: Sister, female peers, and/or relatives

Do you think women have a better chance of getting into college than men? Why?
>   *Probe*: Do you feel you are more at a disadvantage/advantage over the other applicants?

Who do you think are more prepared for college at this high school—male or female students?
>   *Probe*: Why?
>   *Probe*: Support, guidance, encouragement from teachers, parents, friends, and so on

Are male and female students treated differently by teachers, staff, or other students?
>   *Probe*: Procedures, instructions, and communication with male versus female students

PERCEPTIONS OF OPPORTUNITY

How much is tuition at the college(s) you want to attend?
>   *Probe*: Does this influence your decision to attend or not attend one college over the other?

Do you think you will need financial aid when you go to college?

Probe: What do you know about financial aid?

What do you think college will be like for you?
    Probe: Academic and social environment
    Probe: What are your biggest concerns? Who do you talk to about these issues?

CLOSURE

Do you have anything else you would like to add?

Do you have any questions that you would like to ask of me?

May we contact you later this year to follow up with you?

Thank you again for your participation.

Languages Spoken in Asian Countries

Country	Languages (Official, National, and Other)
Afghanistan	Pashtu (Pushtu), Dari Persian
Bangladesh	Bengali (Bangla), English
Bhutan	Bhutanese (Dzongkha), Tshanglakha, Khenkha, Lhotsamkha
Brunei Darussalam	Malay, English, Chinese
Cambodia	Khmer, French, English
China	Putonghua (Mandarin), Wu, Yue (Cantonese), Min, Hakka (Kejia), Gan Xiang
India	Hindi, English, Assamese, Bengali, Gujarati, Kannada, Kashmiri, Malayalam, Marathi, Oriya, Panjabi, Sanskrit, Sindhi, Tamil, Telugu, Urdu
Indonesia	Bahasa Indonesia, English, Dutch, Javanese
Japan	Japanese (Nihongo), Ryukyuan
Korea (North)	Korean (Choso'nmal or Choson'o)
Korea (South)	Korean (Hangungmal); English
Laos	Lao, French, English, and various ethnic languages
Macau	Putonghua (Mandarin), Portuguese, Yue Chinese (Cantonese), English
Malaysia	Bahasa Melayu, English, Chinese dialects, Tamil, Telugu, Malayalam, Panjabi, Thai, Iban, Kadazan.
Mongolia	Khalkha Mongol, Turkic, Russian

Myanmar (Burma)	Burmese, 135 languages of minority ethnic groups
Nepal	Nepali, 70 different dialects and 11 major languages including Tibeto-Burman, Lhotsamkha, Nepalbhasa, Tamang languages; minorities Bhutanese
Pakistan	Urdu, Punjabi, Sindhi, Siraiki, Pashtu, Balochi, Hindko, Brahui, Burushaski
Philippines	Tagalog, English, Cebuano, Ilocan, Hiligaynon or Ilonggo, Bicol, Waray, Pampango, and Pangasinense
Singapore	Chinese, Malay, Tamil, English
Sri Lanka	Sinhala, Tamil, English
Taiwan	Chinese Mandarin (Putonghua), Taiwanese (Min), Hakka dialects
Thailand	Thai, English, ethnic and regional dialects
Vietnam	Vietnamese, French, Chinese, Khmer, Mon-Khmer, Malayo-Polynesian, English

Note. Does not include Pacific Island countries.

Notes

Introduction

1. The term Asian American and Pacific Islander (AAPI) is a socially, politically, and institutionally defined category. In this book I treat the term as a racial category that broadly captures all persons of Asian or Pacific Islander ancestry living in the United States.

2. Preceding the 1980 Census, Pacific Islanders were not included with Asian Americans.

3. While her main focus was on the research published on AAPIs in three journals—*The Review of Higher Education, Research in Higher Education, The Journal of Higher Education*—she also examined their inclusion in other higher education student affairs and practitioner journals, including *Journal of College Student Development, Community College Journal of Research and Practice, Community College Review*, and *NASPA Journal*.

4. The CARE Project was guided by the insight and expertise of a national commission and an advisory board, which included scholars, policy makers, public officials, policy advocates, and community activists. The primary goal of this effort was to engage in realistic and actionable discussions about AAPIs in United States higher education and how societal distinctions of race, ethnicity, language, and other cultural factors are constituted in the day-to-day operations of American schools throughout the educational spectrum. The CARE Project provided needed new data on key issues and trends for Asian Americans and Pacific Islanders in United States higher education.

Chapter 1

1. From 1940 to 1980 the U.S. Census asked about total number of years of schooling completed; since 1990, the census asked about highest level of degree completed.

2. This case was *Gong Lum v. Rice* (1927).

3. *The Daily Princetonian* (2007, January 17) published an opinion column using the pseudonym "Lian Ji" that said, "I so good at math and science . . . Princeton the super dumb college, not accept me . . . I love Yale. Lots of bulldogs here for me to eat."

4. Not only has the U.S. Census Bureau faced challenges with the categorization of AAPIs, it has also had problems associated with undercounting of the population due to language, immigration, and issues associated with access to the population.

Chapter 2

1. The 2000 census allowed, for the first time, the option for respondents to mark more than one racial category to allow for counting of multiracial indviduals.

2. Today, nearly all immigrants gain access to the United States through one of three broad categories: family-sponsored preferences, employment preferences, or diversity. It is important to note that the U.S. government also distinguishes between immigrant and nonimmigrant arrivals. This book mainly focuses on immigrants, but also discuss how nonimmigrant Asians in the United States impact the perception and treatment of AAPIs.

3. Whereas a *refugee* is located outside the United States at the time of application, an *asylee* is located in the United States or at a port of entry at the time of application.

4. The specific categories include F1, H1B, J1, M1, and O1. I also included their spouses and children (and assistants in the case of O1 visas).

5. On March 1, 2003, the United States Immigration and Naturalization Service (INS) transitioned into the Department of Homeland Security (DHS) as INS is now the U.S. Citizenship and Naturalization Services. I provided data from the INS since I am reporting data from prior to this change.

6. In 2000 the poverty threshold for a family of four with two related children was approximately $17,500.

7. Student participants in the qualitative research were selected for interviews based on their academic qualifications (i.e., eligible) for attending a 4-year public university in California. A full description of the selection criteria is described in Appendix A.

8. The difference depends on if children are included as heads of household (larger number) or not (smaller number). Analysis of U.S. Census data, Summary File 3.

Chapter 3

1. South Asian American Policy & Research Institute (SAAPRI) is a nonprofit research institute established in the Chicago area to "facilitate, through the use of research, the formulation of equitable and socially responsible policy affecting South Asian Americans."

2. In 2000 there were large populations of Filipinos in the metropolitan areas of Los Angeles (n = 434,781), the San Francisco Bay Area (n = 379,196), Honolulu (n =191,393), and New York City (n = 62,058).

Chapter 4

1. Lowell High School is a public magnet school located in San Francisco. It is one of only two public schools in the city that selectively admits students based on admissions criteria. In 2008, 52% of the students at Lowell were Chinese American. Through legal channels and community activism, there have been a number of attempts to increase the representation among other racial minorities, which shed new light on how to ensure school desegregation. See Frank Wu (1996) in *Changing America: Three Arguments About Asian Americans and the Law.*

2. Public higher education in California is governed by a Master Plan for Higher Education that guarantees admission for state residents to one of three systems: the University of California (UC), the California State University (CSU), and the community colleges. The rigidity of the Master Plan is most pronounced in how the state is mandated to sort aspiring college students based on specific academic criteria. For example, public 4-year colleges in California require a 15-course sequence in high school for admission.

3. A score of 3 or higher on a 5-point scale is considered passing and can yield college credit and advanced standing for matriculating college students.

Chapter 5

1. The earliest participation of AAPIs in higher education has not been sufficiently documented; however, a few instances may give a sense of the broader history.

2. Yung Wing returned to China after receiving his degree and persuaded the Chinese government to replicate his "study abroad" experience, which resulted in the development of the Chinese Education Movement in 1872. Today this program is considered "the forerunner of the present-day study abroad movement" pursued by the Chinese government. The program, although terminated after 15 years because of concerns that Chinese students were becoming too Americanized, resulted in only two degrees awarded among the 120 program participants (Rhoads, 2005).

3. The regional classification used in this book represents the four regions of the United States as defined by the U.S. Census Bureau. This classification is consistent with that of the U.S. Department of Education.

4. The College Board categorization for AAPIs is inclusive of "Asians, Asian Americans, or Pacific Islanders."

5. The data collected during this particular year was the only year that the Cooperative Institutional Research Program collected demographic data that disaggregated the AAPI category into distinct ethnic subcategories. Although the AAPI students in the sample were offered different ethnic categories from which to choose, some of the possible choices were broad and contain tremendous heterogeneity in ethnicity among them (e.g., "Southeast Asians" and "Other Asian"). It also does not specify a category for Pacific Islanders, nor did the survey request detailed information about nativity, citizenship, and English-language ability. See Appendix A for a description of the survey, data source, research design, and limitations.

6. See Appendix A for a description of the variables, coding, and the methodological procedures.

Chapter 6

1. Research has found that it is important to disaggregate the degree attainment of college students by separating those students who enter college with that goal in mind with those students who have different intentions.

2. See Knapp, Kelly-Reid, Whitmore, and Miller (2007). The graduation rate reflects the total number of completers within 150% of normal time divided by the revised cohort.

3. This is particularly true for foreign-born Asians who arrived with their highest level of education.

4. There are also reports of racial profiling of Southeast Asian students, the treatment of AAPI male students as gang members, harassment of AAPI immigrants by ICE, and placement of AAPI students in the wrong bilingual education courses by school officials.

5. Faculty can have rank (assistant, associate, or full professor), but not a tenured ranking position in some instances.

6. Mellon Mays Undergraduate Fellowship Program was established in 1988. The objective of the program is to increase the number of minority students pursuing PhDs in core fields in the arts and sciences. The program aims to reduce over time the underrepresentation of faculty of color.

The Institute for Recruitment of Teachers was founded in 1990 and is an outreach program of Phillips Academy (Andover, Massachusetts). The purpose of the program is to encourage students from diverse backgrounds to pursue careers in K–12 teaching and academia. More than half of the participants are pursuing PhDs and the rest pursue master's degrees. The program includes mentorship and support in applying to graduate school within the program's 44 consortium colleges and universities. Approximately 10% of student participants in the 2007 cohort were AAPIs.

Conclusion

1. See books by Helen Zia (2001) and others who have written about Vincent Chin, Wen Ho Lee, and other AAPIs who have faced incidents of racism and xenophobia.

2. For example, see *The Bell Curve* (Herrnstein and Murray, 1994) and other biological explanations of the achievement gap.

3. See Knapp, Kelly-Reid, Whitmore, and Miller (2007). The graduation rate reflects the total number of completers within 150% of normal time divided by the revised cohort.

Appendix A

1. Available sample weights were utilized for this stage of the analysis to approximate the national populations of each subgroup. See Sax, Astin, Korn, and Mahoney (1997) for a more comprehensive description of the weighting procedures used with CIRP data.

References

Abboud, S. K., & Kim, J. Y. (2006). *Top of the class: How Asian parents raise high achievers— and how you can too.* New York: The Berkley Publishing Group.

Adelman, C. (1998). *Women and men of the engineering path: A model for analyses of under- graduate careers.* Washington, DC: U.S. Department of Education, National Institute for Science Education.

Adelman, C. (2002). The relationship between urbanicity and educational outcomes. In W. G. Tierney & L. S. Hagedorn (Eds.), *Increasing access to college: Extending possibilities for all students* (pp. 35–64). Albany, NY: State University of New York Press.

Alexander, K., & Eckland, B. (1977). High school context and college selectivity: Institu- tional constraints in educational stratification. *Social Forces, 56,* 166–188.

Alford, R. (1998). *The craft of inquiry: Theories, methods, and evidence.* New York: Oxford University Press.

Allen, W. R. (1992). The color of success: African-American college student outcomes at predominantly white and historically black public colleges and universities. *Harvard Education Review, 62*(1), 26–44.

Allen, W. R. (1999). Missing in action: Race, gender and Black students' educational op- portunities. In D. W. Carbado (Ed.), *Black men on race, gender, and sexuality: A critical reader* (pp. 194–211). New York: New York University Press.

Allen, W. R., Epps, E. G., Guillory, E. A., Suh, S. A., Bonous-Hammarth, M., & Stassen, M. (2000). Outsiders within: Race, gender, and faculty status in U.S. higher education. In W. Smith, P. Altbach, & K. Lomotey (Eds.), *The racial crisis in American higher education* (2nd ed., pp. 189–220). New York: State University of New York Press.

Allport, G. (1954). *The nature of prejudice.* Reading, MA: Addison-Wesley.

American Anthropological Association. (1998, May 17). American Anthropological Asso- ciation Statement on "Race." Retrieved March 16, 2010, from http://www.aaanet.org/ stmts/racepp.htm

Anderson, M., & Hearn, J. (1992). Equity issues in higher education outcomes. In W. E. Becker & D. R. Lewis (Eds.), *The economics of American higher education* (pp. 301–304). Norwell, MA: Kluwer.

Anderson, E., & Massey, D. S. (2001). Problem of the century: Racial stratification in the United States. New York: Russell Sage Foundation.

Antonio, A. L. (2002). Faculty of color reconsidered: Reassessing contributions to scholar- ship. *Journal of Higher Education, 73*(5), 582–602.

Argyris, C., & Schon, D. A. (1996). *Organizational learning II.* Reading, MA: Addison-Wes- ley.

Arifuku, I., Peacock, D. D., & Glesmann, C. (2006). Profiling incarcerated Asian and Pacific Islander youth: Statistics derived from California Youth Authority Administrative Data. *AAPI Nexus* (UCLA Asian American Studies Center), 4(2), 95–109.

Asian American Legal Defense and Education Fund (AALDEF). (2008). *Left in the margins: Asian American students and the No Child Left Behind Act.* New York: Author.

Ascher, C., & Branch-Smith, E. (2005). Precarious space: Majority Black suburbs and their public schools. *Teachers College Record, 107*(9), 1956–1973.

Astin, A. W. (1982). *Minorities in American higher education.* San Francisco: Jossey-Bass.

Astin, A. W. (1985). *Achieving educational excellence.* San Francisco: Jossey-Bass.

Astin, A. W. (1993). *What matters in college: Four critical years revisited.* San Francisco: Jossey-Bass.

Baez, B. (2000). Race-related service and faculty of color: Conceptualizing critical agency in academe. *Higher Education, 39*(3), 363–391.

Baldi, S., Jin, Y., Skemer, M., Green, P. J., & Herget, D. (2007). Highlights From PISA 2006: Performance of U.S. 15-Year-Old Students in Science and Mathematics Literacy in an International Context (NCES 2008–016). National Center for Education Statistics, Institute of Education Sciences, U.S. Department of Education. Washington, DC.

Bankston, C. L., & Zhou, M. (2002). Being well vs. doing well: Self esteem and school performance among immigrant and nonimmigrant racial and ethnic groups. *International Migration Review, 36*(2), 389–415.

Barber, R. (2003). Report to the National Education Association on the trends in foreign teacher recruitment. Washington, DC: The Center for Economic Organizing.

Barringer, H., Gardner, R. W., & Levin, M. J. (1995). *Asian and Pacific Islanders in the United States.* New York: Russell Sage.

Beardsley, L. V. & Teitel, L. (2004). Learning to see color in teacher education: An example framed by the professional development school standard for diversity and equity. *The Teacher Educator, 40*(2), 91–115.

Bell, D. (1987). *And we will not be saved: The elusive quest for racial justice.* New York: Basic Books.

Berthold, S. M. (1999). The effects of exposure to community violence on Khmer Rouge refugees adolescents. *Journal of Traumatic Stress, 12*(3), 455–471.

Besnard, M. (2003). Exploring ethnic identity on a university campus: Filipino American students' perspectives (Doctoral dissertation, University of Southern California, 2001). *Dissertation Abstracts,* AAT3116667.

Blau, P. (1977). *Inequality and heterogeneity: A primitive theory of social structure.* New York: Free Press.

Blau, P. M., & Duncan, O. D. (1967). *The American occupational structure.* New York: John Wiley.

Bobo, L. D., & Massagli, M. P. (2001). Stereotyping and urban inequality. In A. O'Connor, C. Tilly, & L. D. Bobo (Eds.), *Urban inequality: Evidence from four cities.* New York: Russell Sage Foundation.

Bogdan, R. C., & Biklen, S. K. (1998). *Qualitative research for education: An introduction to theory and methods* (3rd ed.). Boston: Allyn & Bacon.

Bowen, H. (1977). *Investment in learning.* San Francisco: Jossey-Bass.

Bowen, W. G., & Bok, D. (1998). *The shape of the river: Long-term consequences of considering race in college and university admissions.* Princeton,NJ: Princeton University Press.

Bowen, W., Kurzweil, M., & Tobin, E. (2005). *Equity and excellence in American higher education.* Charlottesville, VA: University of Virginia Press.

Boyer, E. L. (1987). *College: The undergraduate experience in America.* New York: Harper & Row.

Brand, D. (1987, August 31). Education: The new whiz kids. *Time Magazine.* Retrieved from http://www.time.com/time/magazine/article/0,9171,965326,00.html

Brint, S., & Karabel, J. (1989). *The diverted dream: Community colleges and the promise of educational opportunity in America, 1900–1985.* Oxford: Oxford University Press.

Briscoe, K. (2009). Interrogating race, equity, and access to higher education: A categorical examination. Paper presented at the American Educational Research Association (AERA), San Diego, CA.

Brown, M., Edley, C., Gandara, P., Hayashi, P., Kidder, W., Ledesma, M., Rashida, M., Stark, D., Stern, D., & Stoddart., T. (2006). *California at the crossroads: Confronting the looming threat to achievement, access, and equity at the University of California and beyond.* Berkeley, CA: Chief Justice Earl Warren Institute on Race, Ethnicity and Diversity.

Bryant, A. N. (2001). Community college students: Recent findings and trends. *Community College Review, 29*(3), 77–94.

Carrasco, E. (1996). Collective recognition as a communitarian device: Or, of course we want to be role models! *La Raza Law Journal, 9,* 81–101.

Ceja, M. (2001). *Chicana college choice.* Unpublished doctoral dissertation, University of California–Los Angeles.

Chae, M. H. (2000, August). *Gender and ethnicity development among college students from four ethnic groups.* Paper presented at the Annual Conference of the American Psychological Association, Washington, DC.

Chai, A. Y., & De Cambra, H. (1989). Evolution of global feminism through. Hawaiian feminist politics: The case of the Wai'anae Women's Support Group. *Women's Studies International Forum, 12*(1), 59–64.

Chang, M., Witt-Sandia, D, Jones, J., & Hakuta, K. (Eds.) (1999). *The dynamics of race in higher education: An examination of the evidence.* Stanford, CA: Center for the Comparative Studies on Race and Ethnicity, Stanford University.

Chang, M. J. (2000). The relationship of high school characteristics to the selection of undergraduate students for admission to the University of California–Berkeley. *Journal of Negro Education, 69*(1/2), 49–59.

Chang, M. J. (2003). Haunted by the myth of universal success. In E. Lai & D. Arguelles (Eds.), *The new face of Asian Pacific America: Numbers, diversity and change in the 21st century* (pp. 203–208). San Francisco: AsianWeek Publishing Group.

Chang, M. J., Witt, D., Jones, J., & Hakuta, K. (2003). *Compelling interest: Examining the evidence on racial dynamics in colleges and universities.* Palo Alto, CA: Stanford University Press.

Chang, R. S. (1999). *Disoriented: Asian Americans, law, and the nation-state.* New York: New York University Press.

Chea, T. (2009, April 24). University of California rule angers Asian-Americans. *USA Today.*

Cheng, M., & Yang, P. (2000). The "model minority" deconstructed. In M. Zhou & J. Gatewood (Eds.), *Contemporary Asian America: A multidisciplinary reader* (pp. 459–482). New York: New York University Press.

Chou, R., & Feagin. J. R. (2008). *The myth of the model minority: Asian Americans facing racism.* Boulder, CO: Paradigm Books.

Coleman, J. S. (1966). *Equality of educational opportunity.* Washington, DC: United States Government Printing Office.

Coleman, J. S. (1987). *Public and private high schools: The impact of communities.* New York: Basic Books.

Coleman, J. S. (1988). Social capital in the creation of human capital. *American Journal of Sociology, 94,* 95–120.

College Board. (2006). *College-bound seniors: A profile of SAT Program test-takers.* New York: The College Board.

Coloma, R. S. (2006). Disorienting race and education: Changing paradigms on the schooling of Asian Americans and Pacific Islanders. *Race Ethnicity and Education, 9*(1), 1–15.

Committee of 100. (2005). *The Committee of 100's Asian Pacific Americans in higher education report card.* New York: Author.

Conley, D. (1999). *Being black, living in the red. Race, wealth, and social policy in America.* Berkeley: University of California Press.

Connerly, W. (2006, November 3). We're saying race should not be used. *The Oakland Tribune.*

Connerly, W. (2009, July 2). Study, study, study—A bad career move. *Minding the Campus.* Retrieved May 18, 2010, from http://www.mindingthecampus.com/originals/2009/06/by_ward_connerly_about_five.html

Cooperative Institutional Research Program (CIRP). (2010). Freshman survey. Available at http://heri/ucla/edu/cirpoverview.php

Council of Economic Advisers for the President's Initiative on Race. (1998). *Changing America: Indicators of social and economic well-being by race and hispanic origin.* Washington, DC: U.S. Government Printing Office.

Daily Princetonian. (2007, January 17). Princeton University is racist against me, I mean, non-whites.

Daniels, R. (1997). No lamps were lit for them: Angel Island and the historiography of Asian American immigration. *Journal of American Ethnic History, 17,* 14.

Darling-Hammond, L. (2010). *The flat world and education: How America's commitment to equity will determine our future.* New York: Teachers College Press.

Darling-Hammond, L., & Berry, B. (1999). Recruiting teachers for the 21st century: The foundation for educational equity. *Journal of Negro Education, 68(3),* 254–279.

Delgado, R. (1989). Storytelling for oppositionalists and others: A plea for narrative. *Michigan Law Review, 87,* 2411–2441.

Delgado, R. (1995). *Critical race theory: The cutting edge.* Philadelphia: Temple University Press.

Delgado Bernal, D. (1998). Using a Chicana feminist epistemology in educational research. *Harvard Educational Review, 68*(4), 555–582.

Delgado Bernal, D., & Villalpando, O. (2002). An apartheid of knowledge in academia: The struggle over "legitimate" knowledge of faculty of color. *Equity and Excellence in Education, 35*(2), 169–180.

Dougherty, K. J. (1992). Community colleges and baccalaureate attainment. *The Journal of Higher Education, 63*(2), 188–214.

Dougherty, K. J. (2001). *The contradictory college.* Albany: State University of New York Press.

Du Bois, W. E. B. (2007). *The Philadelphia Negro: A social study.* New York: Cosimo Classics. (Original work published 1899)

Edgert, P. (1994). Assessing campus climate: Implications for diversity. *New Directions for Institutional Research, 81,* 51–62.

Editorial Projects in Education Research Center. (2007). Diplomas Count 2007: Ready for what? Preparing students for college, careers, and life after high school. *Education Week, 26*(40).

Espenshade, T. J., & Chung, C. Y. (2005). The opportunity cost of admissions preferences at elite universities. *Social Science Quarterly, 86*(2), 293–305.

Fann, A. (April, 2009). *Higher education and Native nation building.* Paper presented at the American Educational Research Association annual meeting, San Diego, CA.

Ferguson, R. F. (1999). Racial test-score trends 1971–1996: Popular youth culture and community academic standards. Paper presented at the annual conference of the Institute for Educational Initiatives, Notre Dame, Indiana, November 1999.

Fitzsimmons, W. R. (1991, January–February). Risky business. *Harvard Magazine*, pp. 23–29.

Fleming, J. (1984). *Blacks in college.* San Francisco: Jossey-Bass.

Fong, T. P. (1994). *The first suburban Chinatown: The remaking of Monterey Park, California.* Philadelphia: Temple University Press.

Friedman, T. (2005). *The world is flat: A brief history of the twenty-first century.* New York: Farrar, Straus, & Giroux.

Frey, W. H., & Farley, R. (1996). Latino, Asian, and Black segregation in U.S. metropolitan areas: Are multiethnic metros different? *Demography, 33*(1), 35–50.

Gandara, P. (1995). *Over the ivy walls: The educational mobility of low-income Chicanos.* Albany: State University of New York Press.

Garbarino, J., Dubrow, N., Kostelny, K., & Pardo, C. (1992). *Children in danger: Coping with the consequences of community violence.* San Francisco: Jossey-Bass.

Garcia, R. (1995). Critical race theory and Proposition 187: The racial politics of immigration law. *Chicano-Latino Law Review, 17,* 118–148.

Glazer, N. (1997). *We are all multiculturalists now.* Cambridge, MA: Harvard University Press.

Gong Lum v. Rice, 275 U.S. 78 (1927).

Golden, D. (2006). *The price of admission: How America's ruling class buys its way into elite colleges—and who gets left outside the gates.* New York: Crown.

Goldrick-Rab, S., Harris, D. N., Mazzeo, C., & Kienzl, G. (2009). *Transforming America's community colleges: A federal policy proposal to expand opportunity and promote economic prosperity.* Washington, DC: Brookings Institute Press.

Gordon, J. A. (2002). The color of teaching. *Journal of Teacher Education, 53*(2), 123–126.

Hacker, A. (2003). *Two nations: Black and white, separate, hostile, unequal.* New York: Scribner.

Harris, A. (1994). Forward: The jurisprudence of reconstruction. *California Law Review, 82,* 741–785.

Harvey, W. B. (2001). Minorities in higher education 2000–2001: Eighteenth annual status report. Washington, DC: American Council on Education.

Hassan, T. E. (1987). Asian-American admissions: Debating discrimination. *The College Board Review, 142,* 19–21.

Hearn, J. C. (1984). The relative roles of academic, ascribed, and socioeconomic characteristics in college destinations. *Sociology of Education, 57,* 22–30.

Hearn, J. C. (1991). Academic and nonacademic influences on the college destinations of 1980 high school graduates. *Sociology of Education, 64,* 158–171.

Herrnstein, R., & Murray, C. (1994). *The bell curve: Intelligence and class structure in American life.* New York: Free Press.

Hing, B. O., & Lee, R. (1996). *Reframing the immigration debate.* Los Angeles: LEAP and UCLA Asian American Studies Center.

Hobson-Horton, L. D., & Owens, L. (2004). From freshman to graduate: Recruiting and retaining minority students. *Journal of Hispanic Higher Education, 3*(1), 86–107.

Holley, D. and D. Spencer (1999). The Texas Ten Percent Plan. *Harvard Civil Rights–Civil Liberties Law Review, 34.*

Hossler, D., Schmit, J., & Vesper, N. (1999). *Going to college: How social, economic, and educational factors influence the decisions students make.* Baltimore, MD: The Johns Hopkins University Press.

Holzer, H. (2008). *Workforce development and the disadvantaged: New directions for 2009 and beyond.* Washington, DC: The Urban Institute, Georgetown University.

Horn, L., & Berktold, J. (1999). Students with disabilities in postsecondary education: A profile of preparation, participation, and outcomes (NCES 1999_187). Washington, DC: U.S. Government Printing Office.

Horvat, E. (1996). *African-American students and college choice: Decision-making in social context.* Unpublished doctoral dissertation, University of California–Los Angeles.

Hossler, D., Braxton, J., & Coopersmith, G. (1989). Understanding student college choice. In J. C. Smart (Ed.), *Higher Education: Handbook of Theory and Research, 5,* New York: Agathon Press.

Hossler, D., Schmit, J., & Vesper, N. (1999). *Going to college: How social, economic, and educational factors influence the decisions students make* (vol. 5, pp. 231–288). Baltimore: The John Hopkins University Press.

Hossler, D., & Stage, F. K. (1992). Family and high school experience influences on the postsecondary educational plans of ninth-grade students. *American Education Research Journal, 29*(2), 425–451.

Hune, S., & Chan, K. S. (1997). Special focus: Asian Pacific American demographics and educational trends. In D. Carter & R. Wilson (Eds.), *Annual status report, minorities in higher education* (vol. 15, pp. 39–63). Washington, DC: American Council on Education.

Hurtado, S., Inkelas, K. K., Briggs, C., & Rhee, B. (1995). Differences in college access and choice among racial/ethnic groups: identifying continuing barriers. *Research in Higher Education, 38*(1), 43–75.

Hwang, S. (2005, November 19). The new white flight. *Wall Street Journal,* p. A1.

Jackson, J. F., & Phelps, A. (2004). Diversity in the two-year college academic workforce. *New Directions for Community Colleges, 2004*(27), 79–88.

Jencks, C., Bartlett, S., Corcoran, M., & Elder, G. H. (1979). *Who gets ahead? The determinants of economic success in America.* New York: Basic Books.

Jencks, C., & Phillips, M. (1998). The Black–White test score gap: Why it persists and what can be done. *Brookings Review, 16.*

Joshi, K. Y. (2001). Patterns and paths: Ethnic identity development in second generation Indian Americans (Doctoral dissertation, University of Massachusetts, Amherst, 2001). *Dissertation Abstracts,* AAT 3027215.

Kalbus, J. C. (2000). Path to the superintendency. *Urban Education, 35*(5), 549–556.

Karabel, J., & Astin, A. W. (1975). Social class, academic ability, and college quality. *Social Forces, 53*(3), 381–398.

Karen, D. (1988, April). *Who applies where to college?* Paper presented at the annual meeting of the American Educational Research Association, New Orleans.

Kawaguchi, K. (2003). Ethnic identity development and the collegiate experience of Asian Pacific American students: Implications for practice. *NASPA Journal, 40*(3), 13–29.

Kiang, P. N. (2006). Policy challenges for Asian Americans and Pacific Islanders in education. *Race, Ethnicity, and Education, 9*(1), 103–115.

Kim, C. J. (1999). The racial triangulation of Asian Americans. *Politics and Society, 27*(1), 105–138.

Kim, S. (1993). Understanding Asian Americans: A new perspective. In J. Adams & J. Welsch (Eds.), *Multicutural education: Strategies for implemention in colleges and universities,* (Vol. 3, pp. 83–92) Springfield: Illinois State Board of Higher Education.

Kim, S. C. (1997). Koren American families. In E. Lee (Ed.), *Working with Asian Americans: A guide for clinicians* (pp. 125–135). New York: Guilford.

Kitano, H. L., & Daniels, R. D. (1988). *Asian Americans: Emerging minorities.* Englewood Cliffs, NJ: Prentice Hall.

Knapp, L. G., Kelly-Reid, J. E., Whitmore, R. W., & Miller, E. (2007). *Enrollment in Postsecondary Institutions, Fall 2005; Graduation Rates, 1999 and 2002 Cohorts; and Financial Statistics, Fiscal Year 2005* (NCES 2007-154). Washington, DC: National Center for Education Statistics.

Kou, Y. (2001). The Hmong in America: Twenty-five years alter the U. S. secret war in Laos. *Journal of Asian American Studies, 4*(2), 165–174.

Kozol, J. (1991). *Savage inequalities: Children in America's schools.* New York: Crown.

Kristof, N. D. (2006, May 14). The model students. *New York Times,* p. D13.

Kulis, S., Shaw, H., & Chong, Y. (2000). External labor markets and the distribution of Black scientists and engineers in academia. *The Journal of Higher Education, 71*(2), 187–222.

Kwong, P. (1987). *The new Chinatown.* New York: Noonday Press.

Ladson-Billings, G. (1994). *The dreamkeepers: Successful teachers of African American children.* San Francisco: Jossey-Bass.

Lareau, A. (1989). *Home advantage: Social class and parental intervention in elementary education.* New York: Falmer Press.

Lareau, A. (2003). *Unequal childhoods: Class, race, and family life.* Berkeley: University of California Press.

Le, T., Arifuku, I., Louie, C., & Krisberg, M. (2001a). *Not invisible: Asian Pacific Islander juvenile arrests in Alameda County.* Oakland, CA: National Council on Crime and Delinquency.

Le, T., Arifuku, I., Louie, C., & Krisberg, M. (2001b). *Not invisible: Asian Pacific Islander juvenile arrests in San Francisco County.* Oakland, CA: National Council on Crime and Delinquency.

Lee, S. J. (1996). *Unravelling the "model minority" stereotype: Listening to Asian American youth.* New York: Teachers College Press.

Lee, S. J. (2005). *Up against whiteness: Race, school, and immigrant youth.* New York: Teachers College Press.

Lee, S. M. (2002). Do Asian American faculty face a glass ceiling in higher education? *American Educational Review Journal, 39*(3), 695–724.

Levine, A. (2006). *Educating school teachers.* Washington, DC: The Education Schools Project.

Lew, J. (2004a). *Asian Americans in class: Charting the achievement among Korean American youth.* New York: Teachers College Press.

Lew, J. (2004b). The "other" story of model minorities: Korean American high school dropouts in an urban context. *Anthropology and Education Quarterly, 35*(3), 303–323.

Li, W. (1999). The emergence and manifestation of the Chinese ethnoburbs in Los Angeles' San Gabriel Valley. *Journal of Asian American Studies, 2*(1), 1–28.

Lin, J. (1998). *Reconstructing Chinatown: Ethnic enclave, global change.* Minneapolis: University of Minnesota Press.

Ling, H. (2009). *Asian America: Forming new communities, expanding boundaries.* Piscataway, NJ: Rutgers University Press.

Ling, M. (1998, December). Facing the Asian invasion. *California Monthly.*

Lippmann, W. (1922). *Public opinion.* New York: Macmillan.

Logan, J. (2001). Ethnic diversity grows, neighborhood integration lags behind. Lewis Mumford Center, University Albany, SUNY. Available at http://mumford.albany.edu/census/report

Louie, C. E. (2003). *Predictors of psychological distress among Asian American college students: Cultural identity, minority status stress, and coping.* Unpublished doctoral dissertation, University of Missouri, Columbia.

Louie, V. (2004). *Compelled to excel: Immigration, education, and opportunity among Chinese Americans.* Palo Alto, CA: Stanford University Press.

Lowe, L. (1995). On contemporary Asian American projects. *Amerasia Journal, 21*(1/2), 41–52.

Marshall, G. N., Berthold, S. M, Terry L. Schell, T. L., Elliott, M. N., Chi-Ah Chun, C. A., & Hambarsoomians, K. (2006). Rates and correlates of seeking mental health services among Cambodian refugees. *American Journal of Public Health, 96*(10), 1829–1835.

Massey, D. S. (2003). The American side of the bargain. In T. Jacoby (Ed.), *Reinventing the melting pot: The new immigrants and what it means to be American.* New York: Basic Books.

Massey, D. S. (2008). *Categorically unequal: The American stratification system.* New York: Russell Sage Foundation.

Massey, D. S., Charles, C. Z., Lundy, G. F., & Fischer, M. J. (2003). *The source of the river: The social origins of freshmen at America's selective colleges and universities.* Princeton, NJ: Princeton University Press.

Massey, D. S., & Denton, N. A. (1993). *American apartheid.* Cambridge, MA: Harvard University Press.

Massey, D. S., & Fischer, M. J. (1999). Does rising income bring integration? New results for Blacks, Hispanics, and Asians in 1990. *Social Science Research, 28,* 316–326.

Massey, D. S., Mooney, M., Torres, K. C., & Charles, C. Z. (2007). Black immigrants and Black natives attending selective colleges and universities in the United States. *American Journal of Education, 113,* 243–271.

McDonough, P. M. (1994). Buying and selling higher education: The social construction of the college applicant. *Journal of Higher Education, 65*(4), 427–446.

McDonough, P. M. (1997). *Choosing colleges: How social class and schools structure opportunity.* Albany: State University of New York Press.

McDonough, P. M. & Antonio, A. L. (1996, April). *Racial and ethnic differences in selectivity of college choice.* Paper presented at the annual meeting of the American Educational Research Association, New York.

McDonough, P., & Calderone, S. (2006). The meaning of money: Perceptual differences between collage counselors and low-income families about collage costs and financial aid. *American Behavioral Scientist, 49*(12), 1703–1718.

McNall, M., Dunnigan, T., & Mortimer, J. T. (1994). The educational attainment of the St. Paul Hmong. *Anthropology & Education Quarterly, 25*(1), 44–65.

Mills, C. W. (1959). *The sociological imagination.* New York: Oxford University Press.

Moody, J. (2004). *Faculty diversity: Problems and solutions.* New York: RoutledgeFalmer.

Morrison, L. (1989). The Lubin House experience: A model for the recruitment and retention of urban minority students. In J. C. Elam (Ed.), *Blacks in higher education: Overcoming the odds*. New York: University Press of America.

Murdock, S. H. (1995). *An America challenged: Population change and the future of the United States*. Boulder, CO: Westview Press.

Murdock, S. H., & Ellis, D. R. (1991). *Applied demography: An introduction to basic concepts, methods, and data*. Boulder, CO: Westview Press.

National Center for Education Statistics (NCES). (2008). *The conditions of education* (NCES 2008-031). Washington, DC: Institute for Education Sciences, U.S. Department of Education.

National Center for Education Statistics. (2010a). Common core of data. Available at http://nces.ed.gov/ccd/

National Center for Education Statistics. (2010b). Integrated postsecondary educational data system enrollment survey (IPEDS-E12). Washington, DC: U.S. Department of Education.

National Center for Education Statistics. (2010c). Schools and staffing survey (SASS). Available at http://nces.ed.gov/surveys/sass

National Collaborative on Diversity in the Teaching Force. (2004). *Assessment of diversity in America's teaching force: A call to action*. Washington, DC: National Education Association.

National Commission on Asian American and Pacific Islander Research in Education. (2008). *Facts, not fiction—Setting the record straight: Asian Americans and Pacific Islanders in higher education*. New York: College Board.

National Science Foundation. (2006). U.S. Doctorates in the 20th Century, NSF 06-319. Arlington, VA: Division of Science Resources Statistics.

Newsweek (1971, June 21). Success story: Outwhiting the whites, pp. 24–25.

Niu, S., Tienda, M., & Cortes, K. (2004). College selectivity and the Texas top 10% law. Paper presented at the annual meeting of the Population Association of America, Boston, MA.

Oakes, J. (2005). *Keeping track: How schools structure inequality* (2nd ed.). New Haven, CT: Yale University Press.

Oakes, J., Rogers, J., McDonough, P., Solorzano, D., Mehan, H., & Noguera, P. (2000, January). *Remedying unequal opportunities for successful participation in advanced placement courses in California high schools: A proposed action plan*. An expert report submitted on behalf of the Defendants and the ACLU in the case of *Daniel v. the State of California*.

Oakes, J., Rogers, J., Silver, D., & Goode, J. (2004). *Separate and unequal 50 years after Brown: California's racial "opportunity gap."* Los Angeles: UCLA/IDEA Institute for Democracy, Education, and Access.

Ogbu, J. (1991). Minority coping responses and school experience. *Journal of Psychohistory, 18,* 433–456.

Ogbu, J. (2003). *Black American students in an affluent suburb: A study of academic disengagement*. New York: Routledge.

Olivas, M. (1990). The chronicles, my grandfather's stories, and immigration law: The slave traders' chronicle as racial history. *Saint Louis University Law Journal, 34,* 425–441.

Omi, M. (2000). Racial identity and the state: Contesting the federal standards for classification. In M. Adams, W. Blumenfeld, R. Castaneda, H. Hackman, M. Peters, & X. Zuniga (Eds.), *Readings for diversity and social justice* (pp. 73–78). New York: Routledge.

Omi, M., & Winant, H. (1989). *Racial formation in the United States: from the 1960s to the 1990s.* New York: Routledge.

Omi, M., & Winant, H. (1994). *Racial formation in the United States* (2nd ed.). New York: Routledge.

Ong, P. (2008). *Trajectory of civic and political engagement: A public policy report.* Los Angeles: LEAP Asian Pacific American Public Policy Institute.

Open Doors. (2007). *Report on international educational exchange.* New York: Institute for International Education.

Orfield, G. (1992). Money, equity, and college access. *Harvard Educational Review, 62*(3), 337–372.

Orfield, G. (1993). *The growth of segregation in American schools: Changing patterns of separation and poverty since 1968.* Alexandria, VA: National School Boards Association, Council of Urban Boards of Education.

Orfield, G., & Glass, D. (1994). *Asian students and multiethnic segregation.* Cambridge, MA: Harvard Project on School Desegregation.

Orfield, G., & Lee, C. (2005). *Why segregation matters: Poverty and educational inequality.* Cambridge, MA: The Civil Rights Project, Harvard University.

Orfield, G., & Lee, C. (2006). *Racial transformation and the changing nature of segregation.* Cambridge, MA: Civil Rights Project, Harvard University.

Orfield, G., & Yun, J. T. (1999). *Resegregation in American schools.* Cambridge, MA: Harvard University.

Ortiz, A. M. (1997). Defining oneself in a multicultural world: Ethnic identity in college students (Doctoral dissertation, University of California–Los Angeles, 1997). *Dissertation Abstracts*, AAT 9737325.

Palepu, A., Carr, P. L., Friedman, R. H., Amos, H., Ash, A. S., & Moskowitz, M. A. (1996). Minority faculty and academic rank in medicine. *The Journal of the American Medical Association, 280*(9), 767–771.

Park, G. C. (2001, April). *Multiple dimensions of ethnic persons: Listening to Korean American college students.* Paper presented at the annual meeting of the American Educational Research Association, Seattle, WA.

Perez, W., Espinoza, R., Ramos, K., Coronado, H. M., & Cortes, R. (2009). Academic resilience among undocumented Latino students. *Hispanic Journal of Behavioral Sciences, 31*, 149–181.

Petersen, W. (1966, January 9). Success story, Japanese-American style. *New York Times Magazine.*

Petersen, W. E. (1971). *Japanese Americans: Oppression and success.* New York: Random House.

Pho, T. L., & Mulvey, A. (2003). Southeast Asian women in Lowell: Family relations, gender roles, and community concerns. *Frontiers: A Journal of Women Studies, 24*(1), 101–129.

Poon, O. A. (2006, November). *Asian American college students in education studies: A reivew of three journals, 1996–2006.* Paper presented at the annual conference of the Association for the Study of Higher Education, Anaheim, CA.

Portes, A., & Rumbaut, R. G. (1996). *Immigrant America: A portrait* (2nd ed.). Berkeley: University of California Press.

Post, D. (1990). College-going decisions by Chicanos: The politics of misinformation. *Educational Evaluation and Policy Analysis, 12*, 174–187.

Quiocho, A., & Rios, F. (2000). The power of their presence: Minority group teachers and schooling. *Review of Educational Research, 70*(4), 485–528.

Ramanathan, H. (2006). Asian American teachers: Do they impact the curriculum? Are there support systems for them? *Multicultural Education, 14*(1), 31–35.

Reeves, T., & Bennett, C. (2004). *We the people: Asians in the United States* [Census 2000 Special Reports]. Washington, DC: U.S. Census Bureau.

Rhoads, E. J. (2005). In the shadow of Yung Wing: Zeng Laishun and the Chinese educational mission to the United States. *The Pacific Historical Review, 74*(1), 19–58.

Rong, X. L., & Preissle, J. (1997). The continuing decline in Asian American teachers. *American Educational Research Journal, 34*(2), 267–293.

Rose, M. (2005). *Lives on the boundary: A moving account of the struggles and achievements of America's educationally underprepared.* New York: Penguin Books.

Root, S., Rudawski, A., Taylor, M., & Rochon. R. (2003). Attrition of Hmong students in teacher education programs. *Bilingual Research Journal, 27*(1), 137–165.

Rumbaut, R. G. (1995). Vietnamese, Laotian, and Cambodian Americans. In P. G. Min (Ed.), *Asia Americans: Contemporary trends and issues.* Thousand Oaks, CA: Sage Publications.

Rumbaut, R. G. (1997). Ties that bind: Immigration and immigrant families in the United States. In A. Booth, A. Crouter, & N. Landale (Eds.), *Immigration and the family: Research and policy on United States immigrants.* Hillsdale, NJ: Lawrence Erlbaum Associates.

Rumbaut, T., & Ima, K. (1987). *The adaptation of Southeast Asian refugee youth: A comparative study.* San Diego: San Diego State University.

Sack, W. H., Clarke, G. N., & Seeley, J. (1996). Multiple forms of stress in Cambodian adolescent refugees. *Child Development, 67,* 107–116.

Sax, L. J., Astin, A. W., Korn, W. S., & Mahoney, K. M. (1997). *The American freshman: National norms for fall 1997.* Los Angeles: Higher Education Research Institute, UCLA.

Segal, U. A. (2002). *A framework for immigration: Asians in the United States.* New York: Columbia University Press.

Sheets, R. H., & Chew, L. (2002). Absent from the research, present in our classrooms: Preparing culturally responsive Chinese American teachers. *Journal of Teacher Education, 53*(2), 127–141.

Sikh Coalition. (2007). *Hatred in the hallways: Preliminary report on bias against Sikh students in New York City's public schools.* New York: Author.

Snyder, T. D., Dillow, S. A., & Hoffman, C. M. (2008). *Digest of education statistics 2007* (NCES 2008-022). Washington, DC: National Center for Education Statistics, Institute of Education Sciences, United States Department of Education.

Solorzano, D. G. (1998). Critical race theory, race and gender microaggressions, and the experience of Chicana and Chicano scholars. *Qualitative Studies in Education, 11*(1), 121–136.

Solórzano, D. G., Ceja, M., & Yosso, T. (2000). Critical race theory, racial microaggressions, and campus racial climate: The experiences of African American college students. *Journal of Negro Education, 69*(1/2), 60–73.

Solorzano, D., & Villalpando, O. (1998). Critical race theory, marginality, and the experience of minority students in higher education. In C. Torres & T. Mitchell (Eds.), *Emerging issues in the sociology of education: Comparative perspectives* (pp. 211–224). Albany: State University of New York Press.

Solórzano, D. G., Villalpando, O., & Oseguera, L. (2005). Educational inequalities and Latina/o undergraduate students in the United States: A critical race analysis of their educational progress. *Journal of Hispanic Higher Education, 4*(3), 272–294.

South Asian American Policy & Research Institute. (2005). *Making data count: South Asian Americans in the 2000 census with focus on Illinois.* Author: Chicago, IL.

Southeast Asia Resource Action Center (SEARAC). (2009). *Southeast Asian Americans and health care reform.* Retrieved January 30, 2010, from http://www.searac.org/faq-healthre-form-09.pdf

Spellman, S. O. (1988). Recruitment of minority teachers: Issues, problems, facts, possible solutions. *Journal of Teacher Education, 39*(4), 58–63.

Stage, F., & Hossler, D. (1989). Differences in family influences on college attendance plans for male and female ninth graders. *Research in Higher Education, 30*(3), 301–315.

Stanton-Salazar, R. (1997, Spring). A social capital framework for understanding the socialization of racial minority children and youths. *Harvard Educational Review, 67*(1), 1–41.

Stanton-Salazar, R. (2001). *Manufacturing hope and despair: The school and kin support networks of U.S.-Mexican youth.* New York: Teachers College Press.

Steele, C. M., & Aronson, J. (1995). Stereotype threat and the intellectual test performance of African-Americans. *Journal of Personality and Social Psychology, 68,* 797–811.

Suarez-Orozco, C., & Suarez-Orozco, M. (2001). *Children of immigration.* Cambridge, MA: Harvard University Press.

Sutherland, J. (2008). *Having our say: Exploring the community college transfer process and social networks of black men.* Unpublished doctoral dissertation, New York University, New York.

Suzuki, B. H. (2002). Revisiting the model minority stereotype: Implications for student affairs practice and higher education. *New Directions for Student Services, 97,* 21–32.

Takagi, D. (1992). *The retreat from race: Asian American admissions and racial politics.* New Brunswick, NJ: Rutgers University Press.

Takaki, R. (1998). *Strangers from a different shore: A history of Asian Americans.* Boston: Little Brown.

Tamura, E. H. (2001). Asian Americans in the history of education: An historiographical essay. *History of Education Quarterly, 41,* 1.

Tang, C. S. (1996). Adolescent abuse in Hong Kong Chinese families. *Child Abuse and Neglect, 20,* 873–878.

Tate, W. (1997). Critical race theory and education: History, theory, and implications. *Review of Research in Education, 22,* 195–247.

Teranishi, R. T. (2003). "Raced" perspectives on college opportunity: Examining Asian Americans through critical race theory. *Equity and Excellence in Education, 35*(2), 144–154.

Teranishi, R. T. (2004). Yellow and *Brown*: Residential segregation and emerging Asian American immigrant populations. *Equity and Excellence in Education, 37*(3), 255–263.

Teranishi, R. T. (2005). *Normative approaches to policy research in education: Implications for Asian Americans and Pacific Islanders.* New York: The College Board.

Teranishi, R. T. (2007, May). Race, ethnicity, and high education policy: The use of critical quantitative research. In F. Stage (Ed.), *Using quantitative data to answer critical questions. New Directions for Institutional Research* (No. 133, pp. 37–50). San Francisco: Jossey-Bass.

Teranishi, R. T. (2010). Demography, community, and the education of Asian American and Pacific Islander students. In W. R. Allen (Ed.), *Sociology, demography, and social change.* Oxford: Elsevier.

Teranishi, R. T., Allen, W. R., & Solorzano, D. G. (2004). Opportunities at the crossroads: Racial inequality, school segregation, and higher education in California. *Teachers College Record, 106*(11), 2224–2245.

Teranishi, R. T., & Briscoe, K. (2008). Social capital and the racial stratification of college opportunity. In J. C. Smart (Ed.), *Higher education: Handbook of theory and research* (Vol. 26, pp. 591–614). Dordrecht, Netherlands: Springer.

Teranishi, R. T., & Nguyen, T. K. (2009). Southeast Asian educational mobility: Ethnicity, social capital, and the pursuit of higher education. In W. R. Allen, E. Kimura-Walsh, & K. A. Griffin (Eds.), *Toward a brighter tomorrow: College barriers, hopes, and plans of Black, Latino/a, and Asian American students in California* (pp. 209–232). Charlotte, NC: Information Age Publishing.

Teranishi, R. T., & Parker, T. L. (2010). Social reproduction of inequality: Racial segregation, secondary schools, and postsecondary opportunities. *Teachers College Record, 112*(6), 2–3.

Tilly, C. (1998). *Durable inequality*. Berkeley: University of California Press.

Turner, C. (2003). Incorporation and marginalization in the academy: From border toward center for faculty of color? *Journal of Black Studies, 34*(1), 112–125.

Turner, S. (2004). Going to college and finishing college: Explaining different educational outcomes. In C. Hoxby (Ed.), *College choices: The economics of where to go, when to go, and how to pay* (pp. 13–62). Chicago: University of Chicago Press.

UNESCO Institute for Statistics. (2009). *A global perspective on research and development*. Montreal, Québec, Canada: UNESCO.

University of California, Office of the President. (2000). *Admissions and enrollment information*. Oakland, CA: Author.

U.S. Bureau of Labor Statistics. (2009). College enrollment and work activity of 2008 high school graduates. Retrieved from http://www.bls.gov/news.release/hsgec.nr0.htm

U.S. Census Bureau. (2000a). Summary files. Available at http://factfinder/census.gov/servelet/DatasetMainPageServlet

U.S. Census Bureau. (2000b). *A half-century of learning: Historical statistics in educational attainment in the United States, 1940–2000*. (PHC-T-41). Washington, DC: Author.

U.S. Census Bureau. (2002). Census of population and housing, 2000. American community survey 1-year estimates—United States (Data File). Retrieved from http://factfinder.census.gov/home/en/acs_pums_2008_1yr.html

U.S. Census Bureau. (2003). *Annual estimates of the population by race alone or in combination and Hispanic or Latino origin for the United States and states*. Washington, DC: Author.

U.S. Census Bureau. (2008). *Percent of the projected population by race and Hispanic origin for the United States: 2010 to 2050* (NP2008-T6). Washington, DC: Author.

U.S. Citizen and Immigration Services. (2008). *Characteristics of specialty occupation workers*. Fiscal Year 2007, annual report. Washington, DC: U.S. Department of Homeland Security.

U.S. Department of Health and Human Services (1999). *Surgeon General's Report: Asian Americans/Pacific Islanders*. Washington, DC: Department of Health and Human Services, Surgeon General.

U.S. Department of Health and Human Services, (1999). *Mental health: Culture, race, and ethnicity*. Washington, DC: Department of Health and Human Services, Surgeon General.

U. S. Department of Homeland Security. (2006). *Yearbook of immigration statistics: 2005.* Washington, DC: U.S. Department of Homeland Security, Office of Immigration Statistics.

U.S. Department of Homeland Security. (2008). *Yearbook of immigration statistics: 2007.* Washington, DC: U.S. Department of Homeland Security, Office of Immigration Statistics.

U. S. Department of the Interior. (2008). *Indian entities recognized and eligible to receive services from the U.S. Bureau of Indian Affairs.* Washington, DC: Bureau of Indian Affairs, Interior.

U. S. Immigration and Naturalization Service. (2003). *Estimates of the unauthorized immigrant population residing in the United States: 1990 to 2000.* Washington, DC: U.S. Immigration and Nationalization Service, Office of Policy and Planning.

U.S. News and World Report. (1966, December 26). Success story of one minority in the U.S., pp. 73–78.

Valencia, R. R. (1997). *The evolution of deficit thinking: Educational thought and practice.* London: Falmer Press.

Valenzuela, A., & Dornbusch, S. M. (1994). Familism and social capital in the academic achievement of Mexican origin and Anglo adolescents. *Social Science Quarterly, 75*(1), 18–36.

Villalpando, O. (1994, November). *Comparing the effects of multiculturalism and diversity on minority and white students' satisfaction with college.* Paper presented at the annual meeting of the Association for the Study of Higher Education, Tucson, AZ.

Waters, M. C. (1990). *Ethnic options: Choosing identities in America.* Berkeley, CA: University of California Press.

Wei, D. (1986). The Asian American success myth. *Interracial Books for Children, 17,* 16–17.

Wilds, D., & Wilson, R. (1998). *Annual status report, minorities in higher education* (Vol. 16). Washington, DC: American Council on Education.

Wilson, W. J. (1987). *The truly disadvantaged: The inner city, the underclass, and public policy.* Chicago: University of Chicago Press.

Wing, Y. (1909). *My life in China and America.* New York: H. Holt.

Wong, K. S. (1995). Chinatown: conflicting images, contested terrain. *MELUS, 20*(1), 3–15.

Worthy, E. H. (1965). Yung Wing in America. *Pacific Historical Review, 34,* 265–287.

Wu, F. (1996). Changing America: Three arguments about Asian Americans and the law. *American University Law Review, 45.*

Wu, F. H. (2002). *Yellow: Race in America beyond Black and White.* New York: Basic Books.

Zhou, M. (1992). *Chinatown: The socioeconomic potential of an urban enclave.* Philadelphia: Temple University Press.

Zhou, M., & Bankston, C. L., III. (1998). *Growing up American: How Vietnamese children adapt to life in the United States.* New York: Russell Sage Foundation.

Zhou, M., and Bankston, C. L., III. (1994) Social capital and the adaptation of the second generation: The case of Vietnamese youth in New Orleans. *International Migration Review 18*(4), 821–845.

Zia, H. (2001). *Asian American dreams: The emergence of an American people.* New York: Farrar, Straus, & Giroux.

Index

Abboud, S. K., 104
Ability grouping and tracking practices, 78
Access to quality schooling, 80–85
Adelman, C., 78
Administrators in higher education, 140–142, 141
Advanced placement (AP) program, 78, 83, 97
Affirmative action, 11–12, 102
African Americans, 12, 101, 135. *See also* Blacks
African immigration, 31
Alexander, K., 78, 86
Alhambra (California) (AAPI ethnic enclave), 53ñ54, 75, 84
Allen, W. R., 15, 78, 97, 124, 136, 140
Alport, G., 17
American Anthropological Association, 18
American Apartheid (Denton), 59
"American-born Chinese" (ABC), 71
American-born vs. foreign-born AAPIs, 126
American Samoa, 34
Amos, H., 137
Anderson, E., 10
Antonio, A. L., 105, 139
Argyris, C., 6
Arifuku, I., 68
Aronson, J., 3, 145
Ascher, C., 16
Ash, A. S., 137
Asian American Legal Defense and Education Fund (AALDEF), 38, 134, 135
Asian American Native American Pacific Islander–serving institution (AANAPISI) legislation, 13–14, 143–144
Asian American Pacific Islander (AAPI).
definition of, 163n
creation of racial category, 27
Asian Americans in Class (Lew), 108
Asian Indians (in U.S.)
as Asian American subgroup, 29
educational attainment, 110f, 112, 126
immigration status, 29, 31, 33, 126
residential patterns, 56

socioeconomic status, 35, 36, 46
"Asian Invasion," 2, 58, 130
Asian/Pacific/American Institute at New York University, 6
Asylee
definition of, 164n
legislation, 32

Background characteristics effect on college choice, 121
Baez, B., 140
Baldi, S., 2
Bangladeshis (in U.S.), 56, 125, 126
Bankston, C. L., 6, 50, 55
Barber, R., 131
Barringer, H., 26, 31, 32
Bartlett, S., 35
Beardsley, L. V., 131
Bell, D., 13, 19
Bell Curve, The, (Herrnstein and Murray), 166n
Bennett, C., 46
Berktold, J., 123
Berry, B., 130, 131
Berthold, S. M., 66, 67
Besnard, M., 127, 146
Biklen, S. K., 156
Black and White, Separate, Hostile, and Unequal (Hacker), 11
Blacks
incarceration rate, 68
in K–12 schools, 80, 81
and race in education, 9–14, 17, 21
residential patterns, 58, 59, 61,
students in higher education, 2, 100–102, 102f, 129–131
in teaching, 133, 139
Black-White paradigm, 11, 13, 21
Blau, P. M., 1, 20
"Boat people," 32
Bogdan, R. C., 156
Bok, D., 16
Bonous-Hammarth, M., 136, 140